*Relationship
Counseling and
Psychotherapy*

Relationship Counseling and Psychotherapy

C. H. Patterson

University of Illinois
Urbana–Champaign

Harper & Row, Publishers
New York, Evanston, San Francisco, London

Sponsoring Editor: George A. Middendorf
Project Editor: David Nickol
Designer: June Negrycz
Production Supervisor: Bernice Krawczyk

**Relationship
Counseling and
Psychotherapy**

Scales for measuring empathic understanding in Chapters 4, 5, and 7 reprinted from
*Helping and Human Relations: A Primer for Lay and Professional Helpers, Volume
II, Practice and Research* by Robert H. Carkhuff. Copyright © 1969 by Holt, Rinehart
and Winston, Inc. Reprinted by permission of Holt, Rinehart and Winston, Inc.

Library of Congress Cataloging in Publication Data

Patterson, Cecil Holden, 1912–
   Relationship counseling and psychotherapy.
   1. Psychotherapy. 2. Psychotherapist and patient.
3. Client-centered psychotherapy. I. Title.
[DNLM: 1. Counseling. 2. Interpersonal relations.
3. Psychotherapy. WM420 P317r 1974]
RC480.5.P32   616.8'914   73–20864
ISBN 0–06–045045–2

Self-realization can be encouraged if the therapist has a profound knowledge not of therapeutic theories and formulations but of people and their personal experiences.

Jurgen Ruesch (*Therapeutic Communication.*
New York: Norton, 1961, p. 290)

. . . as man's control of his environment has proceeded . . . he has progressively uncovered more and more complication, but, at the same time he has succeeded in discovering more and more unifying principles which accept the ever increasing variety, but recognize an underlying unity. He has, in short, discovered the many and the one. . . . The diversity . . . is a surface phenomenon: When one looks underneath and within, the universal unity again becomes apparent.

Warren Weaver (Confessions of a Scientist-Humanist,
Saturday Review, May 28, 1966)

Contents

Preface   ix

1 Counseling and/or Psychotherapy   1

2 Goals and Values in Relationship Therapy   15

3 The Nature of Self-Actualization   31

4 The Therapeutic Conditions: I. Responsive Dimensions   49

5 The Therapeutic Conditions: II. Action Dimensions   75

6 Implementing the Conditions:
The Counselor in the Therapy Process   97

7 The Client in the Process   119

8 The Relationship: Placebo, Friendship, or More?   147

9 Diagnosis   163

10 Relationship Group Counseling or Psychotherapy   177

Index of Names   199

Index of Subjects   202

Preface

The days of "schools" in counseling and psychotherapy are drawing to a close. This book is not intended to represent yet another school or approach.

We now have evidence that there are some basic core conditions common to all effective psychotherapy. These conditions are relationship variables—hence the use of the term *relationship counseling* or *relationship therapy* in this book. I have attempted to present the basic elements of counseling or psychotherapy. Whether these are necessary and sufficient conditions for counseling or psychotherapy (they are by my definition) or only necessary but not sufficient, they form the basis for all counseling or psychotherapy.

The term *relationship therapy* is not original. I do not know to whom to credit the first use of the term. Moustakas used it in 1959. I have been using it for several years. Readers familiar with client-centered therapy will wonder what the difference is between it and relationship therapy. The answer, of course, is that there is little, if any, basic difference. The term *relationship therapy* seems to me, at least, to be preferable in that it avoids some of the questionable connotations of the term *client-centered therapy* and at the same time recognizes its essence—the relationship.

The presentation is simple, in the sense of being basic. It is also an integrated or systematic treatment, tied to a theory of human behavior and of interpersonal relationships. Yet it is oriented toward practice, designed to be of concrete help to the student and practitioner. The considerable research supporting this approach is not systematically covered here, although frequent references are made to the evidence. Reviews of the research are already available (Truax and Carkhuff, 1967; Carkhuff and Berenson, 1967; Berenson and Carkhuff,

1967; Carkhuff, 1969; and Truax and Mitchell, 1971 (in Bergin and Garfield, 1971).

This evidence means that it is no longer possible for instructors in counseling or psychotherapy to pretend a neutrality—or objectivity —in their teaching. It does not suffice to expose students to the major theories, telling them that they all appear to be equally effective (or ineffective) and that we have no basis in research on which to make a choice. It is thus no longer possible, in a pseudo-democratic manner, to tell students to take their choice or to construct their own personal theories or approaches. Research has made apparent the commonalities among the apparently widely different approaches and provided evidence that it is these common variables, not unique variables or conditions, that account for the effectiveness of the different approaches. The differences among these approaches are accidental or incidental, at best irrelevant or at worst detrimental. An approach may be effective in spite of, rather than because of, its unique variables.

Such a procedure is no longer justifiable—if it ever was. Professional activity can never be based upon a supposedly democratic principle of personal choice. It can only be based upon knowledge or upon the best professional or scientific judgment of the time and place. It is incumbent upon instructors to be aware of current knowledge or professional judgment and to include it in their instruction. The evidence that now exists regarding the core conditions must be recognized by instructors and communicated to their students. This book provides a convenient method for such communication. It can be used following my *Theories of Counseling and Psychotherapy* (Harper & Row, 1973, 2nd ed.); indeed it may be considered an extension of the final chapter. Or it can be used in a separate course or as the beginning of the supervised practicum.

I have not attempted to cover all the particulars, the topics, or the details of counseling or psychotherapy—no single book could do so. The theory presented is a macrotheory, which no doubt will be eventually spelled out and filled in with more detail by future writers. The book is not simply a presentation of theory, however. An attempt has been made to implement the theory systematically yet in a manner that is useful and practical to the student and beginning counselor. The aspects of implementation that have been developed are those that flow most naturally from the theory.

It will be objected by some, particularly those with a psychodynamic or psychoanalytic orientation, that the approach is oversimplified, too simple to be valid or useful. Certainly, compared to psychoanalysis, it is simple. But it can be argued that while there is an infinite complexity in the details of every science, simplicity is characteristic of the basic ideas, concepts, principles, theorems, or laws. The most widely violated scientific law is the law of parsimony.

The emphasis upon the core relationship conditions cuts through the masses of customs, traditions, social forms, and formal institutions of society, or societies to get to the basis of human experience and interaction—the relations of man to man. It points to these relations, rather than to the superstructure of culture and society, as the source of man's problems and emotional disturbances. The superstructure represents the creation of man in the attempt to live together. It has been developed in an attempt to overcome the problems engendered by the behaviors of those who, because of the lack of, or inadequate, facilitative personal relationships, engage in behaviors that are disruptive, noncooperative, antisocial, or destructive to others. Its methods have been those of control through suppression and punishment, rather than attempts to prevent such behaviors by eliminating their causes.

Man's problems do not stem from some independent, abstract, bad social environment, but from specific bad personal treatment by other men. And it is these problems that create the bad social environment, not vice versa. The remedy, then, is not to change an abstract social environment, but to change the way man relates to man—man's inhumanity to man. The restrictive, repressive, controlling social environment will then be unnecessary. It will wither away.

The solution to our problems, then, lies in the fostering of good interpersonal relationships, the principles of which we now know. These principles transcend time and cultures. "We are all much more basically human than otherwise," wrote Harry Stack Sullivan. Thus, relationship therapy is not time-bound or culture-bound but is a universal approach.

An interpersonal theory or approach to emotional disturbance, is not, of course, new. Sullivan's interpersonal psychiatry is such an approach, perhaps the first and still probably the major one; it is only now being adequately recognized. The present approach, however, does not derive from Sullivan but from client-centered therapy. The human relationship is the most powerful psychological behavior modifier known to man.

Many psychologists and psychotherapists will be horrified at the conclusion that psychotherapy is not a profession but something that can be taught to many persons, persons who lack a college education or a background in psychology. Yet this is the logical extension of the recognition that the essence of psychotherapy is that it is a good human relationship. Rather than responding with horror, we should respond with hope, since it is obvious that the practice of psychotherapy, restricted to those with long professional training built upon four years of undergraduate education, will never be able to reach all those who need help. Nor is a remedial approach through psychotherapy likely to solve the basic problem. It is only when we succeed in teaching the principles of psychotherapy, or the elements of facilitative interpersonal relationships, to everyone that we will resolve the problem and eliminate the need for psychotherapy.

Much of the material included in this book comes from my experience in teaching and supervising students in counseling or psychotherapy. It includes many apparently simple, yet basic, ideas and suggestions that I have found useful in helping beginning counselors. I am indebted to the many students who, over the years, have stimulated me to formulate and express them.

Instructors who are interested in including laboratory work in the core conditions in their teaching, in connection with Chapters 4 and 5, will find materials in Carkhuff's work (*Helping and Human Relations*, Volumes I and II, Holt, Rinehart & Winston, 1969, and *The Art of Helping*, Human Resources Development Press, Amherst, Mass., 1972; the latter is obtainable from the American Personnel and Guidance Association, Washington, D.C.).

The book was written during my tenure as a Fulbright-Hays Lecturer at the University of Aston, Birmingham, England (1972–1973). Much of it was discussed with the students with whom I worked during that year, and I owe the inclusion of many ideas to their questions. I wish to acknowledge my debt to Denis Bury, Lyn Clark, Ivan Ellingham, Tony Hurst, Jennie Kidd, Bryan Lamb, Diane Mottram, Ciaran Oley, Gordon Trimble, Maggie Vicary, and Pat Zaitschek, and to Dr. Richard Nelson-Jones, course tutor, who participated in our classes and seminars.

I am also greatly indebted to Mrs. Vera Green, who translated my handwriting, with its many corrections, rewritings, and insertions, into a legible manuscript.

Relationship Counseling and Psychotherapy

Chapter 1

Counseling and/or Psychotherapy

The debate over whether counseling and psychotherapy are the same or different has been going on for many years. Abeles refers to the issue as an "old saw," taking the position that it is obvious that there is a difference.[1] He does not, however, specify the difference. The continuing concern may represent an "old saw," but it is such precisely because no one has been able to differentiate between counseling and psychotherapy in a way that commands agreement. In this chapter we shall take the position that there are no essential or significant differences between them, thus justifying the use of the terms interchangeably in this book.

DEFINITIONS OF COUNSELING AND PSYCHOTHERAPY

Definitions of counseling and psychotherapy that attempt to differentiate between them make the distinction on several bases.

Differentiation in Terms of Severity of Client Disturbance

One of the earliest attempts to distinguish between counseling and psychotherapy was made at the Ann Arbor Conference on the training of psychological counselors sponsored by the American Psychological Association.[2] The participants were unable to agree on a clear distinction, although they all agreed that there was one. They felt that counseling and psychotherapy were on a continuum, with counseling "concerned with the essentially normal individual," while psychotherapy was concerned with the abnormal or seriously disturbed individual. The Committee on Definition of the Division of Counseling Psychology of the American Psychological Association took essentially the same position a few years later.[3] The counseling psychologist, it says, wants to help essentially normal people "toward overcoming obstacles to their personal growth, wherever these may be encountered, and toward achieving optimum development of their personal resources." Psychotherapy, it states, deals with the more extreme problems presented by "individuals who are in need of emergency treatment" and "whose emotional growth has been severely distorted or stunted" or who represent "psychological disasters."

Hahn and MacLean, in their early text in counseling psychology, accept the concept of severity when they state that part of the unique pattern of the counseling psychologist is "his concern with clients in the 'normal' range." They leave the "deviates" to the therapists.[4] Bordin also adopts a quantitative rather than a qualitative distinction; the client's difficulties, he says, "are certainly less severe, with, therefore, less distortion of reality than the client who requires psychotherapy."[5]

There are a number of difficulties with this distinction between "normal" and severely disturbed (neurotic or psychotic) individuals. Those who propose it recognize that no sharp line can be drawn to separate the two classes of clients. In addition, this position implies that when a client being treated by a psychotherapist reaches normality (assuming that this could be reliably determined), the client would no longer need the psychotherapist but should be transferred to a counselor if he desires further help. In practice, of course, both those who call themselves counselors and those who call themselves psychotherapists start with the client where he is and continue with him until he desires no further help.

Some of those who accept the distinction in terms of severity of disturbance also agree that counseling cannot be limited to the normal person but is also appropriate for the abnormal or severely maladjusted person, insofar as the counseling deals with special problems, such as those in educational or vocational areas. Thus, Super states that counseling deals with "the normalities even of abnormal persons, with locating and developing personal and social resources and adaptive tendencies so that the individual can be assisted in making more effective use of them."[6]

Differentiation in Terms of Problems

In this distinction, several terms are used to designate the nature of problems for which counseling is appropriate. These terms include reality-oriented, environmental, situational, specific, nonembedded, and conscious. Terms applied to problems for which psychotherapy is appropriate include intrapersonal, deep-seated, general, personality disturbances, embedded, and unconscious. Mowrer at one time defined counseling as "the process of giving professional or expert help to persons suffering from fully-conscious conflicts which are accompanied by so-called normal anxiety."[7] Psychotherapy would deal with unconscious conflicts and neurotic anxiety.

Another distinction in this area has been made by Tyler. Counseling deals with decisions related to educational, vocational, or other choices; psychotherapy is concerned with attitudes, feelings, and emotions within the self. Implicit in this is the notion that counseling deals with cognitive problems and psychotherapy with affective problems.

A moment's reflection will reveal the inadequacy of this distinction. Cognition and affect are both involved in all behavior. Choices, even vocational and educational, let alone that of marriage, are never simply cognitive decisions; they are not coldly logical and rational. Reality problems are not all cognitive in nature. And the paranoid person has situational or environmental problems. Interpersonal problems, which in one sense are reality problems, are also personality problems. And it is difficult, if not impossible, to distinguish between normal and neurotic anxiety, or between conscious and unconscious conflicts. Moreover, both may be, and often are, present.

Distinctions Involving Goals

The whole area of the goals of counseling or psychotherapy is confused and will be dealt with in detail in the next chapter. It is only natural that this confusion would be reflected in attempts to distinguish between counseling and psychotherapy in terms of goals.

The Committee on Definition of the APA speaks of counseling as helping individuals to overcome obstacles to personal growth. Many psychotherapists include the removal, reduction, or elimination of blocks as goals of psychotherapy, however.[8] Tyler has stated that it is not the job of the counselor "to remove physical and mental handicaps or to get rid of limitations." Counseling does not attempt "to repair damage done to [the client] in the past, to stimulate inadequate [sic] development of some stunted aspect of his personality," but is a process of "helping a person attain a clear sense of personal identity, along with the acceptance of his limitations."[9] Existentially oriented psychotherapists, however, see as their function the development of personal identity.[10] Psychotherapy, according to Tyler, is directed toward personality change of some sort, while counseling refers to "a helping process, the aim of which is not to change the person but to enable him to utilize the resources he now has for coping with life."[11]

Related to this distinction is the concept of psychotherapy as remedial in nature and of counseling as preventive. Hahn and MacLean[12] and the APA Conference[13] note this distinction. Others, however, would insist that counseling goes beyond prevention, being concerned with facilitating personal development.

Counselors obviously do not refuse to deal with the current problems or difficulties in which clients find themselves. Those who call themselves psychotherapists are certainly concerned with the prevention of more serious future disturbances. What is remedial at one point in time is preventive when considered from a later point. As Blocher notes, "Much of what is attempted in the name of counseling has been as remediative and adjustive as anything attempted in the name of psychotherapy."[14]

Thus the distinction in terms of goals is no more clear-cut than others. It hardly seems possible to separate personality change, even reorganization of the "basic personality" (whatever that is) from changes such as greater utilization of the capacities of the individual. Personality could no more change without the potential being there than can a utilization of resources be achieved without their being present. Tyler rejects a distinction in terms of superficiality versus depth, noting that the way a person sees his work, his religious beliefs, or his relationship to his wife and children, all appropriate concerns of counseling, "are as fundamental a part of him as are his anxieties over sexual or aggressive motivation," which are the concern of psychotherapy.[15] Changes in perceptions, attitudes, beliefs, values, feelings, and emotions all occur as a result of counseling, as Tyler is aware. Who would say that these are not basic personality changes?

Writers who make a distinction between counseling and psychotherapy are not always consistent. Thus Tyler defines what she calls "minimum change therapy" as counseling since it is concerned with the "exploration of resources." Yet she calls it therapy.[16]

Differentiation in Terms of Methods and Techniques

There is little attempt to differentiate counseling from psychotherapy in the literature. Within psychotherapy there is discussion of supportive methods versus uncovering methods or approaches. But both are psychotherapy. Some might claim that techniques such as interpretation, probing, or uncovering are psychotherapeutic techniques. But there is no evidence that these techniques are restricted to those calling themselves psychotherapists.

Counseling is often said to be more cognitively oriented, more rational in its methods and approaches, involving problem-solving techniques. Yet probably the most cognitively oriented approach is that of Ellis, and he does not use the word counseling but calls his approach rational-emotive psychotherapy.[17]

The prevention-remedial distinction is not supported in terms of differences in methods or techniques.

Mowrer writes, "I think it is fair to suppose that the techniques of counseling and psychotherapy are quite different." Counseling, he says, is an attempt "to give information, guidance as to resources, suggestions, perhaps advice and directives."[18] Yet, while counselors would perhaps admit to information-giving and resource guidance, they would reject the idea that this is all counseling is or that this constitutes the essence of counseling. And certainly they would repudiate advice giving and directives as constituting counseling.

One difference between psychotherapists with medical training and counselors is the use of drugs by the former. But the use of drugs can hardly be called psychotherapy, and this difference would also distinguish psychotherapists with medical backgrounds from nonmedically trained psychotherapists.

It appears to be impossible to develop lists of techniques or methods which distinguish psychotherapy from counseling. On the other hand, similarities in methods and techniques are widely recognized. Counseling is increasingly being recognized and defined as a personal relationship. The same is true of what is called psychotherapy. Experience and research indicate that the nature of the relationship is the same. The characteristics of the good psychotherapy relationship are identical with those of a good counseling relationship.

Thus, in all these attempted distinctions, the differences between counseling and psychotherapy exist in the minds of those who want differences to exist rather than in actual fact. Stefflre writes, "In distinguishing counseling from psychotherapy on the basis of differences of methods, we should run counter to the advice of Patterson, who sees no difference between them."[19] He fails, however, to support his "should" by any reasons or evidence.

THE FAILURE TO ESTABLISH SIGNIFICANT DIFFERENCES

It is apparent that efforts to distinguish counseling and psychotherapy have not been successful or convincing. Terms applying to clients or patients, counselors or therapists, problems, goals, methods or techniques, or the process are used by both counselors and psychotherapists. Many authors, beginning with Carl Rogers, use the terms counseling and psychotherapy interchangeably.[20]

Authors of chapters on counseling and on psychotherapy in the *Annual Review of Psychology* have struggled for years to find some way to divide the literature to be reviewed in their respective areas. No satisfactory or meaningful criteria have been found. Articles with "counseling" in their titles have been reviewed in chapters titled "psychotherapy" and vice versa. The only relatively general agreement has been to include studies conducted in a medical setting or studies already published in medical or psychiatric journals in reviews of psychotherapy; studies conducted in nonmedical settings or published in other journals have been included in reviews of counseling. But this distinction is not systematically adhered to.

In actual practice, professionally trained counselors or psychotherapists do not attempt to make distinctions about whether they are engaging in counseling or psychotherapy. They do not attempt fine distinctions about whether a client is abnormal in a pathological sense or is facing a temporary crisis or situational problem. They do not attempt to distinguish between efforts to change basic personality structure or to resolve current problems or dissatisfactions. They do not concern themselves with whether they are engaged in bringing a client with "pathology" up to a "normal" level where they will then terminate or refer the client to someone else, or whether they will only accept a client who is "normal" and work towards helping him increase the use of his potentials. All counselors and psychotherapists within the broad limits of the accessibility of the client to a counseling or psychotherapeutic (interpersonal) approach, take the client where he is and continue with him as far as he can or is willing to go.

There is little or no concern about regulating the depth, intensity, or length of the relationship, at least on the basis of whether one calls himself a counselor or psychotherapist or is engaged in counseling or psychotherapy. Tyler, in her discussion of minimum change therapy, which is supposedly short-term, does not set a limit. She emphasizes that "the experience of having someone really care about him is such an indispensable part of what counseling means for a client that we must be especially careful never to jeopardize it."[21] Setting a time limit, she suggests, may make the client feel he is only worth ten hours or twenty hours or whatever. Likewise, other aspects of the relationship cannot be limited. The counselor cannot enter a relationship that he feels he must carefully limit and still be his real self, genuine and spontaneous. A counselor cannot commit himself only partially to a counseling relationship. You cannot go in swimming without getting wet all over.

Tyler notes that:

> We can best control the duration of counseling contacts [and the present writer would say the depth, intensity, and goals also] by adopting consistently an attitude of respect for what each individual client now is and lending him support and understanding while he comes to terms with this unique self of his. Whether it takes him two hours or two hundred, if he succeeds, the effort will have been worthwhile.[22]

We have been talking about the professionally trained (not necessarily doctorally trained) counselor. The source of much of the confusion of people like Stefflre is the large number of essentially untrained, or inadequately trained, persons who call themselves, or are called, counselors. One may even have completed a master's degree in a counselor education program and not be adequately trained as a counselor. In fact, adequate preparation for professional or psychological counseling (the adjective, though redundant, is necessary because of untrained persons using the title of counselor), requires more than one year of graduate study. Untrained or inadequately trained persons are not psychotherapists—but neither are they counselors, and what they are doing is neither psychotherapy nor counseling.

The persistence of some in claiming a distinction seems to go beyond rationality. There *must* be a difference, it is declared. Hahn notes that, while counseling and psychotherapy cannot be distinguished clearly and while counselors practice what psychotherapists consider to be psychotherapy and psychotherapists practice what counselors consider to be counseling, there is still agreement that they are different![23]

Stefflre insists that "a distinction *must* be made. If it is not present in nature, it must be invented."[24] His reasoning is that since many who have the title of counselor are doing something that is not psychotherapy, there must be something called counseling to cover or define what they are doing. The logic of this seems unfathomable. It might more logically be concluded that such persons are not, in fact, counselors since what they are doing is not counseling under any definition of the term.

A common resolution of the problem for those who, while admitting some similarities, insist that there is a difference, is to assert that counseling and psychotherapy are on a continuum. Then they arbitrarily place counseling on one end and psychotherapy on the other. They then say, "See, it's obvious that there is a difference between two ends of a continuum." Statistically, of course, there is a difference of about six standard deviations between the ends of a normal continuum, and of course this is clearly a significant difference! But in what? The underlying variable is never defined.

Goldman has used a similar analogy to support the continuum argument.[25] Put in logical form, it is as follows:

1. Counseling equals light.
2. Psychotherapy equals darkness.
3. Light is clearly different from darkness, even though they merge at some point.
4. Therefore, counseling is different from psychotherapy.

Stated in this form, the fallacious logic is obvious. It is, however, the kind of argument of most of those who insist on a difference—the conclusion is already included in their premises.

THE CASE FOR THE TERM PSYCHOLOGICAL COUNSELING

In view of the fact that, with all the efforts to differentiate between counseling and psychotherapy, no one has succeeded in proposing important or significant distinctions that command acceptance and agreement, it must be concluded that there are no such essential differences. It might therefore be suggested that it is unnecessary to retain the two words if they are essentially the same. This would appear to be particularly true when the use of the word *counseling* has been extended to cover so many areas. It is used by many according to Humpty Dumpty's definition in Lewis Carroll's *Through the Looking Glass:* "When *I* use a word it means just what I choose it to mean—neither more nor less." Counseling is now to include anything that anyone who is called a counselor does—or can be induced to do. It covers all services to the individual, including a variety of activities beyond the private interpersonal relationship that has been considered the essence of counseling. It has come to cover all helping activities, all methods of attempting to influence and change the behavior of others.

Thus, it is difficult to object when the word is used by those with no professional preparation or training, such as beauty counselors, travel counselors, loan counselors, rug counselors, and so on. We are in a state of confusion in the use of the word and have lost control of its use as limited to a professional function or relationship. As Alice said to Humpty Dumpty: "The question is whether you *can* make words mean so many different things." It is necessary to restrict, or delimit, the meaning of the word so that it has a clear denotative meaning.

It might appear to be desirable to abandon the term counseling altogether because of its ambiguity. But there are practical problems. There appears to be no acceptable alternative term. The term psychotherapy, at least at this time, is not acceptable. It is forbidding to many who can use or are in need of psychotherapy. In addition, the medical practices acts of many states restrict the practice of psychotherapy to persons with a medical degree.

The word *counseling* will continue to be used, then. The fact that it is not legally restricted and is now widely used by persons with no preparation or qualifications to engage in a professional counseling relationship, however, requires that we attempt to distinguish professional counselors from others who call themselves counselors. The efforts to differentiate counseling from psychotherapy leads to a definition that does not differentiate it from the information- and advice-giving of nonprofessionals. Or if it does not go that far, the emphasis on counseling as a cognitive problem-solving, decision-making, testing and test interpretation process, leads to a definition that does not distinguish counseling from teaching.

If the word *counseling* is retained, it would appear to be desirable, if not necessary, to differentiate in some way between professional and nonprofessional counselors. The use of the adjective *psychological* could do this.

RELATIONSHIP THERAPY: A CONTINUUM OF HELPING RELATIONSHIPS

Counseling or psychotherapy may be placed on a continuum. It is not an unlabeled continuum with counseling at one end and psychotherapy at the other. It is a continuum of helping activities or helping relationships. The nature of this continuum is indicated in the figure below.

A Continuum of Psychological Helping Relationships

Information-Giving	Instruction in Subject Matter—Education	Behavior Modification—Teaching	Behavior Therapy—Reeducation	Counseling or Psychotherapy
Cognitive	←		→	Affective
Impersonal	←		→	Personal
Specific	←		→	General
Learning	←		→	Performance
(response not in repertoire)				(response in repertoire)
Relationship as the medium	←		→	Relationship as the essence

There are several variables underlying this continuum. These variations differentiate among the several kinds of helping relationships identified; their exact placement on the continuum is arbitrary, but the order is important. At one end of the continuum are helping relationships that are essentially cognitive rather than highly affective, impersonal rather than highly personal, specific and limited rather than broad and general in their concerns. In learning-theory terms, relationships toward this end of the continuum involve the acquisition of new information, knowledge, or behaviors, while at the other end of the continuum the concern is with freeing or unblocking the use of what is already known or with performing behaviors already learned. A basic variable is the place or importance of the personal relationship in the helping process. A personal relationship—or a psychological relationship—is involved in every helping relationship, even if the information is conveyed in an apparently impersonal manner, as through the printed word. A writer does establish a kind of psychological relationship with the reader, or, perhaps better stated, the reader creates or constructs some kind of relationship. Some kind of relationship is involved in every helping process; that is, a good personal relationship is a necessary part of the process. In many kinds of helping processes, the relationship is not sufficient, however. The helper provides information, direction, guidance, resources, instruction. Thus, in teaching, or reeducation, or remedial education, a good relationship is necessary for effective teaching and learning; it is the medium through which such teaching is achieved. In some teaching—perhaps the best teaching—creating a suitable relationship may be sufficient for some kinds of learning by some learners. Such teaching approaches counseling or psychotherapy. The psychotherapy relationship—a highly affective, personal, open or general relationship—is the necessary and sufficient condition for personality or behavior change of a particular kind or for problems or needs of a particular kind.

For what kind of needs or problems is the therapy relationship necessary and sufficient, or, in other words, specific treatment? The therapy relationship, or *relationship therapy*, is the specific treatment for persons whose problems inhere in or relate to the lack of or inadequacy of good, or facilitative, interpersonal relationships in their past and/or current life experience.

This may seem to be a rather narrow definition of counseling or psychotherapy, and many would not want to restrict the terms so narrowly or would insist that this is only one approach to counseling or psychotherapy—relationship therapy. But it does seem to be desirable to distinguish among the various kinds of helping relationships, and this is one way of doing so. It is perhaps not as narrow or restrictive a definition as it may at first appear. The exact extent of disturbances stemming from inadequate human relationships is not known, but it is certainly great, and may be the most frequent basic reason for seeking counseling or psychotherapy. Burton, while discouraging the search for the single overriding trauma causing emotional disturbance, nevertheless states that "the basic pathogen is, for me, a disordered maternal or care-taking environment rather than any specific trauma as such."[26] Halleck, referring broadly to the client's environment, states that

> at any given moment, the person who identifies himself as a patient is unhappy not only because of a distorted perception of his world, but also because he is experiencing real oppression emanating from his immediate environment. Hardly anyone who is uncomfortable enough to need psychiatric help can be viewed as living in an environment free of malevolence. While the psychiatric patient may be partially or even totally unaware of how he is being influenced, some other person, group or institution is usually contributing to his grief. "Even paranoids have real enemies!"[27]

Many other writers and therapists have suggested that emotional disturbance or neuroses and psychoses are the result of lack of or inadequate love and acceptance in childhood.

That the environments of many people are lacking in good human relationships is indicated by the studies reported by Carkhuff and Berenson on the levels of the basic conditions (on their five-point scales) of a facilitative relationship in various groups in our society.

The levels in samples of the general public, college students, best friends, and teachers were below the minimal level (level 3 is defined as minimal). They conclude that "Most environments simply cannot support and sustain the individual in trouble." Even many professional helpers (high school guidance counselors and experienced counselors and psychotherapists) function below minimal levels.[28]

Of course the environment doesn't completely determine behavior, as will be emphasized in Chapter 3. Nevertheless, the human environment, the way one is treated by others, is a potent influence, particularly in infancy and childhood.

When conditions other than the therapeutic relationship are necessary for solving a person's problems, the relationship is not counseling or psychotherapy, but something else—reeducation, retraining, teaching, advising, and so on. However, the incidental inclusion of other elements, such as information-giving, does not justify calling the process something other than counseling or psychotherapy. A case in point would be the use of tests and occupational information in vocational counseling. "Testing and telling" is not itself counseling, but where the essential process is the relationship, it is counseling.

Three aspects of this definition of relationship therapy deserve attention. First, many people, or clients, need and want more than counseling or psychotherapy—or, at the other end of the continuum, more than information or skill acquisition. Thus, clients may receive more than one kind of help at the same time or over a period of time. Second, a counselor or psychotherapist may engage in other helping relationships besides counseling or psychotherapy. He may engage in skill training, instruction, reeducation, or behavior modification, if he so desires and is qualified. But such helping relationships, under our definition, are not counseling or psychotherapy. Also, a counselor or psychotherapist is justified in restricting himself, if he so desires, to the relationship defined here as counseling or psychotherapy. Third, whatever the nature of the helping process, the relationship is an important, or necessary, condition. Although it becomes increasingly important as one moves toward the counseling or psychotherapy end of the continuum, a good human relationship is facilitative for any helping process.

SUMMARY

Attempts to differentiate between what is called counseling and what is called psychotherapy are reviewed in this chapter. No essential differences upon which there is agreement can be found, in terms of severity of psychological disturbance, problems, goals, or methods and techniques. If the function is performed in a medical setting, or under medical auspices, and with persons having a psychiatric diagnosis, it is called psychotherapy. If it is performed in other, nonmedical settings, it is called counseling. While it would appear to be unnecessary to have two terms to designate the same function, practical reasons, including the prohibition of the practice of psychotherapy by nonmedical personnel or not under medical supervision, lead to the retention of the term counseling to designate the function performed by nonmedical people. In view of the extension of the term counseling to functions performed by nonprofessionals in general, it becomes necessary to distinguish these nonprofessionals from professional counselors. It is suggested that the latter be called psychological counselors.

A continuum of helping relationships is described, with counseling or psychotherapy at one end. Counseling or psychotherapy is defined as the helping process in which the relationship is necessary and sufficient. It is the specific treatment for those persons whose problems inhere in or relate to the lack of or inadequacy of good human relationships. It is the purpose of this book to consider the nature of a facilitative or therapeutic relationship.

NOTES

1 N. Abeles. Review of D. S. Arbuckle (Ed.), Counseling and psychotherapy: An overview. *Personnel and Guidance Journal,* 1968, **46**, 702–704.

2 Institute for Human Adjustment. *Training of psychological counselors.* Ann Arbor: University of Michigan Press, 1950.

3 American Psychological Association, Division of Counseling Psychology, Committee on Definition. Counseling psychology as a speciality. *American Psychologist,* 1956, **11**, 282–285.

4 M. E. Hahn and M. S. MacLean. *Counseling psychology.* New York: McGraw-Hill, 1955.

5 E. S. Bordin. *Psychological counseling* (2nd ed.). New York: Appleton-Century-Crofts, 1968, p. 60.

6 D. E. Super. Transition: From vocational guidance to counseling psychology. *Journal of Counseling Psychology,* 1955, **2**, 3–9.

7 O. H. Mowrer. Anxiety theory as a basis for distinguishing between counseling and psychotherapy. In R. F. Berdie (Ed.). *Concepts and programs of counseling. Minnesota Studies in Student Personnel Work,* No. 1. Minneapolis: University of Minnesota Press, 1951, pp. 7–26. Mowrer has since indicated that he no longer accepts this distinction. See O. H. Mowrer. Changing conceptions of the unconscious. *Journal of Nervous and Mental Diseases,* 1959, **129**, 222–232; reprinted in O. H. Mowrer. *The crisis in psychiatry and religion.* Princeton, N.J.: Van Nostrand, Reinhold, 1961.

8 A. R. Mahrer (Ed.) *The goals of psychotherapy.* New York: Appleton-Century-Crofts, 1967.

9 L. E. Tyler. Theoretical principles underlying the counseling process. *Journal of Counseling Psychology*, 1958, **5**, 3–8.

10 J. F. T. Bugental. *The search for authenticity: An existential approach to psychotherapy*. New York: Holt, Rinehart & Winston, 1965.

11 L. E. Tyler. *The work of the counselor*. (2nd ed.) New York: Appleton-Century-Crofts, 1961, p. 12. In her third edition (1969), however, she makes no clear distinction. She speaks of *choice* counselors and *adjustment* counselors (pp. 12–13); the purpose of counseling is "to facilitate wise choices of the sort on which the person's later development depends" (p. 13). Later, she refers to *choice* counseling and *change* counseling, indicating that the latter is often called therapy (pp. 174–175).

12 Hahn and MacLean, *Counseling psychology*, pp. 31–32.

13 Institute for Human Adjustment, *Training of psychological counselors*.

14 D. H. Blocher. Issues in counseling: Elusive and illusional. *Personnel and Guidance Journal*, 1965, **43**, 796–800.

15 Tyler, *The work of the counselor* (2nd ed.), p. 13.

16 *Ibid.*, p. 213. In the third edition there is no reference to minimum change therapy, however.

17 A. Ellis. *Reason and emotion in psychotherapy*. New York: Lyle Stuart, 1962.

18 Mowrer, Anxiety theory, p. 24.

19 B. Stefflre (Ed.). *Theories of counseling* (2nd ed.). New York: McGraw-Hill, 1972, p. 21. Stefflre is referring to my *Counseling and psychotherapy: theory and practice*. New York: Harper & Row, 1959, p. 10.

20 C. R. Rogers. *Counseling and psychotherapy*. Boston: Houghton Mifflin, 1942; Bordin, *Psychological counseling*; L. M. Brammer and E. L. Shostrom. *Therapeutic psychology*. Englewood Cliffs, N.J.: Prentice-Hall, 1960 (Rev. ed., 1968).

21 L. E. Tyler. Minimum change therapy. *Personnel and Guidance Journal*, 1960, **38**, 475–479.

22 *Ibid.*

23 M. E. Hahn. Conceptual trends in counseling. *Personnel and Guidance Journal*, 1953, **31**, 231–235.

24 Stefflre, *Theories of counseling*, p. 15.

25 L. Goldman. Comment: Another log. *American Psychologist*, 1964, **19**, 418–419.

26 A. Burton. *Interpersonal psychotherapy*. Englewood Cliffs, N.J.: Prentice-Hall, 1972, p. 14.

27 S. L. Halleck. *The politics of therapy*. New York: Science House, 1971, p. 28.

28 R. R. Carkhuff and B. G. Berenson. *Beyond counseling and therapy*. New York: Holt, Rinehart & Winston, 1967, pp. 7–11.

Chapter 2

Goals and Values in Relationship Therapy

Considering the tremendous amount of literature related to counseling or psychotherapy, there is relatively little dealing with the goals of the process. The number of books on counseling or psychotherapy that ignore this topic is amazing. *Goal, objective,* or *purpose* are words missing from the indexes. It is difficult to understand how so much can be written about the process, with so little consideration of the goals, since ends influence, or should influence, means.

Mahrer, in the introduction to *The Goals of Psychotherapy,* writes that "the literature on psychotherapy has little to offer on the goals of psychotherapy—their identification, significance, and organization. On this point clinicians, researchers, and theoreticians have been curiously inarticulate."[1]

One of the contributions of the behavioristic movement in psychology and psychotherapy is that it has brought out clearly the importance of goals. The emphasis of the behaviorists upon stating and defining the objectives of treatment is an example for those who advocate other methods or approaches even though there might be disagreement with the highly specific goals of the behaviorists and their restriction of goals to those which can currently be easily or objectively evaluated.

In Mahrer's book, there appear to be as many goals of psychotherapy as there are authors of chapters. The number and variety of goals are almost endless. Included are such specific goals as the removal or elimination of symptoms, reduction or elimination of test anxiety, phobias, fear of speaking in public, frigidity, impotence, enuresis, alcoholism, and so on. The chapter authors speak of unlearning unadaptive habits and learning adaptive habits,[2] reduction of anxiety, relief from suffering, curing of a mental disease or illness, personality reorganization, effective biological and social functioning, and adjustment to the environment, society, or culture. Still other authors express even broader and more general goals: insight, self-understanding, optimal functioning, maturity, the facilitation of growth, the development of a philosophy of life, and the achievement of meaning in life.[3] Burton, after a survey of the literature, listed forty different aims of psychotherapy, most of them general rather than specific.[4]

It would appear to be almost impossible to combine, or integrate, these and other goals into a generally acceptable goal. The concept of mental health might seem to be an organizing focus. But concepts of mental health vary, being defined in almost as many ways as the goals of psychotherapy. Jahoda, recognizing that "there exists no psychologically meaningful description of what is commonly understood to constitute mental health," examined five criteria: (a) absence of mental disorder, or symptoms; (b) normality of behavior; (c) adjustment to the environment; (d) unity of the personality; and (e) the correct perception of the environment.[5] The first two were discarded, since symptoms are normal or abnormal depending on the cultural context, so that it is difficult to define what is normal in any absolute sense. Adjustment may be "passive acceptance of social conditions to the detriment . . . of mental health," and thus represent conformity (psychotherapy has been accused of being on instrument of social control and for maintaining the status quo[6]). Jahoda proposed a criterion of active adjustment, or "mastery of the environment, involving a choice of what one adjusts to, and a deliberate modification of environmental conditions."[7] Integration, or unity of the personality, or self-consistency, she felt, is useful as a criterion, though it is not acceptable alone, since it doesn't imply freedom from conflicts with the environment. Correct perception of reality, both of the world and of oneself, while difficult to establish (since the majority judgment is not necessarily correct), is still useful as a criterion.[8] (One is reminded of the remark of Nathaniel Lee, the English dramatist, on being confined to the Bedlam insane asylum: "The world and I differed as to my being mad, and I was outvoted."[9]) Jahoda thus proposed a triple criterion, in which Smith concurred.[10]

This proposal, or solution, to the problem of the nature of mental health, or of the goal of counseling or psychotherapy, does not seem to have been adopted or to have influenced the field, though a considerable period of time has elapsed during which it has received attention. Thus, we are still in need of an integrating concept that can encompass the suggested goals, which are of varied degrees of specificity as well as varying widely in nature. A resolution of this problem is offered here.

A LEVELS CONCEPT OF GOALS

One of the difficulties of specifying or agreeing upon the goals of psychotherapy is the fact that the goals stated by different writers vary in specificity, or, to use another term, in level. If goals could be organized in terms of levels, perhaps we would find, or gain, greater agreement. Parloff proposed two levels of goals—mediating and ultimate. Mediating goals, according to his classification, are those that are aspects of the psychotherapy process, for example, recovery of repressed memories. He notes that while there may be great differences in mediating goals, "differences in the stated ultimate goals will in all likelihood be small."[11] Halleck, discussing the need for study of the optimum human condition, writes that "probably no two psychiatrists would agree on what was best for a given patient on any specific issue, but they might eventually discover that there are a few general principles that could provide guidelines for intervention."[12] It is to this problem that the search for, and agreement upon, ultimate goals is directed.

Ultimate Goals

Ultimate goals are broad and general in nature. They are concerned with long-term outcomes. They relate to the questions, What do we want to be? What should people strive to be? What should people be like? What kind of persons do we want and need? These questions have been the concern of philosophers since before Aristotle.

We have noted that Jahoda's concept of positive mental health doesn't appear to be adequate. Two other recent suggested concepts are White's concept of competence[13] and psychological effectiveness. Both Bonner and Maslow have pointed out that competence conceptualizes behavior in the adjustment framework.[14] One must ask, Competence for what? and Effectiveness for what? These questions indicate the need for a criterion of competence and effectiveness, so that these cannot themselves be the criterion. An ultimate goal must itself be the criterion.

There are a number of terms or concepts which appear to transcend these limitations and to constitute an ultimate goal. These terms include self-realization, self-enhancement, the fully functioning person, and self-actualization. Perhaps the most commonly used term is the last. It is proposed here that self-actualization is the ultimate goal of counseling or psychotherapy.

There are a number of aspects, or significant characteristics of this concept, in addition to its constituting a criterion in the sense that it is not vulnerable to the question, For what? First, it is a goal that avoids the problems of the adjustment model. It eliminates the criticism that counseling or psychotherapy is a process that is establishment-oriented and conformity-inducing. Second, it eliminates the conflict between intrapersonal and interpersonal goals. Self-actualization involves both aspects of the person. Third, when adequately defined and understood, it eliminates the individual-versus-society dilemma. Williamson's objection that self-actualization is unacceptable because the individual might actualize his potentialities for evil, or his bestial aspects, is based upon a misconception of the nature of self-actualization, confusing it with selfishness or uninhibited self-expression.[15] But the individual lives with other people and in the society at large. He needs other people. He has a basic need or desire to associate with others, and he needs them if he is to exist in society. Rogers says that there is no need to be concerned about controlling man's aggressive, antisocial impulses in a society of self-actualizing persons. The individual's need for affection or companionship, for example, will balance any aggressive reaction or extreme need for sex, or other needs that would interfere with the satisfaction of fellow individuals. He "will live with others in the maximum possible harmony, because of the rewarding character of reciprocal positive regard."[16] Thus, "we do not need to ask who will socialize him, for one of his own deepest needs is for affiliation and communication with others. As he becomes more fully himself, he will become more realistically socialized."[17]

A fourth important characteristic of self-actualization is that it is not an isolated goal of counseling or psychotherapy, a treatment for disturbed or abnormal individuals. It is a goal that goes beyond the absence of disturbance, disorder, mental "illness," and the like. It is a positive goal, a goal for the so-called "normal" person who feels dissatisfied, unhappy, unfulfilled, and seeks the help of counseling or psychotherapy. In fact, self-actualization is a goal for all persons. It is the goal of life. And as such it is, or should be, the goal of society and of all its institutions—religion, education, marriage, the family, and occupations or vocations. Thus, counseling or psychotherapy is of a piece with the rest of life. Its purpose is to contribute with other social institutions to the personal development and fulfillment of the individual. In fact, counseling or psychotherapy is an institution which has been developed in and by society to provide special assistance to those whose progress toward self-actualization has been blocked or interrupted in a particular way, specifically by the lack of good human relationships.

A fifth significant aspect of self-actualization as a goal is that it is not static. It is not something to be achieved once and for all. It is a process, the process of becoming. Self-actualizing is a better term to designate this continuing process. The goal, then, is the development of self-actualizing persons. This aspect brings the concept of self-actualization within the existential framework. It is not an end—or rather, the end is the process.

There is a final aspect of self-actualization that is particularly significant. We have been talking in terms of goals. Yet goals are related to drives or motives. Thus, when we talk about the goal of life, we become involved in drives, motives, or needs, since goals are influenced by, if not determined by, needs. The ultimate goal of counseling or psychotherapy—and of life itself—should be directly related to the basic need of human beings. *Self-actualization is not only the goal of life—it is the basic motive of human beings.* Goldstein was perhaps the first to use this term to indicate basic motivation when he stated that "an organism is governed by a tendency to actualize, as much as possible, its individual capacities, its 'nature' in the world."[18] Combs and Snygg, in their perceptual theory of human behavior, refer to the maintenance and enhancement of the self, which they equate with self-actualization, as the "all inclusive human need which motivates all behavior in all times and in all places."[19] Rogers has said that "the organism has one basic tendency and striving—to actualize, maintain and enhance the experiencing organism."[20] This single basic drive appears to be inherent in the human organism and, though based upon a value orientation, to have a biological basis. Ashley Montagu, the distinguished anthropologist, emphasizes a biological basis for human values:

> We can here demonstrate that there are certain values for human life which are not matters of opinion, but which are biologically determined. If we do violence to these inbuilt values, we disorder our lives, as persons, as groups, as nations, and as a world of human beings.[21]

Self-actualization is the basic inbuilt value in human beings.

Thus, the concept of self-actualization provides a single universal goal, or common need, not only for counseling or psychotherapy and all helping relationships, but for life. Counseling or psychotherapy is thus consistent with life and living, and its goal is not something apart from life and everyday living but inherent in it. This goal is implicit, if not explicit, in the writings of many counselors and psychotherapists. Mahrer recognizes it in his attempt to summarize the apparently diverse goals of the authors represented in his book when he included "achieving optimal functioning" as a common characteristic of many of their statements.[22] Rollo May states that "the goal of therapy is to help the patient actualize his potentialities."[23]

The concept of self-actualization provides an integrating term for incorporating many, if not most, of the broad, general goals of psychotherapy expressed by writers in the field, as well as for the goals and objectives of life developed by many philosophers. It can encompass Freud's genital man, Jung's individuation, Adler's perfection, Binswanger's authentic one, even Frankl's will to meaning. For although Frankl suggested that self-actualization is a by-product of the attainment of meaning, it would seem that it is actually self-actualization that gives life itself meaning. Even the behaviorists recognize that these are desirable outcomes beyond their specific objectives. Wolpe, in describing the results of his treatment, includes general changes such as "increased productiveness, . . . improved interpersonal relationships—and ability to handle psychological conflict and reasonable stresses."[24]

Many philosophers in their search for the ultimate good have arrived at concepts closely resembling self-actualization. Aristotle's highest or supreme good was in effect self-actualization; man's basic function (or motivation) is to exercise his highest capacities.[25] This concept of the development of one's potentials as the goal of life has persisted in the writings of other philosophers (for example, Locke and Rousseau) as well as in those of many psychologists.

The Immediate Goal and Mediate Goals

The immediate goal in counseling or psychotherapy is to set in motion and to continue the process that will lead to the client's achievement of the ultimate goal. The mediating goals of Parloff are aspects of the process and thus would be considered immediate goals. The counseling or therapy process as the immediate goal will be considered in detail in Chapters 6 and 7.

As the model presented here was being developed, a third level of goals, designated mediate goals, was included.

A category of mediate goals was considered desirable for two reasons. First, the ultimate goal is a common goal, universal for all clients, in all situations and cultures. It was felt that there should be a level of goals that would allow for the presence of individual differences, or the various ways in which individuals might actualize themselves. Second, such a level would meet the demand of the behaviorists and others for more specific, concrete goals, which again would vary among individuals. In an earlier model, mediate goals were considered to be subgoals, or steps toward the ultimate goal. In turn, the ultimate goal of self-actualization would serve as a criterion for the acceptance or rejection of mediate goals as justifiable or desirable goals.

Examples of mediate goals would be such things as achieving educational levels necessary for the full utilization of one's potentials (thus, not dropping out of school) ; obtaining employment (since holding a job is usually considered necessary for self-actualization in our society) ; saving or, if desirable, terminating a marriage; and other more specific goals such as eliminating phobias, examination anxiety, and fear of public speaking.

Two things became apparent, however, as the model developed. First, many of the more specific goals were the objectives of other helping processes, in terms of the continuum presented in Chapter 1; that is, they involved education or reeducation or skill training. Second, it became apparent that, in many cases at least, these specific goals or subgoals can be considered not only as steps toward self-actualization but as by-products of self-actualization. That is, as the person becomes more self-actualized—more open, free, independent or autonomous, more aware of himself, others, and his environment, and more capable in interpersonal relationships—he is able to achieve these goals himself, on his own, or to seek and obtain the specific assistance—such as tutoring, skill instruction, information, education or reeducation—necessary to achieve them.

The by-products of self-actualization are different for individual clients. As by-products, they are not necessarily goals to be directly achieved or specifically sought. Indeed, they need not be considered or planned for in advance as outcomes, thus avoiding the problem of determining in advance specific outcomes, which may only be developed by the client during or even following therapy.

It thus appears to be sufficient, at least in some cases, to provide the conditions leading to the development of self-actualizing persons. As the individual becomes more self-actualizing, he develops, seeks, and achieves his own more specific goals. That this actually does occur is indicated by research showing that a good therapeutic relationship leads to a wide variety of changes, including the achievement of specific goals, in a wide variety of clients with a wide variety of problems (see Chapter 9).

VALUES AND PSYCHOTHERAPY

Goals are values. Therefore, in his choice or acceptance of a goal, or goals, the values of the therapist enter into psychotherapy.

The view that the values of the therapist should be kept out of therapy is no longer accepted. Indeed, it is now recognized that the therapist's values cannot be kept out of therapy, if only because goals are values and all therapists are concerned with goals. Since methods are related to goals, as means to ends, values also enter into the therapy process. A therapist who values independence, or client responsibility, for example, will behave differently in the therapy relationship than a therapist who does not value these goals.

The influence of the therapist's values goes beyond this, however, entering into the nature of what the client discusses and into the reactions of the therapist in this direction. If therapists value dreams, their clients dream and report their dreams; if therapists value sexual material, or any other particular kind of content, their clients produce it, thus "validating" the theories of their therapists. Moreover, therapists respond to the client's productions from a value orientation, whether they are aware of it or not. It might even be contended that if the therapist were amoral (and especially if defensively so), he would be unable to empathize with a client in a moral conflict and thus be unable to help him. Further, this value orientation is communicated to some extent, at least, in words, tone of voice, or nonverbal ways, whether the therapist intends to or not. Thus therapists are not neutral in their values, and it is not possible for them to conceal their values from the client.

Ingham and Love were among the earliest to recognize the intrusion of the therapist's values into the therapy:

> The existence of the therapeutic relationship puts the therapist in a position in which he does, without choice, influence values in the mind of the patient. It is almost impossible for a therapist to avoid giving some impression of whether he favors such things as general law and order, personal self-development, and emotional maturity. The development of the relationship partly depends on the expression of such standards, because if the therapist were able to withdraw to such an extent that no evaluative attitudes would be apparent, he would not be able to participate sufficiently. But in an area in which the therapist does avoid

revealing his ideas, the patient will project some onto him. So even if he could keep complete silence, he would still represent judgmental attitudes in the mind of the patient. If they have discussed an issue that involves moral values for a period of time, it is evident that the patient will have a concept of what the therapist thinks. His attitudes about right and wrong, or good and bad, are likely to be particularly influential for the patient.[26]

Wolberg, in a comment on a paper by Ginsburg, writes that:

> No matter how passive the therapist may believe himself to be, and no matter how objective he remains in an attempt to permit the patient to develop his own sense of values, there is an inevitable incorporation within the patient of a new super-ego patterned after the character of the therapist as he is perceived by the patient. There is almost inevitably an acceptance by the patient of many of the values of the therapist as they are communicated in the interpretation or through direct suggestion, or as they are deduced by the patient from his association with the therapist.[27]

Parloff notes that "the disclosure of many of the therapist's values is inevitable . . . such disclosure and communication may occur without the therapist being aware of it."[28] It might be expected that the therapist, by reason of his position and prestige, would be an example or model for the client, who would tend to pattern himself after the therapist, intentionally or unintentionally.

An early study by Rosenthal provides evidence for the therapist's influence. Rosenthal studied 12 patients with a wide variety of diagnoses, ages 18 to 46, with from three weeks to one year of psychotherapy. The patients and their therapists were given a series of tests early in therapy and at the conclusion of treatment. Patients' scores on a test of moral values changed over therapy; those patients rated as improved became more like their therapists, while those rated as unimproved tended to become less like their therapists.[29] Parloff and his associates also found similar results. Observers listed topics discussed by two schizophrenic patients. The patients and therapists ranked them from most to least important after each therapy hour. After nine months, therapists and patients predicted each others' rankings. At the beginning of therapy the values (as indicated by the ranking of topics) of both patients differed from those of the therapist. As therapy progressed, the patients' values came closer to those of the therapist, though for one patient no further convergence occurred after the first six weeks.[30]

The recognition that the values of the therapist cannot be kept out of psychotherapy and do influence the client makes it incumbent on the therapist to decide how he will deal with his values. In the first place, he must be aware of his values, not only as they are represented in his goals, but in other areas of behavior. Second, he must decide whether or not he should deliberately attempt to influence the client's values, and if so, which values and in what ways.

There is disagreement upon whether the therapist should attempt to inculcate specific values in his client. Wilder, commenting upon Ginsburg's paper, states that "it has been taken for granted that the analyst must not try to impose his value systems on the patient, and I still think this to be true." Wilder recognizes that there are "rising voices to the effect that the analyst not only does but should transmit his own value system to the patient" and notes that "a patient often says 'Doctor, after all, you seem to have found a measure of peace and stability, why don't you shorten the therapy by simply telling me your philosophy.' "[31] Weisskopf-Joelson proposes that the inculcation of a philosophy of life be considered as one of the objectives of psychotherapy.[32] Thorne includes reeducation in a philosophy of life as a method of counseling.[33] Ellis' rational-emotive psychotherapy is essentially instruction in a philosophy of life.[34] Viktor Frankl also instructs clients in values and an approach to life.[35]

There are a number of reasons why it might be undesirable for a therapist to indoctrinate clients or attempt to inculcate a philosophy of life in his clients.

First of all, while there are no doubt some generally, or even universally, accepted principles or ethical standards or rules, these do not constitute a philosophy of life. Each individual's philosophy, while sharing much in common with others, particularly in his culture, is unique. No individual's philosophy is adequate for another individual.

Second, it is too much to expect all counselors or psychotherapists to have a fully developed, adequate, generally accepted philosophy of life ready to be impressed on clients. Murphy, while admitting that "no one knows enough to construct an adequate philosophy of life," says that "it is not true that the wise man's sharing of a philosophy of life is an arrogant imposition upon a defenseless client."[36] Unfortunately, all counselors are not "wise men."

Third, it may be questioned whether the counseling relationship is the appropriate place for direct instruction in ethics and a philosophy of life. The home, the church, and the school are more appropriate places for such instruction. Particularly appropriate for the consideration of alternative philosophies and ethical systems is the school.

Fourth, an individual usually does not adopt a system or code of ethics or a philosophy of life from one source and at a particular time. These are products of many influences over a long period of time.

Fifth, it would appear to be best for each individual to develop his own unique philosophy from many sources and not to be deprived of the experience of doing so. Such a philosophy will probably be more meaningful and useful than one adopted readymade from someone else, no matter how wise a man he may be. It cannot be imposed from without but must be developed from within.

Sixth, we must still accept the right of the client to refuse to accept or develop any system of ethics or any philosophy of life and to accept or suffer the consequences.

This does not mean that the counselor should refuse to discuss ethics, values, or a philosophy of life. In the process of doing so, he may, sometimes at the request of the client, disclose and discuss his own values, always clearly identifying them as his own preferences and avoiding the implication that the client ought to accept them. There may also be times when the counselor, whether by request of the client or not, feels it necessary not only to state his own attitudes and values but to inform the client of the attitudes, ethics, or values of society— or some part of society.

The counselor is not amoral or neutral, and he should not pretend to be. To do so may lead to the danger of appearing not only to accept the client's unethical or immoral behavior but of approving or condoning it.

This approach to values has several advantages. By recognizing that the counselor's moral attitudes and values do enter into counseling, it prevents the counselor from erroneously believing that he is neutral. Freed of this belief and the feeling that it is necessary or desirable to be neutral, he is better able to recognize and accept his own values. He can then be aware of them in the counseling relationship; and, when he feels that the relationship would be improved by his expressing his own attitudes and feelings, he can do so. That is, he can freely be himself, without guilt about being so or without feeling that he should not have any feelings. Thus, this approach contributes to the openness and honesty of the counseling relationship. When the counselor's attitudes, beliefs, and feelings are unexpressed (and even unrecognized by the counselor), they may (and apparently do) have a pressuring influence on the client. Where they are expressed by the counselor and labeled as his own values or point of view or identified as those of others or of society in general, there is less coerciveness about them.

This approach also distinguishes counseling or psychotherapy from the didactic teaching of values or a philosophy of life and from religious proselytization.

But it must be recognized that the therapist does influence the client—that he does teach in the sense that being a model is teaching.

The important question then becomes, What should the counselor be a model for? The answer is that the counselor should be a model for what he wants his client to become—a self-actualizing person. He should be a model of facilitative interpersonal relationships, since this is what the client needs to become a self-actualizing person. The characteristics of this model will be considered in the next chapter.

WHO DETERMINES GOALS?

Whether the client or the counselor should determine goals has been a troublesome question, with the behaviorists insisting that the client should determine his own goals. Yet, the therapist has his own goals. Many feel, however, that the therapist should not impose his own goals on the client. Should the therapist abandon his own goals and accept those of the client?

The model presented here provides a solution to this dilemma. The problem of the therapist imposing his own goals on the client arises when therapists have a variety of relatively specific goals, which may not be relevant to all clients. The acceptance of a single, broad, ultimate goal applicable to all clients would change this situation. The reluctance of therapists to adopt such a goal is based upon the difficulties of defining a goal that appears to be applicable or best for all clients. Halleck points out that "philosophers, theologians, political scientists, and psychologists have struggled with this problem for centuries, searching for value systems founded upon religious beliefs, social utility, ethical relativism, or human biology."[37] Self-actualization is a goal that more and more psychologists and psychotherapists appear to be adopting.

If self-actualization is seen not only as a goal but as the basic, dominant motive of life, then its acceptance as a goal does not mean that the therapist is imposing an external, arbitrary goal upon his clients. He is recognizing and accepting a goal that is inherent in the client himself. The ultimate goal is not determined by either the therapist or the client but by life itself.

Within the context of the ultimate goal, the client has the freedom to determine subgoals. Therapists who disclaim any ultimate goal or who are unaware of their implicit (and more specific) goals, may impose their own goals on the client without being aware of it. This may be encouraged by the fact that many clients, when they enter therapy, have no clear or explicit goals. Halleck notes that "if the therapist takes time to investigate a patient's social situation, he will usually find that when the patient enters therapy he doesn't have a clear idea of what he wants. The patient comes to the therapist in the role of a supplicant."[38] Therapists sometimes disagree with or refuse to accept the stated goals of the client. The behaviorists often appear to direct or force the client into having a problem or goal which their technique can deal with, ignoring or rejecting other problems or goals as being too vague, general, or not susceptible of operational definition.

The specific goals of therapy are selected by the client, in terms of their contribution toward his becoming a more self-actualizing person, or, from another point of view, they are by-products of his increasing self-actualization. As a more fully self-actualizing person, he is then more capable of achieving these specific goals. If he requires assistance from others—information, education, training, or reeducation—he seeks and obtains it, or he may be referred by the therapist to sources of such specific help.

Self-actualization is the goal not only of psychotherapy, but, since it is the basic motivation of the human being, it is, or should be, the goal of society and all its institutions—the family, the school, the church. It is the goal of all helping relationships. The various kinds of helping relationships referred to in Chapter 1 are concerned, each in its own way, with facilitating self-actualization. Counseling or psychotherapy is only one way of facilitating self-actualization. It is appropriate for those individuals whose self-actualization is prevented or inhibited by the lack of, or the inadequacy of, good human relationships.

SUMMARY

This chapter is concerned with the goals of counseling or psychotherapy. Since goals are values, the place of values in psychotherapy is also considered.

Two levels of goals are proposed, an ultimate goal and an immediate goal. The ultimate goal is the development of self-actualizing persons. This is a goal that is inherent in the human organism and is common to all clients. The possibility of an intermediate level of goals, which might be called subgoals, varying with different clients, is considered and rejected. It is proposed instead that the more specific behavior changes that are often considered to be goals or outcomes of therapy (and that do vary among clients) are by-products of self-actualization. The person who, as a result of the therapy relationship, becomes a more self-actualizing person, moves toward the achievement of these goals or changes on his own, seeking and obtaining where necessary or desirable the specific kinds of help he wants.

The immediate goal of counseling or psychotherapy is the initiating and continuing of the therapeutic process or relationship, which leads to the client becoming a more self-actualizing person.

NOTES

[1] A. R. Mahrer (Ed.). *The goals of psychotherapy*. New York: Appleton-Century-Crofts, 1967, p. 1.

[2] J. Wolpe. Behavior therapy and psychotherapeutic goals. In Mahrer, *Goals of psychotherapy*, pp. 129–144.

[3] V. E. Frankl. *The doctor and the soul* (2nd ed.). New York: Knopf, 1965.

[4] Arthur Burton. *Interpersonal psychotherapy*. Englewood Cliffs, N.J.: Prentice-Hall, 1972, pp. 10–11.

[5] Marie Jahoda. Toward a sociology of mental health. In M. J. E Senn (Ed.). *Symposium on the healthy personality*. Supplement II. *Problems of infancy and childhood*. New York: Josiah Macy Foundation, 1950.

[6] S. L. Halleck. *The politics of therapy*. New York: Science House, 1971.

[7] Jahoda. Toward a sociology of mental health.

[8] Marie Jahoda. *Current concepts of positive mental health*. New York: Basic Books, 1958.

[9] Cited in S. De Grazia. *Errors in psychotherapy*. Garden City, N.Y.: Doubleday, 1952, p. 146.

[10] M. B. Smith. Optima of mental health: A general frame of reference. *Psychiatry*, 1950, **13**, 503–510.

[11] M. B. Parloff. Goals in psychotherapy: Mediating and ultimate. In Mahrer, *Goals of psychotherapy*, pp. 5–19.

[12] Halleck, *Politics of therapy*, pp. 197–198.

[13] R. W. White. Motivation reconsidered: The concept of competence. *Psychological Review*, 1959, **66**, 297–333.

[14] H. Bonner. *On being mindful of man*. Boston: Houghton Mifflin, 1965, p. 190. A. H. Maslow. *Toward a psychology of being*. Princeton, N.J.: Van Nostrand Reinhold, 1962, pp. 168–169.

[15] E. G. Williamson. A concept of counseling. *Occupations*, 1950, **29**, 182–189; E. G. Williamson. Value orientation in counseling. *Personnel and Guidance Journal*, 1958, **37**, 520–528; E. G. Williamson. The societal responsibilities of counselors. *Illinois Guidance and Personnel Association Newsletter*, 1963, Winter, 5–13.

[16] C. R. Rogers. A theory of therapy, personality and interpersonal relations. In S. Koch (Ed.). *Psychology: A study of science. Study I: Conceptual and systematic. Vol. 3: Formulations of the person and the social context*. New York: McGraw-Hill, 1959, pp. 184–256.

[17] C. R. Rogers. A therapist's view of the good life: The fully functioning person. In C. R. Rogers (Ed.). *On becoming a person*. Boston: Houghton Mifflin, 1961, p. 194.

[18] K. Goldstein. *The organism*. New York: Harcourt Brace Jovanovich, 1939, p. 196.

[19] A. W. Combs and D. Snygg. *Individual behavior*. New York: Harper & Row, 1959, p. 38.

[20] C. R. Rogers. *Client-centered therapy*. Boston: Houghton Mifflin, 1951, p. 195.

[21] Ashley Montagu. *On being human*. New York: Hawthorn Books, 1950.

[22] Mahrer, *Goals of psychotherapy*.

[23] Rollo May. *Psychology and the human dilemma*. Princeton, N.J.: Van Nostrand Reinhold, 1967, p. 109.

24 J. Wolpe. *Psychotherapy by reciprocal inhibition.* Stanford: Stanford University Press, 1958, p. 200.

25 Aristotle, *Ethics,* I, 7, 1098a.

26 H. V. Ingham and Leonore R. Love. *The process of psychotherapy.* New York: McGraw-Hill, 1954, pp. 75–76.

27 S. W. Ginsburg and J. L. Herma. Values and their relationship to psychiatric principles and practice. *American Journal of Psychotherapy,* 1953, **7,** 546–473.

28 M. B. Parloff. Communication of values and therapeutic change. Paper presented at the Annual Convention, American Psychological Association, New York, August 31, 1957; M. B. Parloff. Therapist-patient relationship and outcome of psychotherapy. *Journal of Consulting Psychology,* 1961, **25,** 29–38.

29 D. Rosenthal. Changes in some moral values following psychotherapy. *Journal of Consulting Psychology,* 1955, **19,** 431–436.

30 M. B. Parloff, B. Iflund and N. Goldstein. Communication of "therapy values" between therapist and schizophrenic patients. *Journal of Nervous and Mental Disease,* 1960, **130,** 193–199.

31 Ginsburg and Herma, Values.

32 Edith Weisskopf-Joelson. Some suggestions concerning Weltanschauüng and psychotherapy. *Journal of Abnormal and Social Psychology,* 1953, **48,** 601–604.

33 F. C. Thorne. *Psychological case handling.* Brandon, Vt.: Clinical Psychology Publishing Co., 1968.

34 A. Ellis. *Reason and emotion in psychotherapy.* New York: Lyle Stuart, 1953.

35 V. E. Frankl. *The doctor and the soul* (2nd ed.) . New York: Knopf, 1965.

36 G. Murphy. The cultural context of guidance. *Personnel and Guidance Journal,* 1955, **34,** 4–9.

37 Halleck, *Politics of therapy,* p. 196.

38 *Ibid.,* p. 80.

Chapter 3

The Nature
of Self-Actualization

A major criticism of goals such as self-actualization is that they are too general, broad, and amorphous to be useful. The behaviorists, particularly, ask for operational definitions in terms of specific behaviors. This is a legitimate question. If a concept is significant and pertinent, it can, at least in principle or eventually, be reduced to specific, objective, or measurable variables. However, the process of doing so may require considerable time and effort. It is indefensible to reject out of hand, as the behaviorists sometimes do, any concept or objective that cannot be immediately, easily, and objectively measured. Simplicity, or ease of measurement, is not an appropriate criterion. To refuse to be concerned with anything that cannot now be objectively measured is to rule out of consideration many potentially significant and important concepts and to delay progress in attempts to define, objectify, and measure them.

Some progress has already been made in defining and objectifying the concept of self-actualization. This chapter is concerned with the results of efforts in this direction. First, however, it is desirable that we consider the theoretical background from which the concept of self-actualization has developed.

THE NATURE OF MAN

Man as an Active as Well as a Reactive Being

Allport has described three concepts or images of man.[1] The first concept is that of man as a reactive being. Man is an object, a biological organism, responding to the stimuli in his environment. His behavior is determined by the stimuli to which he is exposed. Past stimuli have made him what he is. His present and future are determined by past stimuli and the potential stimuli that he will encounter. Thus, he is not free to determine his own behavior. His behavior is reflexive, reactive, or responsive to external stimuli, rewards, or reinforcements. Though it may exist, consciousness—thinking and feeling—is irrelevant in the study of man's behavior. This is the traditional or "scientific" approach to man, the view of stimulus-response psychology and of the behaviorists, exemplified by J. B. Watson and B. F. Skinner.

The second concept is that of man as a reactive being in depth. Man is a result of his past experiences, and his past as well as present and future are determined by his internal drives or instincts. Chief among these drives or instincts are sex or libido and death or aggression. This is the view of depth psychologies, chief among which is psychoanalysis.

Allport contrasts a third concept of man with these two, which he calls man in the process of becoming. This model sees man as proactive, as personal, conscious, and future-oriented. He is in control of his behavior and of his destiny (within limits, of course). This is the model of existentialism and humanistic psychology.

These three concepts or images of man can be reduced to two apparently opposing models. The first two concepts are similar, presenting man as a reactive being, whether in response to his environment or to his instincts and drives. He reacts to stimuli from without and from within. Thus, in the first model, man is controlled by stimuli, a victim of his environment and his innate drives. The second model, of man in the process of becoming, reverses this view. Man is a determiner, not determined; he is not controlled but controls, both his environment and himself. He has something to say about what he shall do or become.

Man's behavior is less controlled by instinct than is any other animal's. Rather than being manipulated by his environment, he manipulates his environment for his own purposes. He is not a creature of instinct or of environmental stimuli alone—of the past and of the present alone. Unlike the animals, he has a future and is forward-looking, influenced by anticipation, expectation, and foresight. In fact, he creates, to some extent at least, his own environment, his own world.

He is free, within limits, of course, and since he is free, he can and must make choices. And since he is free to choose, he is responsible for his choices and his behavior.

These two models of man are in conflict. They appear to be antithetical, so that one is compelled to choose one or the other. The prevailing view of man, the one that is fostered by our current scientific approach, is that of man as a reactive being, as determined. The concept of freedom appears to be inconsistent with the assumption of determinism. Moreover, there is overwhelming support in psychology for the view that man is a reactive being. We cannot reject or deny this view. But must we then, as the behaviorists insist, reject the existentialist or humanistic view?

The difficulty is stating the problem as an either/or choice. It is not necessary to accept one view and reject the other. The solution is to recognize that neither model alone is a complete or accurate model of man. Each, by itself, gives us only a partial view. The reactive model is a limited one, a "nothing but" model. But man is this and "something more." This something more is significant, even crucial, in understanding man and his behavior and in developing an adequate theory of human behavior. The danger of the reactive model is not that it is true, but that it is regarded as the whole truth. If man is treated as nothing but a reactive object, he will in fact become one.

A major difficulty in accepting the humanistic view is the freedom-determinism dilemma. Philosophy has never—and may never—resolve this dilemma, and it is not possible here, nor necessary, to go into its philosophical aspects. Science has accepted determinism—at least at this point it appears to be a necessary assumption. But science, especially psychology, must recognize and deal with human experience. A major aspect of human experience is the influence of beliefs—or assumptions—on human behavior. There are two factors related to the freedom-determinism dilemma that must be recognized. The first is the fact of the psychological existence of the feeling or experience of freedom and choice in the individual. This feeling or experience must be recognized and included in any theory of human behavior. Second, and of perhaps more importance, is the fact that beliefs exert an influence upon behavior. It makes a tremendous difference in our conception of man and in the way human beings act and in the way they deal with each other whether the assumption of determinism or of freedom is accepted. To view a man as free means that we treat him differently than if we view him as completely determined, and our different treatment of him leads to different behavior on his part.

To accept the existence of freedom does not necessitate rejection of the existence of causation, or control, or order. Freedom would be

meaningless without the existence of control. Freedom is not an absolute, but a matter of degree. Freedom in the psychological sense is the
introduction of the individual himself as a causal or controlling factor
in his behavior.

The behaviorists emphasize that the environment, through its
rewards, selects and molds the individual's behavior. Yet, from another
point of view, it is the individual who selects the responses that produce what to him is rewarding or desirable. And this is often done in a
conscious manner, with the experience of choice. The term "instru-
mental response" carries this connotation of choice and purpose. This
view is represented by the cartoon of the rat in a Skinner box pressing
a bar to receive pellets. The caption read (if my memory is correct)
something like this: "Look how I've got him conditioned. Every time
I press this bar he gives me a pellet." The insistence of the behaviorists that everything is externally determined, while at the same time
they talk about the control and creation of environments also illustrates the paradox, or the importance of the point of view one takes.
Behavior is determined, but not entirely by the environment. Man
is also a determiner of his own behavior.

Man is a living, active being, not an inactive object waiting to be
stimulated. He searches for stimuli and seeks experiences. He orga-
nizes stimuli and the environment, the world, in terms of his needs, or
actually in terms of his single basic need, the preservation and enhancement of himself—self-actualization.

Man Is Inherently Good

In Chapter 1 we touched upon the problem of whether self-
actualization might not include the actualization of a selfish, antisocial self. We suggested that, because man's needs involve other
persons, he would not find it possible to become self-actualizing
without obtaining from others their companionship and cooperation.
However, this can be seen as the conditioning of man's behavior
through positive and negative reinforcement, leaving open the issue
of whether man is innately bad.

Many, if not most, religions view man as innately depraved. Freud
was pessimistic regarding man's nature. He believed that the individual's instincts were antisocial and must be controlled by culture or
society:

It does not appear certain that without coercion the majority of
human individuals would be ready to submit to the labour necessary for acquiring new means of supporting life. One has, I think,
to reckon with the fact that there are present in all men destruc-

tive, and therefore anti-social and anti-cultural, tendencies, and that with a great number of people these are strong enough to determine their behavior in society.[2]

Man is not only antisocial but actually hostile to other men, according to Freud:

> Civilized society is perpetually menaced with disintegration through this primary hostility of men toward one another. . . . Culture has to call up every possible reinforcement in order to erect barriers against the aggressive instinct of man.[3]

Aggression has long been considered an instinct. Adler originally proposed that aggression was the single basic motive or instinct of man.[4] The strength and practical universality of aggression argue for its innateness. However, many have questioned its innateness or instinctiveness. Anthropologists have found societies with little trace or evidence of aggression.[5] Ashley Montagu writes:

> My own interpretation of the evidence, strictly within the domain of science, leads me to the conclusion that man is born good and is organized in such a manner from birth as to need to grow and develop his potentialities for goodness. . . . [The view that aggressiveness is inherited] is not scientifically corroborated. In fact, *all* the available evidence gathered by competent investigators indicates that man is born without a trace of aggressiveness.[6]

He refers to Lauretta Bender's finding that hostility in the child is a symptom complex resulting from deprivation in development. Charlotte Buhler in her studies of infants also found that there is "evidence of a primary orientation toward 'reality' into which the baby moves with a positive anticipation of good things to be found. Only when this reality appears to be hurtful or overwhelming does the reaction become one of withdrawal or defense."[7] Maslow also declares that impulses of hate, jealousy, hostility, and so on are acquired. "More and more," he writes, "aggression is coming to be regarded as a technique or mode of compelling attention to the satisfaction of one's need."[8] There is no instinct of aggression that seeks expression or discharge without provocation or without regard to circumstances.

In other words, aggression is not primary but is a reaction to deprivation, threat, or frustration. This is the frustration-aggression hypothesis put forward in 1939 by the Yale anthropologist Dollard and his psychologist associates.[9] A more general term for the stimuli that provoke aggression is threat. Aggression is universal because threat, in some form or other, is universal. The psychoanalyst Bibring, in criticizing Freud's theories, questions "whether there are any phenomena of aggression at all outside the field of the ego-preservative functions" and notes "the empirical fact that aggressiveness appears only or almost only when the life instincts or the ego instincts are exposed to harm."[10] A popular novel purporting to demonstrate the innateness of aggressiveness in man inadvertently supports the view that aggression is the result of threat, since the development of aggression in the group of castaway boys occurs under conditions of fear and feelings of being threatened.[11]

There is evidence that man is inherently good in the continual striving toward an ideal society, with the repeated and independent development of essentially similar religious and ethical systems whose ideals have withstood the test of time. In spite of deprivation, threat, and frustration, these ideals have been held and practiced by many individuals. Mankind has developed systems of government and law that, though imperfectly, especially in their applications, represent these ideals.

It might actually be argued that goodness or cooperation has a survival value[12] and that innate aggression would be selectively eliminated by evolution. If there were not an inherent drive toward good in man, or if aggression were innate, it is difficult to understand how the human race could have continued to survive. The potential for good has survived in the face of continued threat and frustration. When we can reduce deprivation and threat, the manifestations of good will increase and aggression will decrease. It is important to add that aggression does not include assertive behavior, initiative behavior, nor even much of competitive behavior. The confusion of these kinds of behavior with aggression has perhaps contributed to the belief that aggression is innate.

Emotional disturbance, an important manifestation of which, in many people, is aggression, is the result of the frustration of the drive toward self-actualization by a threatening, deprived, or misunderstanding social environment.

Man Has a Single Basic Motivation

In Chapter 2 we stated that the single basic motivation of all human beings is the actualization of one's potentials. A number of psychologists have reached this conclusion, apparently independently, including Goldstein, Angyal, Rogers, and Combs and Snygg. Angyal defines life as a "process of self-expansion" and adds that "the tendency of the organism is toward increased autonomy," or a tendency toward self-determination. He also refers to self-realization as being the intrinsic purpose of life.[13] Lecky, impressed by the integration and organization of the self, felt that a need for self-consistency and its preservation is the single basic need of the organism.[14]

Self-actualization is a part of Rogers' general organismic actualizing tendency: "The organism has one basic tendency and striving—to actualize, maintain, and enhance the experiencing organism."[15] Rogers also uses terms such as independence, self-determination, integration, and self-actualization. Thus, although writers use different terms—self-enhancement, self-fulfilment, self-realization, self-actualization—to designate the single basic motivation of all human beings, they all seem to be referring to the same concept or phenomenon. Man is by nature engaged in the process of actualizing his potentials.

Combs and Snygg have perhaps developed the unitary theory of motivation most extensively:

> From birth to death the maintenance of the phenomenal self is the most pressing, the most crucial, if not the only task of existence. . . . Man seeks not only the maintenance of *a* self. . . . Man seeks both to maintain and enhance his perceived self.[16]

The use of the terms preservation and maintenance along with enhancement and actualization poses the question of whether there aren't actually two motives. Maslow perhaps was influenced by some such consideration in his concept of deficiency motivation and growth motivation.[17]

But preservation or maintenance, and enhancement or actualization, may be seen as two aspects of the same motive operating under different conditions. Adler recognized the different expression of the same motive in neurotics and normals. The neurotic, threatened and compensating for deep feelings of inferiority, reacts to preserve or restore his self-esteem, or to overcome his inferiority with superiority through a striving for power. The normal individual, on the other hand, free of threat and without feelings of inferiority, can strive for completeness or perfection.[18] For the unhealthy, disturbed, or abnormal individual under stress and threatened, enhancement or positive striving is impossible. He must defend himself against attack or threat, and strive to safeguard, defend, or secure what he is or has. His energies are absorbed in preservation. Goldstein has made the same point. He considers the drive for self-preservation a pathological phenomenon. The drive for self-actualization, he suggests, undergoes a change in the sick (or threatened) individual, in whom the scope of life is reduced so that he is driven to maintain (or defend) a limited state of existence. Preservation or maintenance of the self is thus the pathological form of self-actualization, the only form of self-actualization left to the disturbed or threatened individual (or, in Goldstein's work, the brain-damaged individual[19]).

A more serious question about the concept of a single basic motive is raised by those who contend that man has many motives and who propose various hierarchical orderings of them. Maslow's hierarchy is the most widely known proposal of this kind. It starts with the basic physical needs, which are prepotent and take precedence, when they are unmet, over all other needs. When these basic needs are met, the safety needs emerge. Then come the belongingness need, the love need, the esteem need, and then the need for self-actualization.[20] The problem is that the order is not invariant, as Maslow himself recognizes. It is not always true that the lower, more basic physiological needs take precedence over the higher, less prepotent needs. A man may sacrifice his life for his honor. We need, therefore, some organizing principle to explain this apparent inconsistency.

The concept of self-actualization as the single basic need provides this organizing principle. It clarifies, or eliminates, the confusion we face when we attempt to understand and order, or integrate, the multiplicity of often contradictory or opposing specific drives or motives that are attributed to human beings. There is no need to attempt to order drives or needs in a hierarchy. There *is* no hierarchy in the sense that certain needs always take precedence over other needs. All the specific needs are subservient to the basic tendency for the preservation and enhancement of the self. The individual's specific needs are organized and assume temporary priority in terms of their relationship to the basic need for self-actualization. At any one time, the most relevant specific need assumes priority or prepotence or, to use Gestalt terminology, becomes the figure against the ground of other needs.[21] When it is satisfied, the next most relevant need in terms of self-actualization assumes prepotence or becomes the figure, while the others recede into the background. All are organized by the basic need for self-actualization, and their significance or relevance is determined by this basic need.

Man Is a Social Being

In our discussion of the confusion of self-actualization with selfishness, we indicated that man needs other men to actualize himself. Man is, as Aristotle noted, a social animal. Because of his prolonged infancy, man learns to become dependent on others and remains dependent on others for affection. Man becomes a person and develops a self only in a society or a group.

In most societies most people typically want to receive a maximum degree of warmth and tenderness from another person and to express such feelings toward another person. When man is unable to develop intimate relationships with others, he is miserable and his physical well-being is threatened. Children can be permanently damaged if they have no intimacy. Even if they receive adequate nourishment and shelter, infants who have no contact with loving adults become ill.[22]

Occasionally, reports are published about the discovery of a child, or even an adult, who has been extremely neglected, isolated from human contact, and treated worse than an animal. Such persons, if they have been treated this way for a long time, are barely human. There are stories, some of them documented, of children who, though lost for a long time have managed to survive. But when they have been found, they are no longer human. The "wild boy" of Aveyron discovered in a forest in France in the early 1800's, never became human, though the French physician Itard spent much time and effort with him. While it is suspected that he was mentally retarded, his dehumanization went beyond his supposed mental deficiencies. Patients in mental institutions often deteriorate when they are not treated as real persons or human beings. Men confined in prison become "stir crazy" from lack of human relationships.

It would seem to be clear that one cannot be a self-actualizing person except in a group or society. The condition for self-actualizing persons is a facilitative relationship with other persons. Men contribute to each other's self-actualization in a group or society characterized by such relationships. These relationships are reciprocal. Rogers notes that the enhancement of the self "inevitably involves the enhancement of other selves as well. . . . The self-actualization of the organism appears to be in the direction of socialization, broadly defined."[23]

THE SELF-ACTUALIZING PERSON

A number of writers have contributed to the description and definition of the self-actualizing person, sometimes using other designations for such a person. Combs and Snygg discuss the characteristics of the *adequate* person, the person who has developed an adequate self. The adequate person perceives himself in positive ways: he has a positive self-concept, he accepts himself. The adequate person also accepts others:

> We are so entirely dependent upon the goodwill and cooperation of others in our society that it would be impossible to achieve

feelings of adequacy without some effective relationship with them. The adequate personality must be capable of living effectively and efficiently with his fellows.[24]

In addition, the adequate person is aware of and able to accept all his perceptions without distortion. From a behavioral point of view, the adequate person is characterized by efficient behavior, since he is not handicapped by defensiveness and is more open to experience. He is spontaneous and creative because, being secure, he can take chances, experiment, and explore. Being secure and accepting himself, he is capable of functioning independently; he finds his own feelings, beliefs, and attitudes adequate guides to behavior. Finally, the adequate person is compassionate. He can relate to others with concern rather than with the hostility and fear of defensiveness.

In discussing the actualizing tendency, Rogers notes that it leads to or is manifested by growth and motivation, differentiation, independence and autonomy, and self-responsibility. Rogers' concept of the fully functioning person is similar to the adequate-person concept of Combs and Snygg. Rogers describes three major characteristics of the fully functioning person: (a) He is open to his experience, to all external and internal stimuli. He has no need to be defensive. He is keenly aware of himself and his environment. He experiences both positive and negative feelings without repressing the latter. (b) The fully functioning person lives existentially. Each moment is new. Life is fluid, not fixed. He is changing, in process, flexible and adaptive. (c) "This person [finds] his organism a trustworthy means of arriving at the most satisfying behavior in each existential situation."[25] His behavior is determined from within; the locus of control is internal. Since he is open to all his experience, he has available the relevant data on which to base his behavior. Behavior is not always perfect, since some relevant data may be missing. But the resulting unsatisfying behavior is corrected on the basis of feedback. Such a person is a creative and self-actualizing person.

Earl Kelley describes the fully functioning person in similar terms. Such a person thinks well of himself and feels able or competent while being aware of his limitations. He also thinks well of others, recognizing their importance to him as opportunities for self-development. The fully functioning person develops and lives by human values rather than by external demands. He is creative. A characteristic not mentioned by Rogers or Combs and Snygg is the ability of the fully functioning person to recognize the value of mistakes as a source of learning and to profit from them.[26]

These descriptions of the self-actualizing person were developed through observation, experience, and, in Rogers' case, research in education and psychotherapy. Maslow, in a study devoted to self-actualization, lists these same characteristics as well as some others and so provides a comprehensive picture of the self-actualizing person.[27] Maslow used an accepted and sound method in his study of self-actualization. He selected a criterion group of persons (living and dead) who, on the basis of professional judgment were deemed outstanding self-actualizing persons. As a general definition, he used the following:

> . . . the full use and exploitation of talents, capacities, potentialities, etc. Such people seem to be fulfilling themselves and to be doing the best that they are capable of doing. They are people who have developed or are developing the full stature of which they are capable.[28]

The subjects were studied intensively to ascertain the characteristics they had in common that differentiated them from ordinary or average people. Fourteen characteristics emerged.

1. *More efficient perception of reality and more comfortable relations with it.* This characteristic includes the detection of the phoney and dishonest person and the accurate perception of what exists rather than a distortion of perception by ones' needs. *Self-actualizing people are more aware of their environment,* both human and nonhuman. They are not afraid of the unknown and can tolerate the doubt, uncertainty, and tentativeness accompanying the perception of the new and unfamiliar. This is clearly the characteristic described by Combs and Snygg and Rogers as awareness of perceptions or openness to experience.

2. *Acceptance of self, others, and nature.* Self-actualizing persons are not ashamed or guilty about their human nature, with its shortcomings, imperfections, frailties, and weaknesses. Nor are they critical of these aspects of other people. *They respect and esteem themselves and others.* Moreover, they are honest, *open, genuine, without pose or facade.* They are not, however, self-satisfied but are concerned about discrepancies between what is and what might be or should be in themselves, others, and society. Again, these characteristics are those which Kelley, Rogers, and Combs and Snygg include in their descriptions.

3. *Spontaneity.* Self-actualizing persons are not hampered by convention, but they do not flout it. *They are not conformists,* but neither are they anticonformist for the sake of being so. They are not externally motivated or even goal-directed—rather their motivation is the internal one of growth and development, the actualization of themselves and their potentialities. Rogers and Kelley both speak of growth, development and maturation, change and fluidity.

4. *Problem-centering.* Self-actualizing persons are not ego-centered but focus on problems outside themselves. They are *mission-oriented,* often on the basis of a sense of *responsibility, duty, or obligation* rather than personal choice. This characteristic would appear to be related to the security and lack of defensiveness leading to compassionateness emphasized by Combs and Snygg.

5. *The quality of detachment; the need for privacy. The self-actualizing person enjoys solitude and privacy.* It is possible for him to remain unruffled and undisturbed by what upsets others. He may even appear to be asocial. This is a characteristic that does not appear in other descriptions. It is perhaps related to a sense of security and self-sufficiency.

6. *Autonomy, independence of culture and environment.* Self-actualizing persons, though dependent on others for the satisfaction of the basic needs of love, safety, respect and belongingness, "are not dependent for their main satisfactions on the real world, or other people or culture or means-to-ends, or in general, on extrinsic satisfactions. *Rather they are dependent for their own development and continued growth upon their own potentialities* and latent resources."[29] Combs and Snygg and Rogers include independence in their descriptions, and Rogers also speaks of an internal locus of control.

7. *Continued freshness of appreciation.* Self-actualizing persons repeatedly, though not continuously, experience awe, pleasure, and wonder in their everyday world.

8. *The mystic experience, the oceanic feeling.* In varying degrees and with varying frequencies, *self-actualizing persons have experiences of ecstasy, awe, and wonder* with feelings of limitless horizons opening up, followed by the conviction that the experience was important and had a carry-over into everyday life. This and the preceding characteristic appear to be related and to add something not in other descriptions, except perhaps as it may be included in the existential living of Rogers.

9. *Gemeinschaftsgefühl. Self-actualizing persons have a deep feeling of empathy, sympathy, or compassion for human beings in general.* This feeling is, in a sense, unconditional in that it exists along with the recognition of the existence in others of negative qualities that provoke occasional anger, impatience, and disgust. Although empathy is not specifically listed by others (Combs and Snygg include compassion), it would seem to be implicit in other descriptions, including acceptance and respect.

10. *Interpersonal relations. Self-actualizing people have deep interpersonal relations with others.* They are selective, however, and their circle of friends may be small, usually consisting of other self-

actualizing persons, but the capacity is there. They attract others to them as admirers or disciples. This characteristic, again, is at least implicit in the formulations of others.

11. *The democratic character structure. The self-actualizing person does not discriminate* on the basis of class, education, race, or color. He is humble in his recognition of what he knows in comparison with what could be known, and he is ready and willing to learn from anyone. *He respects everyone* as potential contributors to his knowledge, but also just because they are human beings.

12. *Means and ends.* Self-actualizing persons are highly ethical. *They clearly distinguish between means and ends* and subordinate means to ends.

13. *Philosophical, unhostile sense of humor.* Although the self-actualizing persons studied by Maslow had a sense of humor, it was not of the ordinary type. Their sense of humor was the spontaneous, thoughtful type, intrinsic to the situation. Their humor did not involve hostility, superiority, or sarcasm. Many have noted that a sense of humor characterizes people who could be described as self-actualizing persons, though it is not mentioned by those cited here.

14. *Creativeness.* All of Maslow's subjects were judged to be creative, each in his own way. The creativity involved here is not the special-talent creativeness. It is a creativeness potentially inherent in everyone but usually suffocated by acculturation. *It is a fresh, naive, direct way of looking at things.* Creativeness is a characteristic most would agree to as characterizing self-actualizing persons.

The description of the self-actualizing person is a description of the kind of individual who functions at a high level, using his potentials and experiencing personal satisfaction. He is also a desirable member of society. In fact, it can be said that, unless there are enough individuals possessing to a minimal degree the characteristics of the self-actualizing person, society cannot survive. These characteristics, in Skinner's terminology, are the conditions that lead to the "ultimate strength of men."

> If a science of behavior can discover those conditions of life which make for the ultimate strength of men, it may provide a set of 'moral values' which, because they are independent of the history and culture of any one group, may be generally accepted.[30]

Historically, such self-actualizing men have been the major contributors to the development of civilization, and where societies have disintegrated or disappeared, it was probably because of the lack of enough such men.

These characteristics can be defined and stated in ways that permit their being evaluated and measured. They are observable in men. In fact, we observe and evaluate them continuously in our everyday interpersonal relationships. At the very least, they can be rated by judges on the basis of observation of a person's behavior. In fact, some of these characteristics can be measured by instruments now available. We shall consider these measurements in our discussion of the nature of the therapy relationship.

It is interesting to compare the description of the self-actualizing person with the young child. Young children are naturally self-actualizing, providing evidence for the innateness or naturalness of this state. The infant and young child are curious and exploratory of their environment. They don't have to be stimulated to be active. As Skinner says, "No one asks how to motivate a baby. A baby naturally explores everything he can get at, unless restraining forces have been at work. . . ."[31] The young child is naturally open, generous, spontaneous, honest, trusting, accepting, creative. His behavior is positive, cooperative, and loving, rather than negative, competitive, or aggressive —until he is taught the latter.

THE NATURE OF EMOTIONAL DISTURBANCE

If the goal of psychotherapy is the development of self-actualizing persons, then it follows that the problem, or the "pathology," for which psychotherapy is the remedy is the inability of the client to become a self-actualizing person. As indicated in Chapter 1, the client fails at this task because he has not and/or does not now have the personal environment that allows and encourages him to be self-actualizing. Specific problems are aspects of, indications of, or "symptoms" of this failure to be self-actualizing. Anxiety and guilt, and aggression, are results of the frustration of the drive toward self-actualization. The discrepancy between what a person is and what he is capable of being is the source of anxiety and guilt. The person who is not self-actualizing is lacking in some or all of the characteristics of self-actualizing persons. He does not accept himself; he has low self-esteem. He is not open to his environment and the experience of his organism and his senses; his relationship with reality is disturbed. He does not accept others, or respect them, and is disturbed in his interpersonal relationships. He is self-centered rather than problem-centered (in the sense of devoting himself to a problem or cause outside himself). He is dependent, inhibited rather than spontaneous, and wears a mask or facade rather than being real and genuine. His creativity is suppressed, so that he is unable to utilize and develop his potentials.

This concept of the nature of self-actualization as the goal of psychotherapy, and of life, and of its frustration as the source of, and constituting the nature of, emotional disturbance, avoids the problems connected with the term mental hygiene and the nature of "good" or "positive" mental hygiene. We start with the positive, with a goal inherent in the nature of man, so that its lack, its frustration, or its blocking is the problem or the "pathology."

Perhaps it should be reiterated here that many things can impede the development of self-actualizing persons. Impediments include physical deprivation, physical illness, lack of education, training, experience, and opportunities for the development of one's potentials. Psychotherapy is concerned with a particular class of impediments to self-actualization—the lack of or inadequacy of the appropriate personal environment or personal or psychological conditions for self-actualization, what might be called emotional deprivation. Other kinds of treatment or help are appropriate for dealing with other kinds of impediments to self-actualization. Counseling or psychotherapy is the specific treatment for the lack of self-actualization resulting from emotional deprivation.

SUMMARY

This chapter begins with a consideration of the nature of man as background for developing a description of the self-actualizing person. Man is an active as well as a reactive being. He is inherently good rather than bad. Aggression is a reaction to threat rather than an instinct expressed regardless of conditions in the environment. Man has a single basic motivation, the preservation and enhancement of the self, or the drive toward self-actualization. Man is by nature a social being; he becomes human only in a group or society of other persons. He is able to actualize himself most adequately in a society of other self-actualizing persons as a result of reciprocal influence.

The characteristics of the self-actualizing person are explored, drawing heavily from the research of Maslow. Among other characteristics of the self-actualizing person is the ability to develop good interpersonal relationships. This involves acceptance of and respect for others, understanding or empathy with others, and openness, genuineness, or honesty in interpersonal relationships. The self-actualizing person accepts himself and his human nature with its fallibilities. He is secure and thus does not have to be defensive; he is not easily threatened. He is in close touch with his environment, being sensitive and aware of stimuli. His locus of control is internal rather than external, so that he is autonomous, independent, and develops his own value system.

These characteristics are observable and thus in principle can be defined operationally so that they can be measured. In fact, it is now possible to measure some of them.

It is the inability to become a self-actualizing person because of a deprived social and emotional environment that constitutes emotional disturbance or psychological pathology. It is this disturbance, or this source of the frustration of the drive toward self-actualization, toward which counseling or psychotherapy is directed and for which it is the specific treatment.

NOTES

[1] G. W. Allport. Psychological models for guidance. *Harvard Educational Review*, 1962, **32**, 373–381.

[2] S. Freud. *The future of an illusion*. London: Hogarth Press, 1949, pp. 10–11.

[3] S. Freud. Civilization and its discontents. New York: Harrison Smith, n.d. Quoted in D. E. Walker. Carl Rogers and the nature of man. *Journal of Counseling Psychology*, 1956, **3**, 89–92.

[4] H. L. Ansbacher and Rowena R. Ansbacher (Eds.). *The individual psychology of Alfred Adler*. New York: Basic Books, 1956, p. 34.

[5] For an excellent survey by an anthropologist of the problem of aggression, see A. Alland, Jr. *The human imperative*. New York: Columbia University Press, 1972.

[6] Ashley Montagu. *The humanization of man*. Cleveland, Ohio: World Publishing, 1962.

[7] Charlotte Buhler. *Values in psychotherapy*. New York: Free Press, 1961, p. 71.

[8] A. Maslow. Our maligned human nature. *Journal of Psychology*, 1949, **28**, 273–278.

[9] J. Dollard, L. W. Doob, N. E. Miller, O. H. Mowrer and R. R. Sears. *Frustration and aggression*. New Haven: Yale University Press, 1939.

[10] E. Bibring. The development and problems of the theory of instincts. In C. L. Stacy and M. F. Martino (Eds.). *Understanding human motivation*. Cleveland: Howard Allen, 1958, pp. 474–498.

[11] William Golding. *Lord of the flies*. New York: Coward McCann, 1955.

[12] Ashley Montagu. *On being human*. New York: Henry Schuman, 1950.

[13] A. Angyal. *Foundations for a science of personality*. New York: Commonwealth Fund, 1941, pp. 29, 47, 354.

[14] P. Lecky. *Self-consistency: A theory of personality*. New York: Island Press, 1945.

[15] C. R. Rogers. *Client-centered therapy*. Boston: Houghton Mifflin, 1951, p. 487.

[16] A. W. Combs and D. Snygg. *Individual behavior* (Rev. ed.). New York: Harper & Row, 1959.

[17] A. H. Maslow. Deficiency motivation and growth motivation. In M. R. Jones (Ed.). *Nebraska symposium on motivation, 1955*. Lincoln, Nebraska: University of Nebraska Press, 1955, pp. 1–30.

[18] Ansbacher and Ansbacher, *Adler*, p. 114.

[19] K. Goldstein. *The organism*. New York: Harcourt Brace Jovanovich, 1939.

[20] A. H. Maslow. *Motivation and personality* (2nd ed.). New York: Harper & Row, 1970, pp. 35–47.

21 F. S. Perls. *Ego, hunger and aggression.* New York: Random House, 1969.

22 S. L. Halleck, *The politics of therapy.* New York: Science House, 1971, p. 204. Halleck refers to a summary of research by L. J. Yarrow. Separation from parents during early childhood. In M. Hoffman and L. Hoffman (Eds.). *Child development research.* New York: Russell Sage Foundation, 1964, pp. 89–136.

23 Rogers, *Client-centered therapy,* pp. 150, 488.

24 Combs and Snygg, *Individual behavior,* p. 246.

25 C. R. Rogers. *Freedom to learn.* Columbus, Ohio: Merrill, 1969, p. 286.

26 Earl C. Kelley. The fully functioning self. In A. W. Combs (Ed.). *Perceiving, behaving, becoming.* Washington, D.C.: National Education Association, 1962, pp. 9–20.

27 A. H. Maslow. Self-actualizing people: A study of psychological health. In C. E. Moustakas (Ed.). *The self: Explorations in personal growth.* New York: Harper & Row, 1956, pp. 160–194.

28 *Ibid.,* pp. 161–162.

29 *Ibid.,* p. 176.

30 B. F. Skinner. *Science and human behavior.* New York: Macmillan, 1953, p. 445.

31 B. F. Skinner. *Walden two.* New York: Macmillan, 1948, p. 101.

Chapter 4

The Therapeutic Conditions: I. Responsive Dimensions

The theme of this book is that psychotherapy is a relationship. It is assumed that providing a facilitative or therapeutic relationship is the necessary and sufficient condition for helping those persons who are failing to develop or progress toward self-actualizing behavior. Such individuals, it is assumed, are not in need of direct instruction, skill training, control, and guidance. Rather, it is assumed, if they are provided with the appropriate kind of relationship, their inherent capacity to grow, develop, and become a self-actualizing person will manifest itself. They will be capable of making necessary choices and decisions and of implementing them in action. If they have these capacities, then they have the right to exercise them, and should be given the freedom to do so.

Concern with the nature of the therapeutic relationship has been evident in every theory or approach to psychotherapy. There have been many attempts to identify the characteristics of effective therapists. In 1957, Carl Rogers presented, as hypotheses, necessary and sufficient conditions for therapeutic personality change.[1] The three conditions involving the therapist have become the focus of considerable writing and research since then[2] and have come to be known as the core conditions for facilitative interpersonal relationships. Truax and Carkhuff review the evidence for the recognition and acceptance of these conditions by a wide variety of therapists from Freud to current behaviorists.[3]

Truax, Carkhuff, and Berenson have proposed several additional conditions, some of which have been designated as action dimensions, in distinction to responsive dimensions. One of the action dimensions, concreteness of expression, is also included among the responsive dimensions

In this chapter we deal with the three basic core dimensions and with concreteness; in the next chapter, we consider the action dimensions.

EMPATHIC UNDERSTANDING

The Nature of Empathy

In English, the word *understanding* has come to mean knowledge *of,* or understanding *about,* something. One of the goals of science is understanding—understanding of objects and the results of their manipulation. This is not the kind of understanding we refer to when we use the word in counseling or psychotherapy. Here we are concerned not with knowing *about* the client but knowing how he feels and thinks and perceives things—himself and the world about him. It is understanding from the internal frame of reference, rather than from the external or so-called objective frame of reference. Some languages, for example French and German, have two verbs for *to know,* one meaning to know from the external frame of reference and the other simply to know, subjectively. Because English does not make this distinction, we need a modifier for the word *understanding;* empathic is used for this purpose.

Empathic understanding has long been recognized as an important element in psychotherapy.

Empathy should not be confused with sympathy. It does not involve identification with the client. This is clear in Rogers' definition: ". . . an accurate, empathic understanding of the client's world as seen from the inside. To sense the client's private world as if it were your own, but without losing the 'as if' quality—this is empathy. . . ."[4] A phrase in the language of some American Indians expresses it: "to walk in his moccasins." Great novelists are experts in empathic understanding, leading their readers to empathize with their characters. The theme of one novel, *To Kill a Mockingbird,* is dependent on the concept of empathy. At one point in the story Atticus Finch, the lawyer, trying to help his two young children to understand people's behavior toward him, says: "If . . . you can learn a simple trick. . . . you'll get along a lot better with all kinds of folks. You never really understand a person until you consider things from his point of view—until you climb into his skin and walk around in it."[5]

Empathy, of course, is not a trick, nor is it simple. Our society is externally oriented; we do not normally or easily see things from another person's point of view. We are too preoccupied with our own frame of reference. On the other hand, once we know what it means, most of us can relatively easily assume temporarily another's point of view. Students in counseling or psychotherapy seem to have relatively little difficulty in understanding the nature of empathy and putting themselves in the place of another person—at least momentarily. It seems that the capacity for empathy is present, to some extent at least, in many people in our society, certainly in most of those who are seriously interested in becoming counselors or psychotherapists.

But it is difficult to persist in this frame of reference, since it is not our usual behavior in everyday human relationships. Students easily pop out of the internal into the external frame of reference, and it takes considerable time to overcome the habits of everyday interactions with others. Students are also often bothered by the apparent subjectivity of empathic understanding. They are obsessed with the need to obtain "objective facts." But the so-called facts are nothing more than the subjective perceptions and impressions of other observers, usually with added evaluative or judgmental aspects. The real "facts" in counseling or psychotherapy are the perceptions, ideas, beliefs, attitudes, and feelings of the client; he is the expert on these facts, and the counselor must attempt to see and understand them.

The question is sometimes raised regarding discrepancies between the client's perceptions and those of others—shouldn't the counselor check the client's perceptions against those of his associates, family, or teachers? If the client's perceptions are greatly out of line with others', this will usually be apparent; often it will be brought to the counselor's attention by those in the client's environment. In cases where the discrepancies are less evident, the counselor will usually become aware of them as counseling continues. The real question is what the counselor should or can do about such discrepancies. Usually he should do nothing about them immediately, since there is nothing effective he can do until a relationship is established. When this is achieved, it is likely that the client will recognize, or admit, discrepancies that he has been aware of, or become aware of them, and then therapy can deal with them. Or, if they are apparent, and the client does not seem to be progressing toward awareness of them, the counselor can respond to them through confrontation. (Chapter 5.)

Empathy involves at least three aspects or stages. Assuming that the client is willing to allow the counselor to enter his private world and attempts to communicate his perceptions and feelings to the counselor, the counselor must be receptive to the communication. Second, the counselor must understand the communication of the client. To do this he must be able to put himself in the place of the client, to take the role of the client. Third, he must be able to communicate his understanding to the client.

Since we cannot actually be another person, we are inevitably outside, in an "as if" situation. This is not necessarily a negative situation, but can be positive if we responsively engage in an exploration with the client of his perceptions, emotions, and experiences. It is also a protection against too close an identification and against empathy becoming sympathy. "Being empathic, we assume the role of the other person, and in that role initiate ourselves the process of self-exploration as if we were the other person himself."[6] In trying to understand him and in feeling and experiencing with him, we help him in the process of expressing, exploring, and understanding himself.

Differences between counselors and their clients are barriers to empathy. Differences in sex, age, religion, socioeconomic status, education, and culture impede the development of empathic understanding. Of course, no one can completely understand another person. Everyone is unique, a product of a unique series of experiences. The wider a person's background, the more varied his experiences, the greater his understanding of a wider variety of other people. Yet it is impossible for any one individual to have the variety of experiences necessary for understanding all other persons, if identical or similar experiences were necessary for empathy. No male can really experience what it is like to be a female; no white can really experience what it is to be black. But it is not necessary for one to be exactly like another or to have had similar experiences to understand another. It may help in understanding a psychotic to have been psychotic oneself, but it is not necessary.

We can empathize to some extent at least, and sometimes to a great extent, with any other person on the basis of our commonalities as human beings. As Sullivan put it, "We are all much more simply human than otherwise."[7]

Fortunately, it is not necessary that we understand or empathize completely with another to be able to help the other person through relationship therapy. If we are really trying to understand, with at least occasional success in the beginning of therapy, therapy has a chance of continuing and of being successful. Indeed, the client will try to help the therapist understand him and sometimes will show remarkable persistence with an obtuse therapist.

It is certainly desirable that counselors should prepare themselves in any way they can to understand potential clients. A counselor who wants to work with a particular age, sex, social, or ethnic group should make some effort to gain an understanding of the particular group. It is frequently recommended that such persons take a course in the social and behavioral sciences, particularly anthropology, for this purpose. However, such courses are not particularly helpful, and they may be harmful. Anthropology is, or strives to be, a science. It is the hallmark of science that it is objective—that is, it studies objects or makes objects out of what it studies. Thus, the approach of anthropology, as it is usually taught, does not lead to a human understanding but to the viewing of other peoples as curious objects, sometimes barely human. To be sure, some anthropologists do develop a deep understanding of the peoples they study, but this is not usually conveyed in an anthropology course. In addition, anthropology is concerned with commonalities of cultures, with groups, rather than with individuals. It thus is in danger of fostering stereotypes, particularly in the minds of students, who are taking only a course or two. Stereotypes are harmful rather than helpful in dealing with or understanding individuals. A counselor who has had a course on the poor whites of Appalachia or the blacks in the deep rural South is likely to be hindered rather than helped when he encounters a poor Appalachian white or a southern rural black as a client.

There are two useful ways in which counselors can prepare themselves, to some extent at least, to work with clients from other groups than their own. One is to acquire as much vicarious experience as possible. People who really know the other group can be of help. But one widely available source is literature. The student should steep himself in the literature of the group—poetry, novels, biographies, and autobiographies. The second way in which the serious student can develop understanding of another group is to live with them—not as a visitor or as a professional person but as a person without any special identity except perhaps as a worker of some kind with them. Perhaps it is not too much to require that prospective counselors have some such experience for from six months to a year.

Measuring Empathic Understanding

In 1961, Truax developed a Tentative Scale for the Measurement of Accurate Empathy. This is a nine-point scale with definitions of each point and examples.[8] Carkhuff revised the scale and converted it into a five-level system for measuring empathic understanding.

EMPATHIC UNDERSTANDING IN INTERPERSONAL PROCESSES[9]

Level 1

The verbal and behavioral expressions of the first person either *do not attend to* or *detract significantly* from the verbal and behavioral expressions of the second person(s) in that they communicate significantly less of the second person's feelings than the second person has communicated himself.

EXAMPLES: The first person communicates no awareness of even the most obvious, expressed surface feelings of the second person. The first person may be bored or uninterested or simply operating from a preconceived frame of reference which totally excludes that of the other person(s).

In summary, the first person does everything but express that he is listening, understanding, or being sensitive to even the feelings of the other person in such a way as to detract significantly from the communications of the second person.

Level 2

While the first person responds to the expressed feelings of the second person(s), he does so in such a way that he *subtracts noticeable affect from the communications* of the second person.

EXAMPLES: The first person may communicate some awareness of obvious surface feelings of the second person, but his communications drain off a level of the affect and distort the level of meaning. The first person may communicate his own ideas of what may be going on, but these are not congruent with the expressions of the second person.

In summary, the first person tends to respond to other than what the second person is expressing or indicating.

Level 3

The expressions of the first person in response to the expressed feelings of the second person(s) are essentially *interchangeable* with those of the second person in that they express essentially the same affect and meaning.

EXAMPLE: The first person responds with accurate understanding of the surface feelings of the second person but may not respond to or may misinterpret the deeper feelings.

In summary, the first person is responding so as to neither subtract from nor add to the expressions of the second person; but he does not respond accurately to how that person really feels beneath the surface feelings. Level 3 constitutes the minimal level of facilitative interpersonal functioning.

Level 4

The responses of the first person add noticeably to the expressions of the second person(s) in such a way as to express feelings a level deeper than the second person was able to express himself.

EXAMPLE: The facilitator communicates his understanding of the expressions of the second person at a level deeper than they were expressed, and thus enables the second person to experience and/or express feelings he was unable to express previously.

In summary, the facilitator's responses add deeper feeling and meaning to the expressions of the second person.

Level 5

The first person's responses add significantly to the feeling and meaning of the expressions of the second person(s) in such a way as to (1) accurately express feelings levels below what the person himself was able to express or (2) in the event of ongoing deep self-exploration on the second person's part, to be fully with him in his deepest moments.

EXAMPLES: The facilitator responds with accuracy to all of the person's deeper as well as surface feelings. He is "together" with the second person or "tuned in" on his wave length. The facilitator and the other person might proceed together to explore previously unexplored areas of human existence.

In summary, the facilitator is responding with a full awareness of who the other person is and a comprehensive and accurate empathic understanding of his deepest feelings.

Examples of Empathy

Carkhuff and Berenson describe the movement from low to high empathy:

> The emphasis, then, is upon movement to levels of feeling and experience deeper than those communicated by the client, yet within the range of expression which the client can constructively employ for his own purposes. The therapist's ability to communicate at high levels of empathic understanding appears to involve the therapist's ability to allow himself to experience or merge in the experience of the client, reflect upon this experience while suspending his own judgments, tolerating his own anxiety, and communicating this understanding to the client.[10]

At low levels of empathy the counselor is obtuse to the client's expressions, and is responding to, or with, his own feelings and perceptions. He is not in the client's frame of reference, but may be evaluating and judging the client and his behavior, reacting with suggestions, advice, moralizations, and so on. His responses are irrelevant to the feelings and perceptions of the client.

CLIENT: Sometimes I get so depressed I don't know where I'm going.
THERAPIST: Well, you know, its around exam time and lots of kids get feeling a little down at this time of year.
CLIENT: Yes, but this has nothing to do with exams. That's not even bothering me.
THERAPIST: You mean none of the exams is bothering you? Surely one of them must be bothering you![11]

At a minimally facilitative level the counselor is with the client and the client feels this.

CLIENT: Sometimes I get so depressed I just don't know what to do.
THERAPIST: Sometimes you feel like you're never going to get up again.
CLIENT: Right. I just don't know what to do with myself. What am I going to do?[12]

At a highly facilitative level, the therapist goes beyond the words or even expressed feelings of the client to the implications of his statements. He is still responding to the client and not intruding his own feelings or perceptions. The client's feelings may be blurred and confused so that he does not recognize all their meanings or implications, which are clarified by the therapist.

CLIENT: Gee, those people! Who do they think they are? I just can't stand interacting with them any more. Just a bunch of phonies. They leave me so frustrated. They make me so anxious. I get angry at myself. I don't even want to be bothered with them anymore. I just wish I could be honest with them and tell them all to go to hell! But I just can't do it.

THERAPIST: Damn, they make you furious! But it's not just them. It's with yourself too, because you don't act on how you feel.[13]

It is impossible for a therapist to maintain the highest level of empathy continuously. And it is unnecessary. In fact, it is probably undesirable. At the beginning of therapy an extremely high level of empathy can be threatening and inhibit the communications of the client. He may well feel that the counselor understands him better than he does himself and that it is unnecessary for him to continue to express himself. Carkhuff suggests that in the early stage the therapist is most effective if he focuses on level 3 (the minimal level) of the facilitative conditions.[14]

Discrimination Versus Communication

Carkhuff makes an important distinction between the ability to discriminate an accurate empathic response and the ability to communicate empathically. If one is presented with a number of responses at various levels of empathy, one is able relatively easily, or with relatively little training, to recognize or identify the better or best responses. It is much more difficult to construct or compose a good response. Discrimination is a necessary but not sufficient condition for communication. Individuals who are able to make accurate discriminations are not necessarily able to communicate accurately. Those who can communicate accurately can also discriminate accurately, however.[15]

RESPECT

The Nature of Respect

In his 1957 article, Rogers included unconditional positive regard as one of the conditions for constructive personality change. Rogers credits Standal with originating this term.[16] Positive regard is unconditional in that it doesn't depend on the client's behavior. The client is regarded as a person, not as a collection of behaviors. Rogers has used other terms to describe this condition, including acceptance of the client as a person, with his negative as well as positive aspects.

Caring, prizing, valuing, and liking are other terms for the respect condition. It is a nonpossessive caring. The client is regarded as a person of worth; he is respected. The counselor's attitude is nonevaluative, nonjudgmental, without criticism, ridicule, depreciation, or reservations. This does not mean that the counselor accepts as right, desirable, or likeable, all aspects of the client's behavior or that he agrees with or condones all his behavior. "In the nonjudgmental attitude the [therapist] does not relinquish his own sense of values, his personal or social ethics."[17] Yet the client is accepted for what he is, as he is. There is no demand or requirement that he change or be different in order to be accepted or that he be perfect. Imperfections are accepted, along with mistakes and errors, as part of the human condition.

Respect is expressed in the therapist's listening to the client and in his effort to understand the client, as well as in his communication of that understanding. On the other hand, respect increases with understanding. While there should be a basic respect for the client simply as a person, a human being, respect is augmented with understanding of his uniqueness.

Nonpossessive warmth is another term which has been applied to the respect condition. There is a real interest in the client, a sincere concern for him, a trust, a love. It "does not imply passivity or unresponsivity; nonpossessive warmth is an outgoing positive action involving active, personal participation."[18] Although initially respect is expressed by communicating "in at least minimally warm and modulated tones" the potential for warmth,[19] respect can be communicated in many different ways.

> We must emphasize that it is not always communicated in warm, modulated tones of voice; it may be communicated for example, in anger. In the final analysis, it is the client's experience of the expression that counts, and the client may experience the therapist's attempt to share his own experience fully as an indication of the therapist's respect for the client's level of development.[20]

Being open and honest—real and genuine—with the client is also often a manifestation of respect for him.

The question of whether respect must be unconditional has been raised. Rogers has expressed some doubt about this, on the basis of a study by Spotts, which indicated that unconditionality contributed no variance apart from positive regard.[21] Barrett-Lennard has developed a relationship inventory for completion by clients, which contains separate scales for positive regard and unconditional positive regard.[22] However, they do not appear to be independent. This does not resolve the issue of unconditionality, however; unconditionality may be the basic factor in both.

Carkhuff and Berenson feel that unconditional positive regard, as well as nonpossessive warmth, are misnomers. "Unconditionality would, instead, appear to be nothing more than the initial suspension of potentially psychonoxious feelings, attitudes, and judgments."[23] It would appear, however, that the nonjudgmental and nonevaluative attitude and the distinction between acceptance of the client as a person worthy of respect regardless of his (unacceptable) behaviors constitute what is indicated by the word unconditional.

Measuring Respect

Truax developed a five-point Tentative Scale for the Measurement of Nonpossessive Warmth in 1962.[24] The variable of unconditionality is defined as an acceptance of the experience of the client without imposing conditions. Warmth involves a nonpossessive caring for him as a separate person and, thus, a willingness to share equally his joys and aspirations or his depressions and failures. It involves valuing the patient as a person, separate from any evaluation of his behavior or thoughts."[25] Carkhuff's revision of the scale follows:

THE COMMUNICATION OF RESPECT IN INTERPERSONAL PROCESSES[26]

Level 1

The verbal and behavioral expressions of the first person communicate a clear lack of respect (or negative regard) for the second person(s).

EXAMPLE: The first person communicates to the second person that the second person's feelings and experiences are not worthy of consideration or that the second person is not capable of acting constructively. The first person may become the sole focus of evaluation.

In summary, in many ways the first person communicates a total lack of respect for the feelings, experiences, and potentials of the second person.

Level 2

The first person responds to the second person in such a way as to communicate little respect for the feelings, experiences, and potentials of the second person.

EXAMPLE: The first person may respond mechanically or passively or ignore many of the feelings of the second person.

In summary, in many ways the first person displays a lack of respect or concern for the second person's feelings, experiences and potentials.

Level 3

The first person communicates a positive respect and concern for the second person's feelings, experiences and potentials.

EXAMPLE: The first person communicates respect and concern for the second person's ability to express himself and to deal constructively with his life situation.

In summary, in many ways the first person communicates that who the second person is and what he does matter to the first person. Level 3 constitutes the minimal level of facilitative interpersonal functioning.

Level 4

The facilitator clearly communicates a very deep respect and concern for the second person.

EXAMPLE: The facilitator's responses enable the second person to feel free to be himself and to experience being valued as an individual.

In summary, the facilitator communicates a very deep caring for the feelings, experiences, and potentials of the second person.

Level 5

The facilitator communicates the very deepest respect for the second person's worth as a person and his potentials as a free individual.

EXAMPLE: The facilitator cares very deeply for the human potentials of the second person.

In summary, the facilitator is committed to the value of the other person as a human being.

Examples of Respect

CLIENT: I just can't wait to get out of school—I'm so excited. I just want to get out and get started on my career. I know I'm going places.
THERAPIST: What's the matter, don't you like school?[27]

Here it is obvious that the therapist shows complete lack of respect and warmth for the client but is evaluative.

The next example also involves disapproval of the client's behavior as well as evaluation and lack of warmth:

THERAPIST: . . . another part here too, that is, if they haven't got a lot of schooling, there may be a good argument, that, that they—are better judges, you know.
CLIENT: Yeah . . .
THERAPIST: Now, I'm not saying that, that's necessarily true, I'm—just saying that's *reality*.
CLIENT: Yeah.
THERAPIST: And you're in a *position* that you can't argue with them. Why is it that these people burn you up so much?
CLIENT: They *get by with* too many things . . .
THERAPIST: Why should that bother you?
CLIENT: 'Cause I never got by with anything.
THERAPIST: They're papa figures, aren't they?[28]

Now contrast these with the following dialogue, in which the words can only give an indication of the warmth present:

CLIENT: . . . ever recovering to the extent where I could become self-supporting and live alone. I thought that I was doomed to hospitalization for the rest of my life and seeing some of the people over in the main building, some of those old people who are, who need a lot of attention and all that sort of thing, is the only picture I could see of my own future. Just one of (Therapist: Mhm) complete hopelessness, that there was any . . .
THERAPIST: (Interrupting) You didn't see any hope at all, did you?
CLIENT: Not in the least. I thought no one really cared and I didn't care myself, and I seriously—uh—thought of suicide; if there'd been any way that I could end it all *completely* and not become a burden or an extra care, I would have committed suicide, I was that low. I didn't want to live. In fact, I hoped that I—I would go to sleep at night and not wake up, because I, I really felt there was nothing to live for. (Therapist: Uh, huh. [very softly]) Now I, I truly believe that this drug they are giving me helps me a lot, I think, I think it is one drug that really does me *good*. (Therapist: Uh, hm).

THERAPIST: But you say that, that during that time you, you felt as though no one cared, as to what (Client: That's right) what happened to you.

CLIENT: And, not only that, but I hated *myself* so that I didn't *deserve* to have anyone care for me. I hated myself so that I, I, I not only felt that no one did, but I didn't see any reason why they *should*.

THERAPIST: I guess that makes some sense to me now. I was wondering why it was that you were shutting other people off. You weren't *letting* anyone else care.

CLIENT: I didn't think I was *worth* caring for.

THERAPIST: So you didn't ev—maybe you not only thought you were—hopeless, but you wouldn't allow people . . . (Therapist's statement drowned out by client) .[29]

THERAPEUTIC GENUINENESS

The Nature of Genuineness

One of the conditions postulated by Rogers in 1957 was congruence, or integration in the relationship. Rogers wrote that "it means that within the relationship he [the therapist] is freely and deeply himself, with his actual experiences accurately represented by his awareness of himself."[30]

This condition has since become known as genuineness. The therapist is "for real," an open, honest, sincere person. He is involved in the relationship and not simply a mirror, a sounding board, or a blank screen. He is a real person in a real encounter. And that is the reason why the exact nature of the relationship cannot be predicted or controlled in advance. He is freely and deeply himself, without a facade, not phony. He is not thinking and feeling one thing and saying something different. He is, as the existentialist would say, authentic, or, to use Jourard's term, transparent.[31] He is not playing a role. Berne writes:

> If the therapist plays the role of a therapist, he will not get very far with perceptive patients. He has to *be* a therapist. If he decides that a certain patient needs Parental reassurance, he does not play the role of a parent; rather he liberates his Parental ego state. A good test for this is for him to attempt to "show off" his Parentalism in the presence of a colleague, with a patient toward whom he does not *feel* parental. In this case he is playing a role and a forthright patient will soon make clear to him the difference between *being* a reassuring Parent and playing the role of a reassuring parent. One of the functions of psychotherapeutic training es-

tablishments is to separate trainees who want to play the role of therapist from those who want to be therapists.[32]

Genuineness appears to have become the major emphasis of many approaches to psychotherapy. The major theories have given it a more important place. Even psychoanalysis, in which the therapist is a rather ambiguous figure, a blank screen, has moved from this position to the acceptance of the therapist as a real person. If there is one thing that unites many of the apparently extremely diverse innovations in psychotherapy, it is the concept of genuineness—of doing one's own thing.

There is a real danger here, however, involving a misinterpretation of genuineness as supporting an "anything goes" policy. Genuineness is not always therapeutic. It is unlikely that a highly authoritative, dogmatic person is highly therapeutic. Carkhuff and Berenson comment on this problem:

> However, a construct of genuineness must be differentiated from the construct of facilitative genuineness. Obviously, the degree to which an individual is aware of his own experience will be related to the degree to which he can enable another person to become aware of his experience. However, many destructive persons are in full contact with their experience; that is, they are destructive when they are genuine. The potentially deleterious effects of genuineness have been established in some research inquiries. Hence the emphasis upon the therapist's being freely and deeply himself in a nonexploitative relationship incorporates one critical qualification. When his only genuine responses are negative in regard to the second person, the therapist makes an effort to employ his responses constructively as a basis for further inquiry for the therapist, the client and their relationship. In addition, there is evidence to suggest that whereas low levels of genuineness are clearly impediments to client progress in therapy, above a certain minimum level, very high levels of genuineness are not related to additional increases in client functioning. Therefore, while it appears of critical importance to avoid the conscious or unconscious facade of "playing the therapeutic role," the necessity for the therapist's expressing himself fully at all times is not supported. Again, genuineness must not be confused, as is so often done, with free license for the therapist to do what he will in therapy, especially to express hostility. Therapy is not for the therapist. [Later on, they comment as follows:] . . . under some circumstances, the honesty of communication may actually constitute a limitation for the progress of therapy. Thus, with pa-

tients functioning at significantly lower levels than the therapist, the therapist may attend cautiously to the client's condition. He will not share with the client that which would make the client's condition the more desperate.[33]

Genuineness does not require that the therapist always express all his feelings; it only requires that whatever he does express is real and genuine and not incongruent. And at a minimal level genuineness is not being insincere, dishonest, phony, or incongruent. Genuineness is not impulsiveness, though the two appear to be equated in the minds of many, instructors as well as students.

Truax and Mitchell make an important point (and Carkhuff and Berenson would appear to agree in their comment just quoted) :

> From the research evidence and an examination of the raw data itself relating genuineness to outcome, as well as collateral evidence, it is clear that what is effective is an absence of defensiveness and phoniness—a lack of evidence that the therapist is not genuine. In other words, it is not the positive end of the genuineness scale that contributes to therapeutic outcome. Instead it is a lack of genuineness which militates against positive client change. The highest levels of the genuineness scale do not discriminate between differential outcomes. The scale itself and the evidence concerning genuineness would be more precise if we dropped the term genuineness and call[ed] it instead by some negative term that would include both defensiveness and being phony.[34]

This is an important point, in view of the increasing emphasis on being genuine. It would appear that the great effort to be genuine is leading to the phenomenon of phony genuineness. This may be an explanation for the inconsistent results with the genuineness scale in some studies (such as Bergin and Garfield's) .[35]

This caution has apparently not been heeded, especially in group therapy or encounter groups. Genuineness has been distorted to condone the therapist who reacts off the top of his head. Gendlin discusses the facilitating of therapy with nonverbal schizophrenics through the expression of the therapist's feelings. But he emphasizes the need for the therapist to take "a few steps of self attention" before expressing himself, as well as to clearly identify his feelings as his own. Genuineness, then, does not mean unhibited expression of feelings. The therapist doesn't unthinkingly blurt out such things as "You bore me," as seems to be encouraged and practiced in the name of genuineness. Rather, if he feels bored, he looks at himself and the relationship to see if he is contributing to the feeling. He might end up by saying: "Somehow I feel rather bored by your emotionless recital of events," or something similar.[36]

This confusion is probably related to some of the puzzling and inconsistent results of research. The three basic core conditions are usually positively correlated, often quite highly. But in some instances genuineness has shown no correlation or even a negative correlation with the other two. Garfield and Bergin, in a study which led them to question the applicability of the three core conditions to other than client-centered therapy, found that genuineness correlated negatively with empathy $(-.66)$ and with warmth $(-.75)$.[37] None of the three correlated significantly with several outcome measures, so while it is not possible to say that empathy and warmth were therapeutic, it is obvious that genuineness was not therapeutic in this study.

Measuring Therapeutic Genuineness

Truax constructed a five-point Tentative Scale for the Measurement of Therapist Genuineness or Self-Congruence in 1962.[38] He stated that this was the most difficult scale to develop. Examination of the scale suggests that a high rating would not necessarily represent therapeutic genuineness. It was this scale that Garfield and Bergin used in their 1971 study. Carkhuff's revision of the scale appears to correct this deficiency .

FACILITATIVE GENUINENESS IN INTERPERSONAL PROCESSES[39]

Level 1

The first person's verbalizations are clearly unrelated to what he is feeling at the moment, or his only genuine responses are negative in regard to the second person(s) and appear to have a totally destructive effect upon the second person.

EXAMPLE: The first person may be defensive in his interaction with the second person(s) and this defensiveness may be demonstrated in the content of his words or his voice quality. Where he is defensive he does not employ his reaction as a basis for potentially valuable inquiry into the relationship.

In summary, there is evidence of a considerable discrepancy between the inner experiencing of the first person and his current verbalizations. Where there is no discrepancy, the first person's reactions are employed solely in a destructive fashion.

Level 2

The first person's verbalizations are slightly unrelated to what he is feeling at the moment, or when his responses are genuine they are negative in regard to the second person; the first person does not appear to know how to employ his negative reactions as a basis for inquiry into the relationship.

EXAMPLE: The first person may respond to the second person(s) in a "professional" manner that has a rehearsed quality or a quality concerning the way a helper "should" respond in that situation.

In summary, the first person is usually responding according to his prescribed role rather than expressing what he personally feels or means. When he is genuine his responses are negative and he is unable to employ them as a basis for further inquiry.

Level 3

The first person provides no "negative" cues between what he says and what he feels, but he provides no positive cues to indicate a really genuine response to the second person(s).

EXAMPLE: The first person may listen and follow the second person(s) but commits nothing more of himself.

In summary, the first person appears to make appropriate responses that do not seem insincere but that do not reflect any real involvement either. Level 3 constitutes the minimal level of facilitative interpersonal functioning.

Level 4

The facilitator presents some positive cues indicating a genuine response (whether positive or negative) in a nondestructive manner to the second person(s).

EXAMPLE: The facilitator's expressions are congruent with his feelings, although he may be somewhat hesitant about expressing them fully.

In summary, the facilitator responds with many of his own feelings, and there is no doubt as to whether he really means what he says. He is able to employ his responses, whatever their emotional content, as a basis for further inquiry into the relationship.

Level 5

The facilitator is freely and deeply himself in a nonexploitative relationship with the second person(s).

EXAMPLE: The facilitator is completely spontaneous in his interaction and open to experiences of all types, both pleasant and hurtful. In the event of hurtful responses the facilitator's comments are employed constructively to open a further area of inquiry for both the facilitator and the second person.

In summary, the facilitator is clearly being himself and yet employing his own genuine responses constructively.

Examples of Genuineness

CLIENT: . . . So that's how I got home from C——. I was kind of lucky.
THERAPIST: Yeah, that is, that's quite a story. (long pause) .
CLIENT: Can I ask you a question?
THERAPIST: Yeah, I guess so.
CLIENT: Do you think I'm crazy?
THERAPIST: Oh no—not in the sense that *some* of the patients you see out in the ward, perhaps.
CLIENT: I don't mean *mentally*, not—where I don't know anything, but I mean, am I out of my head? Do I do things that are foolish for people to do?
THERAPIST: Well, I'd say you do things that you might say are—foolish, in a sense. You do things that aren't . . . (Pause)
CLIENT: (Filling in for therapist)   *Normal.*
THERAPIST: Yeah, well, they aren't usual by any means, of course.

The therapist is clearly being evasive, rather than open and honest.[40] Contrast this with the following dialogue:

CLIENT: I'm so thrilled to have found a counselor like you. I didn't know any existed. You seem to understand me so well. It's just great! I feel like I'm coming alive again. I have not felt this in so long.
THERAPIST: Hey, I'm as thrilled to hear you talk this way as you are! I'm pleased that I have been helpful. I do think we still have some work to do yet, though.[41]

CONCRETENESS

These three basic core conditions—empathy, respect, and genuineness —have been recognized for some time and subjected to considerable study. There is research evidence for their effectiveness, most of which is summarized by Truax, Carkhuff and Berenson in the references cited in the preceding pages. In 1964, Truax and Carkhuff proposed another variable, concreteness, as an important facilitative condition.[42]

Nature of Concreteness

Concreteness, or specificity, involves the use of specific and concrete terminology, rather than general or abstract terminology, in the discussion of feelings, experiences, and behavior. It avoids vagueness and ambiguity. It leads to differentiation of feelings and experiences rather than generalization. Concreteness or specificity is not necessarily practicality nor is it objectivity. It does not apply to impersonal material—it is *personally relevant* concreteness. It is "the fluent, direct and complete expression of specific feelings and experiences, regardless of their emotional content."[43]

Specificity is the opposite of much of the verbalization of many counselors, who attempt to generalize, categorize, and classify with broad general labels the feelings and experiences of the client. Many interpretations are generalizations, abstractions, or higher level labeling (or the inclusion of a specific experience under a higher level category). Concreteness is the opposite of such labeling. It suggests that such interpretation is not useful but harmful. In addition to being threatening, abstract interpretations cut off client exploration. Rather than permitting an analysis of a problem into its specific aspects, labeling leads to the feeling that the problem is solved and the issue closed. A simple, though perhaps extreme, example would be applying the label Oedipus complex to a client's description of his feelings and attitudes regarding his father and mother. The client might well feel that this solves his problem, that he has insight, and that nothing further need be done—or can be done.

Concreteness serves three important functions: (a) it keeps the therapist's response close to the client's feelings and experiences; (b) it fosters accurateness of understanding in the therapist, allowing for early client corrections of misunderstanding; and (c) it encourages the client to attend to specific problem areas.[44]

By responding in specific and concrete terms to long, general, vague ramblings of the client, the therapist helps the client to sift out the personally significant aspects from the irrelevant aspects. Although it might appear that questions of the who, what, when, where and how type would be useful, Carkhuff believes that

> such questions should serve the function of entry and follow-through in an area only when the helpee cannot himself imple-

ment entry and follow-through in that area. In no way should questions and probing dominate helping because of the stimulus response contingencies that it develops. . . .[45]

In other words, questions should perhaps be limited to situations where the therapist doesn't understand or cannot follow the client and must ask for clarification.

It is possible that the level of concreteness should vary during different phases of the therapy process. It should be high in the early stages, but later, when the client moves into deeper and more complex material, a high level may be undesirable or even impossible until confused and mixed feelings and emotions are expressed and become clearer. Later, in the ending phases when the client is planning and engaging in action, high levels would again be desirable. In the early stages, concreteness can contribute to empathic understanding.

Measuring Concreteness

Carkhuff's revision of the completeness scale follows:

CONCRETENESS OR SPECIFICITY OF EXPRESSION IN INTERPERSONAL PROCESSES[46]

Level 1

The first person leads or allows all discussion with the second person(s) to deal only with vague and anonymous generalities.

EXAMPLE: The first person and the second person discuss everything on strictly an abstract and highly intellectual level.

In summary, the first person makes no attempt to lead the discussion into the realm of personally relevant specific situations and feelings.

Level 2

The first person frequently leads or allows even discussions of material personally relevant to the second person(s) to be dealt with on a vague and abstract level.

EXAMPLE: The first person and the second person may discuss the "real" feelings but they do so at an abstract, intellectualized level.

In summary, the first person does not elicit discussion of most personally relevant feelings and experiences in specific and concrete terms.

Level 3

The first person at times enables the second person(s) to discuss personally relevant material in specific and concrete terminology.

EXAMPLE: The first person will make it possible for the discussion with the second person(s) to center directly around most things that are personally important to the second person(s), although there will continue to be areas not dealt with concretely and areas in which the second person does not develop fully in specificity.

In summary, the first person sometimes guides the discussions into consideration of personally relevant specific and concrete instances, but these are not always fully developed. Level 3 constitutes the minimal level of facilitative functioning.

Level 4

The facilitator is frequently helpful in enabling the second person(s) to fully develop in concrete and specific terms almost all instances of concern.

EXAMPLE: The facilitator is able on many occasions to guide the discussion to specific feelings and experiences of personally meaningful material.

In summary, the facilitator is very helpful in enabling the discussion to center around specific and concrete instances of most important and personally relevant feelings and experiences.

Level 5

The facilitator is always helpful in guiding the discussion, so that the second person(s) may discuss fluently, directly and completely specific feelings and experiences.

EXAMPLE: The first person involves the second person in discussion of specific feelings, situations, and events, regardless of their emotional content.

In summary, the facilitator facilitates a direct expression of all personally relevant feelings and experiences in concrete and specific terms.

Examples of Concreteness

CLIENT: I don't know just what the problem is. I don't get along with my parents. It's not that I don't like them, or that they don't like me. But we seem to disagree on so many things. Maybe they're small and unimportant, but . . . I don't know, we never have been close . . . there has never, as far as I can remember, been a time when they gave me any spontaneous affection . . . I just don't know what's wrong.

THERAPIST: It seems that your present situation is really of long standing and goes back to a long series of difficulties in your developmental process.

Clearly, this kind of general, abstract response will not help the client to focus upon the specifics of the problem. Compare this with the following concrete response to the same client statement:

THERAPIST: Although you say you don't know what's wrong, and although you say your parents like you, they never seem to have given any specific evidence of love or affection.

SUMMARY

Three basic conditions of a facilitative or therapeutic interpersonal relationship have been implicit if not explicit in most if not all theories or approaches to counseling or psychotherapy. In the currently accepted terminology, they are empathic understanding, respect or warmth, and therapeutic or facilitative genuineness. Considerable evidence for their effectiveness in facilitating a variety of client personality and behavior changes has been accumulated. A fourth condition is described by Truax and Carkhuff: personally relevant concreteness. Some evidence of its effectiveness has been obtained. These four conditions are grouped by Carkhuff and Berenson under the term core facilitative conditions. They are the conditions that appear to be the common elements in all or most existing systems or approaches to counseling or psychotherapy. Their definitions or description, together with scales that enable their measurement, are presented in this chapter.

These conditions interrelate with each other, both in terms of contributing to each other in the therapy process and in being statistically correlated (in most studies). Rogers and Truax suggest that genuineness is basic, since warmth and empathy can be threatening or meaningless without it. In turn, empathy must be based upon warmth and respect.[47] However, warmth and respect are known to increase with the depth of understanding of another, and the attentiveness and listening characterizing the attempt to understand another is evidence of respect for the client. Truax and Carkhuff write: "We begin to perceive the events and experiences of his life 'as if' they were parts of our own life. It is through this process that we come to feel warmth, respect and liking for a person who in everyday life is unlikeable, weak, cowardly, treacherous, vile, or despicable."[48]

Thus, it is likely that the core conditions interact to facilitate or increase each other. Some degree of all the core conditions is necessary to begin with and then they grow together, each one contributing to the increase in level of the other conditions.

NOTES

[1] C. R. Rogers. The necessary and sufficient conditions of therapeutic personality change. *Journal of Consulting Psychology*, 1957, **21**, 95–103.
[2] C. B. Truax and R. R. Carkhuff. *Toward effective counseling and psychotherapy.* Chicago: Aldine, 1967; R. R. Carkhuff and B. G. Berenson. *Beyond counseling and therapy.* New York: Holt, Rinehart & Winston, 1967; R. R. Carkhuff. *Helping and human relations.* Vol. I, *Selection and training.* Vol. II, *Practice and research.* New York: Holt, Rinehart & Winston, 1969.
[3] Truax and Carkhuff, *Toward effective counseling,* pp. 23–43.
[4] C. R. Rogers. *On becoming a person.* Boston: Houghton Mifflin, 1961, p. 284.
[5] Harper Lee. *To kill a mockingbird.* Philadelphia: Lippincott, 1960, p. 24.
[6] C. B. Truax and K. M. Mitchell. Research on certain therapist interpersonal skills in relation to process and outcome. In A. E. Bergin and S. L. Garfield (Eds.). *Handbook of psychotherapy and behavior change: An empirical analysis.* New York: Wiley, 1971, pp. 299–344.
[7] H. S. Sullivan. *Conceptions of modern psychiatry.* Washington, D.C.: William Allanson White Psychiatric Foundation, 1947, p. 7.
[8] Truax and Carkhuff, *Toward effective counseling,* pp. 46–58.
[9] Carkhuff, *Helping,* Vol. II, pp. 315–317.
[10] Carkhuff and Berenson, *Beyond counseling,* p. 27.
[11] *Ibid.,* p. 32.
[12] *Ibid.,* p. 31.
[13] Carkhuff, *Helping,* Vol. I, p. 119.
[14] *Ibid.,* pp. 216, 202.
[15] *Ibid.,* pp. 113–132.
[16] Rogers, *On becoming a person,* p. 283.
[17] F. P. Biestek. The nonjudgmental attitude. *Social Casework,* 1953, **34**, 235–239.
[18] Truax and Mitchell, Research on interpersonal skills, p. 317.
[19] Carkhuff, *Helping,* Vol. I, p. 205.
[20] Carkhuff and Berenson, *Beyond counseling,* p. 28.
[21] C. R. Rogers. The interpersonal relationship: The core of guidance. *Harvard Educational Review,* 1962, **32**, 416–429.
[22] G. T. Barrett-Lennard. Dimensions of therapist response as causal factors in therapeutic change. *Psychological Monographs,* 1962, **76** (43, Whole No. 562).
[23] Carkhuff and Berenson, *Beyond counseling,* p. 28.
[24] Truax and Carkhuff, *Toward effective counseling,* pp. 58–68.
[25] *Ibid.,* p. 58.

26 Carkhuff, *Helping*, Vol. II, pp. 317–318.
27 Carkhuff and Berenson, *Beyond counseling*, p. 37.
28 Truax and Carkhuff, *Toward effective counseling*, p. 61.
29 *Ibid.*, p. 67.
30 Rogers, Necessary and sufficient conditions, p. 97.
31 S. Jourard. *The transparent self.* Princeton, N.J.: Van Nostrand Reinhold, 1964.
32 E. Berne. *Transactional analysis in psychotherapy.* New York: Grove Press, 1961, p. 233.
33 Carkhuff and Berenson, *Beyond counseling*, pp. 29, 81.
34 Truax and Mitchell, Research on interpersonal skills, p. 316.
35 S. L. Garfield and A. E. Bergin. Therapeutic conditions and outcome. *Journal of Abnormal Psychology*, 1971, **77**, 108–114.
36 E. T. Gendlin. Client-centered developments in work with schizophrenics. *Journal of Counseling Psychology*, 1962, **9**, 205–211.
37 Garfield and Bergin, Therapeutic conditions.
38 Truax and Carkhuff, *Toward effective counseling*, pp. 68–72.
39 Carkhuff, *Helping*, Vol. II, pp. 319–320.
40 Truax and Carkhuff, *Toward effective counseling*, p. 69.
41 Carkhuff, *Helping*, Vol. I, p. 121.
42 C. B. Truax and R. R. Carkhuff. Concreteness: A neglected variable in the psychotherapeutic process. *Journal of Clinical Psychology*, 1964, **20**, 264–267.
43 Carkhuff and Berenson, *Beyond counseling*, p. 29.
44 *Ibid.*, p. 30.
45 Carkhuff, *Helping*, Vol. I, p. 207.
46 Carkhuff, *Helping*, Vol. II, pp. 323–324.
47 Truax and Carkhuff, *Toward effective counseling*, p. 32. But see also p. 42 where the order understanding, respect, and genuineness is suggested. Truax and Mitchell (Research on interpersonal skills, p. 314) also state this order but say that in practice empathic listening results in understanding, leading to liking, which then leads to genuineness on the part of the therapist.
48 Truax and Carkhuff, *Toward effective counseling*, p. 42.

Chapter 5

The Therapeutic Conditions: II. Action Dimensions

Carkhuff and Berenson distinguish two phases of the counseling or therapy process—the inward and downward phase, or the responsive phase, and the outward and upward phase, or the initiative and action phase. According to them, most traditional therapies consist of only the first phase. It is in this phase that the basic core conditions are essential and the therapeutic relationship firmly established. It is characterized by the responsiveness of the therapist to the client. In the second phase, the therapist, on the basis of the understanding developed in the first phase, assumes more initiative in helping the client make and act upon choices and decisions. In the first phase, the client achieves insights; in the second phase, the therapist attempts to change the client's behavior toward more effective functioning.[1]

The second phase involves conditions in addition to those of the first phase. Chapter 4 explains that concreteness is involved in both the responsive phase and the action, or problem-solving phase. In addition to concreteness, three other conditions are needed to facilitate the second phase.

CONFRONTATION

The Nature of Confrontation

Confrontation is an expression by the therapist of his experience of discrepancies in the client's behavior. Carkhuff distinguishes three broad categories of confrontation: (a) discrepancy between the client's expression of what he is and what he wants to be (real self, or self-concept, versus ideal self); (b) discrepancies between the client's verbal expressions about himself (awareness or insight) and his behavior either as it is observed by the therapist or reported by the client; and (c) discrepancies between the client's expressed experience of himself and the therapist's experience of him.[2] A fourth catgory might be added to cover discrepancies between the client's experiences of himself and others as reported at different times, either in the same session or in different sessions.

Confrontation may be viewed as the attempt to bring to awareness the presence of cognitive dissonance or incongruence in the client's feelings, attitudes, beliefs, or behaviors. It may also lead to the discovery of ambivalence in feelings and attitudes toward persons in the client's life.

In the early stages of therapy, the therapist is tentative in his confrontations, usually formulating them as questions since he will not be too confident about them. "Premature direct confrontations may have a demoralizing and demobilizing effect upon an inadequately prepared helpee."[3] The therapist may say something like, "You seem to be saying two different things" or "Now you say this, but earlier you seemed to be saying that."

Later in the therapy, more direct confrontations may focus specifically upon discrepancies. "The increasing specificity will lead to the development of an understanding of the distortions in the helpee's assumptive world and, hopefully, to a reconstruction of that world."[4] Direct confrontations precipitate an awareness of a crisis in the client that, when faced, leads to movement to higher levels of functioning. The goal is to enable the client to confront himself and, when desirable, others. *Confrontation of self and others is prerequisite to the healthy individual's encounter with life.*"[5] An important use of confrontation is to point out to the client that insight is not enough and that, although he has insight, his behavior has not changed. Confrontation enables the client to go beyond insight and to recognize the need to change his behaviors.

Confrontation is not limited to negative aspects of the client or to facing him with his limitations. It also includes pointing out discrepancies involving his resources and assets that are unrecognized or unused.

Research indicates that therapists functioning at high levels on the core conditions use confrontation more frequently than low-level functioning therapists, and, significantly, high-level functioning therapists confront their clients more often with their assets and resources than with their limitations. Low-level functioning therapists do the reverse.[6]

The association of confrontation with high levels of the core conditions, including empathy, suggests that confrontation may be useful or effective only in the context of high levels of empathy and respect.

There has been an avoidance of confrontation among therapists of most of the major approaches. Direct confrontation has been limited to clients who are aggressive, manipulative, or confronting themselves; thus, the therapist reacts to rather than initiates confrontation. Certainly there is a risk in confrontation. In addition to the possible dangers when it is not associated with empathy and warmth or concern, confrontation, like genuineness, can be used to vent the therapist's aggressiveness and internal anger, frustration, and other negative feelings. The word itself is perhaps not a felicitous one, with its connotations of aggressiveness and face-to-face conflict. It would be helpful if a more appropriate word could be found.

It is possible that confrontation should not be considered as a separate condition or dimension of psychotherapy. Perhaps it could be included in empathic understanding. The recognition and communicating of discrepancies in the client's verbalizations and behaviors does seem to be an aspect of empathy.

Measuring Confrontation

Carkhuff has developed a scale for measuring confrontation, one in which there is no differentiation between levels 1 and 2. This could be taken as supporting the idea that confrontation is an aspect of high empathy and should be incorporated into the empathy scale.

CONFRONTATION IN INTERPERSONAL PROCESSES[7]

Level 1

The verbal and behavioral expressions of the helper disregard the discrepancies in the helpee's behavior (ideal versus real self, insight versus action, helper versus helpee's experiences).

EXAMPLE: The helper may simply ignore all helpee discrepancies by passively accepting them.

In summary, the helper simply disregards all of those discrepancies in the helpee's behavior that might be fruitful areas for consideration.

Level 2

The verbal and behavioral expressions of the helper disregard the discrepancies in the helpee's behavior.

EXAMPLE: The helper, although not explicitly accepting these discrepancies, may simply remain silent concerning most of them.

In summary, the helper disregards the discrepancies in the helpee's behavior, and, thus, potentially important areas of inquiry.

Level 3

The verbal and behavioral expressions of the helper, while open to discrepancies in the helpee's behavior, do not relate directly and specifically to these discrepancies.

EXAMPLE: The helper may simply raise questions without pointing up the diverging directions of the possible answers.

In summary, while the helper does not disregard discrepancies in the helpee's behavior, he does not point up the directions of these discrepancies. Level 3 constitutes the minimum level of facilitative interpersonal functioning.

Level 4

The verbal and behavioral expressions of the helper attend directly and specifically to the discrepancies in the helpee's behavior.

EXAMPLE: The helper confronts the helpee directly and explicitly with discrepancies in the helpee's behavior.

In summary, the helper specifically addresses himself to discrepancies in the helpee's behavior.

Level 5

The verbal and behavioral expressions of the helper are keenly and continually attuned to the discrepancies in the helpee's behavior.

EXAMPLE: The helper confronts the helpee with helpee discrepancies in a sensitive and perceptive manner whenever they appear.

In summary, the helper does not neglect any potentially fruitful inquiry into the discrepancies in the helpee's behavior.

Examples of Confrontation

In the following dialogue, the therapist avoids a confrontation with the client. This dialogue also illustrates lack of openness and honesty on the therapist's part, which suggests that instances of avoidance of client confrontations may be included in genuineness.

THERAPIST: I think it is very important to be completely open and honest with each other.

CLIENT: Well, how do I seem to you, how do I come across when you listen to me?

THERAPIST: Well, er umm . . . I like you. You're a nice woman.

CLIENT: Don't equivocate!

THERAPIST: Maybe we need to get to know each other better.

CLIENT: Maybe.[8]

The next example illustrates a high level of confrontation, but it is difficult to distinguish this from a high level of empathy.

CLIENT: I now understand what my father has done to me. It's all very clear to me. I think I've got the situation licked.

THERAPIST: But you're still getting up at 5 o'clock in the morning for him when he could get rides from a lot of other men.

CLIENT: Well, uh, he is still my father.

THERAPIST: Yeah, and you're still scared to death of him . . . scared that he'll beat you up or disapprove of you and you're thirty-five years old now. You still fear him like you were a kid.

CLIENT: No, you're wrong, because I don't feel scared of him right now.

THERAPIST: You're scared right now—here—with me—he's here . . .

CLIENT: (Pause)   I guess I understand him better for what he is, but when I'm around him, I'm still scared, and always think of standing up to him after I leave him. Then I talk myself out of doing what I really want to do.[9]

The following dialogue illustrates a positive confrontation, facing the client with an unrecognized or unaccepted strength.

CLIENT: I know I sound weak and mousy. My question is—am I?

THERAPIST: I get your question, but you don't really come across as being this upset over it, and I don't experience you as a weak person.

CLIENT: I don't really feel weak, but somehow. . . .

THERAPIST: You don't like being seen as a weak person.

CLIENT: I know people like me better when I act weak.

THERAPIST: Maybe you're afraid people won't like you if you come on strong.[10]

Again it would appear that positive confrontation involves empathy, with an aspect of immediacy.

SELF-DISCLOSURE

The Nature of Self-Disclosure

O. H. Mowrer has for some time emphasized self-disclosure on the part of the therapist, leader, or facilitator in groups. Barrett-Lennard found therapist self-disclosure to have some effect in therapy.[11] Dickenson also found evidence for positive effects of therapist self-disclosure in groups; he developed a scale for therapist self-disclosure.[12] However, little other research has been done on therapist self-disclosure in individual therapy, and little is known of its effects.

Therapist self-disclosure involves a particular kind of respect for the client. It also is an index of the closeness of the relationship. Both may be indicative of the therapist's acceptance of the client as similar to himself, which may be a late development in therapy as the client improves his functioning. In self-disclosure, the therapist reveals information about himself, his ideas, values, feelings, and attitudes. He may reveal that he has had experiences or feelings similar to those of the client; both the similarities and differences may be emphasized.

Self-disclosure must be for the benefit of the client. The therapist doesn't disclose himself to make himself feel better. He doesn't impose himself on the client. Therapy is for the client, not the therapist. For this reason, as in the case of genuineness, we must think in terms of facilitative or therapeutic self-disclosure.

Just as there is some question about whether confrontation is not a part of empathy (with perhaps an aspect of genuineness), so there is some question as to whether self-disclosure is not a part of honesty and genuineness (with perhaps an aspect of empathy). Carkhuff notes that "The dimension of self-disclosure is one facet of genuineness. . . . Spontaneous sharing on the part of both parties is the essence of a genuine relationship."[13]

Measuring Self-Disclosure

Carkhuff has developed a scale to measure self-disclosure, based upon Dickenson's scale.

FACILITATIVE SELF-DISCLOSURE IN INTERPERSONAL PROCESSES[14]

Level 1

The first person actively attempts to remain detached from the second person(s) and discloses nothing about his own feelings or personality to the second person(s), or if he does disclose himself, he does so in a way that is not tuned to the second person's general progress.

EXAMPLE: The first person may attempt, whether awkwardly or skillfully, to divert the second person's attention from focusing upon personal questions concerning the first person, or his self-disclosures may be ego shattering for the second person(s) and may ultimately cause him to lose faith in the first person.

In summary, the first person actively attempts to remain ambiguous and an unknown quantity to the second person(s), or if he is self-disclosing, he does so solely out of his own needs and is oblivious to the needs of the second person(s).

Level 2

The first person, while not always appearing actively to avoid self-disclosures, never volunteers personal information about himself.

EXAMPLE: The first person may respond briefly to direct questions from the client about himself; however, he does so hesitantly and never provides more information about himself than the second person(s) specifically requests.

In summary, the second person(s) either does not ask about the personality of the first person, or, if he does, the barest minimum of brief, vague, and superficial responses are offered by the first person.

Level 3

The first person volunteers personal information about himself which may be in keeping with the second person's interests, but this information is often vague and indicates little about the unique character of the first person.

EXAMPLE: While the first person volunteers personal information and never gives the impression that he does not wish to disclose more about himself, nevertheless, the content of his verbalizations is generally centered upon his reactions to the second person(s) and his ideas concerning their interaction.

In summary, the first person may introduce more abstract, personal ideas in accord with the second person's interests, but these ideas do not stamp him as a unique person. Level 3 constitutes the minimum level of facilitative interpersonal functioning.

Level 4

The facilitator freely volunteers information about his personal ideas, attitudes, and experiences in accord with the second person's interests and concerns.

EXAMPLE: The facilitator may discuss personal ideas in both depth and detail, and his expressions reveal him to be a unique individual.

In summary, the facilitator is free and spontaneous in volunteering personal information about himself, and in so doing may reveal in a constructive fashion quite intimate material about his own feelings and beliefs.

Level 5

The facilitator volunteers very intimate and often detailed material about his own personality, and in keeping with the second person's needs may express information that might be extremely embarrassing under different circumstances or if revealed by the second person to an outsider.

EXAMPLE: The facilitator gives the impression of holding nothing back and of disclosing his feelings and ideas fully and completely to the second person(s). If some of his feelings are negative concerning the second person(s), the facilitator employs them constructively as a basis for an open-ended inquiry.

In summary, the facilitator is operating in a constructive fashion at the most intimate levels of self-disclosure.

Examples of Self-Disclosure

Examples of facilitative therapist self-disclosure are difficult to come by. Low levels of self-disclosure simply do not need to be illustrated—they represent the absence of the therapist's discussion of himself. However, low levels would also be represented by the refusal of the therapist to reveal himself when it would be therapeutic. Thus:

CLIENT: After I left here the last time I began to feel depressed and to wonder if I would ever get better. I guess I began to doubt your ability to help me. After all, you're so much younger than I am—you can't have had much experience. . . . What about your training and experience? Do you have medical training or a doctor's degree?

THERAPIST: I don't think that my training or experience is relevant here. Your doubts are probably related to your own inadequacies and problems.

A simple self-disclosure is illustrated in the following dialogue:

CLIENT: I just don't think anyone can understand what I am going through unless he has gone through the same thing—or something close to it. I'm not sure you understand—or that I should expect you to. Do you at all know how I feel?

THERAPIST: Yes, I do; as a matter of fact I went through something very similar when my mother died.

A very different kind of self-disclosure is reconstructed by one of Carkhuff's clients:

THERAPIST: Last hour you wondered why I'd make myself available for counseling you. Now I know. Now I can say it. I think I can learn from you.

CLIENT: I honor you for saying that. It makes you more vulnerable.

THERAPIST: You don't know *how* vulnerable.

CLIENT: I know. (I tried to make an intellectual discussion about it.)

THERAPIST: Let's just leave it at what I said.

CLIENT: O.K., we'll do it your way.[15]

IMMEDIACY OF RELATIONSHIP

The Nature of Immediacy

Immediacy refers to the current interaction of the therapist and the client in the relationship. Concern with immediacy is significant because the client's behavior and functioning in the therapy relationship are indicative of his functioning in other interpersonal relationships. Gestalt therapy recognizes this in the concern with the here and now.[16] The Adlerians also focus on immediate behavior in the counseling situation. Kell and Mueller emphasize what they call the "eliciting behaviors" of clients in the counseling relationship, particularly self-defeating behaviors.[17] If the essence of counseling is a relationship, and we are concerned about the functioning of the client in interpersonal relationships—indeed, it is because of inadequate functioning in interpersonal relationships that most clients come to a counselor—then the client's functioning in the counseling relationship should be important.

> The way he relates to the counselor is a snapshot of the way he relates to others. . . . Clients come to counseling manipulating, hostile, rejecting, testing. They invest or do not invest; they are afraid; they present weakness; they attempt to seduce; they stay in a shell; they hide; they try to force the counselor to be responsible; they try to force punishment from the counselor; they apologize for being human. If the counselor does not focus on trying to understand these things, growth possibilities for clients can be missed.[18]

The counselor has the opportunity to deal directly with the client's problem behavior, and the client has the opportunity to learn and to change his behavior.

Carkhuff suggests that immediacy bridges the gap between empathy and confrontation, making possible

> a translation in the immediate present of the helper's insights into the helpee's expressions. The helper in responding immediately to his experience of the relationship with the helpee not only allows the helpee to have the intense experience of two persons in interaction but also provides a model of a person who understands and acts upon his experience of both his impact upon the other and the other's impact upon him.[19]

The therapist must be sensitive toward the feelings of the client toward him and deal with them rather than ignore them. It is particularly difficult for the therapist to recognize negative feelings as related to himself or, if he does recognize them, to respond to them. The difficulty is increased by the fact that the client's message may be, and often is, indirect; that is, it is concealed in references to other persons than the therapist. Carkhuff gives as an example the statement by a client that she has difficulty relating to her physician, which is a way of stating that she has difficulty relating to the therapist.[20] It is obvious that this is an inference, or even an interpretation, that is based upon the therapist's feeling or intuition—or, if he is accurate, on his sensitivity. There is the danger that the therapist may be mistaken, that he is imposing his own interpretation, or projecting, rather than being sensitive to the client. In addition to depending on his own experiencing of the client, the therapist is going beyond, or ignoring, the content of the client's communication to respond to the unspoken message. "Usually when the helpee cannot express himself directly, it is not so much a function of his inability to express himself as it is of the attitudes he holds about the helper in relation to himself."[21] While an accurate response by the therapist can facilitate progress, an inaccurate response can be threatening and damaging.

While the relationship at every moment can be examined in terms of its immediacy, it is not always appropriate to respond to this, and it is, of course, impossible for the therapist to focus continuously on the immediacy of the relationship. It is perhaps most appropriate to focus on immediacy when the therapy seems to be stalled or going nowhere—though this may be simply the result of the client "taking a rest." But it may be because of factors in the immediate relationship and focusing upon the relationship may help. If the counselor is unable to identify precipitating factors, he can ask the client for help—to say what he feels is impeding the relationship. It is possible that the impasse involves feelings, attitudes, or behavior of the counselor of which he is unaware. But it is also useful to look specifically at the relationship in terms of immediacy when things seem to be going well, that is, its positive aspects.

Immediacy, while involving the relationship of the client to the therapist, is not a transference relationship. It involves the therapist as he really is, rather than simply, or mainly, as a representative of some other important figure in the client's experience. However, his relationship with the therapist is related to and influenced by his habits or methods of relating to others, though not necessarily in the manner of the psychoanalytic transference.

As in the case of the other action dimensions, therapist responses of immediacy at a high level are not suddenly presented to the client. Before the therapist knows and understands the client, he cannot be too certain of his experience of the client. And before the client has developed a good relationship with the therapist, he is not prepared for the disclosure. Therefore, the therapist's expression of immediacy is tentative: "Are you trying to tell me how you feel about me and our relationship?" As the relationship develops, the therapist becomes more sure of his inferences, and the client more ready to accept them. But also, as the client improves and functions at higher levels, he becomes more open in his communications, and interpretations of immediacy are then unnecessary.

As in the cases of confrontation and self-disclosure, it may be questioned whether immediacy is independent of or qualitatively different from the conditions considered in Chapter 4. To be sensitive to the client's perceptions, feelings, and attitudes toward the therapist or to how he is relating to the therapist, would appear to be a part of empathy. Carkhuff refers to immediacy as "one of the most critical variables in terms of communicating a depth of understanding of the complex interactions between the parties in the relationship."[22] The expression of the therapist's experiences of the client appears to be an aspect of genuineness. The pointing out of the meaning of the client's words or behavior in terms of his relationship with the therapist appears to be similar to confrontation. Thus immediacy may be empathy and/or genuineness and/or confrontation that involves a particular content—the relationship between the therapist and the client. Since empathy, warmth, and genuineness are no doubt complex variables, it is probably desirable to attempt to analyze them into components. How this can best be done is a problem: Is it desirable to do so in terms of content areas, such as the client's behavior in therapy as distinguished from his behavior outside the relationship?

Measuring Immediacy

Carkhuff's scale is a revision of scales by the Mitchells and by Leitner and Berenson.[23]

IMMEDIACY OF RELATIONSHIP IN INTERPERSONAL PROCESSES[24]

Level 1

The verbal and behavioral expressions of the helper disregard the content and effect of the helpee's expressions that have the potential for relating to the helper.

EXAMPLE: The helper may simply ignore all helpee communications, whether direct or indirect, that deal with the helper-helpee relationship.

In summary, the helper simply disregards all of those helpee messages that are related to the helper.

Level 2

The verbal and behavioral expressions of the helper disregard most of the helpee expressions that have the potential for relating to the helper.

EXAMPLE: Even if the helpee is talking about helping personnel in general, the helper may, in general, remain silent or just not relate the content to himself.

In summary, the helper appears to choose to disregard most of those helpee messages that are related to the helper.

Level 3

The verbal and behavior expressions of the helper, while open to interpretations of immediacy, do not relate what the helpee is saying to what is going on between the helper and the helpee in the immediate moment.

EXAMPLE: The helper may make literal responses to or reflections on the helpee's expressions or otherwise open-minded responses that refer to no one specifically but that might refer to the helper.

In summary, while the helper does not extend the helpee's expressions to immediacy, he is not closed to such interpretations. Level 3 constitutes the minimum level of facilitative interpersonal functioning.

Level 4

The verbal and behavioral expressions of the helper appear cautiously to relate the helpee's expressions directly to the helper-helpee relationship.

EXAMPLE: The helper attempts to relate the helpee's responses to himself, but he does so in a tentative manner.

In summary, the helper relates the helpee's responses to himself in an open, cautious manner.

Level 5

The verbal and behavioral expressions of the helper relate the helpee's expressions directly to the helper-helpee relationship.

EXAMPLE: The helper in a direct and explicit manner relates the helpee's expressions to himself.

In summary, the helper is not hesitant in making explicit interpretations of the helper-helpee relationship.

Examples of Immediacy

CLIENT: I'm not sure I should continue these sessions. I don't feel I'm getting anywhere. You—they don't seem to be helping me. I don't get the feeling you are very concerned.

THERAPIST: You're pretty discouraged and feel like quitting and giving up trying.

CLIENT: Yeah . . . it doesn't seem worthwhile to continue.

Here, the therapist ignores the client's feelings about himself (the therapist), focusing instead on his general reaction of discouragement. Contrast this with the following dialogue, where the therapist responds with a high level of immediacy (as well as confrontation) to the client's (implicit or explicit) feelings of aggression toward the therapist:

THERAPIST: John, you really want to destroy our relationship here.

CLIENT: It's more than that.

THERAPIST: You want to kill me.

CLIENT: No, not really, I. . . .

THERAPIST: John, you want to kill me.

CLIENT: Yes, I want to kill you. I know you haven't earned it, but I want to kill you, maybe for everyone I hate.

THERAPIST: That's too easy.

CLIENT: All I know is I want to kill you.

THERAPIST: You can't.

CLIENT: I can! I can! One way or another I will. So I can't take you this way but I'll find another. I'll fail you. I'll lead you astray. You'll think I'm improving but I'll fail. I'll be your failure case. You'll be responsible.

THERAPIST: You'll do anything you have to, to undermine me, to destroy me, even something that hurts you.

CLIENT: Yes, Yes.

THERAPIST: If you can in some way defeat me, you won't have to change your way of living. You do stupid things to protect a stupid way of life, and that's stupid.

CLIENT: Oh, I want to change. I do, I can't help it. I can't help it. God, I've been wrong to hurt you.

THERAPIST: You had to find out whether you could take me. If you could, I couldn't help you, and I can.[25]

The following dialogue illustrates the therapist's inference that the client's statement about others also applies to the therapist:

CLIENT: I'm never sure where I stand with anyone.

THERAPIST: That applies here as well, right, Jim?

CLIENT: Yeah, I guess it does. I've been thinking of bringing it up—guess I was afraid to learn that you, too, would give some meaningless bunch of words.

THERAPIST: You're telling me you're not sure you trust me enough to go further—even though we have shared a great deal.

CLIENT: Guess I was sure you'd think I was crazy—earlier I felt I might shock you.

THERAPIST: Look—at this moment I experience this: Whatever Jim fears most does not cause me *any* anxiety—I'm not sure I can get it all into words—but your impulses don't scare me—and I trust that. I feel good with you, Jim, and when our meetings are over I do not feel drained of energy. Damn it, you have your own strength—have it, for crying out loud—then you will know.[26]

THE INTEGRATION OF RESPONSIVE AND ACTION DIMENSIONS

The separation of the therapeutic conditions into two groups, the understanding, or responsive, conditions and the initiating, or action, conditions is not a hard and fast separation. To some extent all the conditions are or can be present throughout the therapy process. Concreteness can be a responsive or an action dimension. Genuineness may be a responsive or an action dimension. Understanding or empathy is essential for confrontation and immediacy. Warmth or respect also are essential as a base for the action conditions. The action conditions must have a context of warmth and understanding. This is important, particularly for the beginning counselor, who may be tempted (or encouraged by a misunderstanding of the place of the action conditions) to quickly move into high levels of action conditions without adequate understanding or without the basis of empathy and warmth or respect.

The division of therapy into dimensions or conditions that lead to insight and dimensions or conditions that lead to action is probably not warranted.[27]

The understanding conditions, in addition to providing the basis for action, also may contribute directly to action or make action possible for the client whose therapeutic relationship lacks high levels of the action conditions. On the other hand, the action conditions can stimulate and contribute to client insight.

It is possible, as has been indicated earlier, to consider the action conditions not as new or different conditions but as extensions of the understanding conditions to new areas. Thus, therapist self-disclosure is genuineness or openness applied to the therapist's personal life. Immediacy is empathy applied to the therapist-client relationship of the moment. In addition, the action conditions may be to some extent, if not entirely, essentially high levels of the understanding conditions. That this is the case seems to be recognized, implicitly, by Carkhuff.[28]

THE ESSENCE OF THE CONDITIONS

When one brings together the various aspects of the facilitative conditions—empathy, warmth, respect, concern, valuing and prizing, openness, honesty, genuineness, transparency, intimacy, self-disclosure, confrontation—it becomes apparent that they constitute love in the highest sense or *agape,* to use the Greek term. A loving relationship is the therapy for all disorders of the human spirit and of disturbed interpersonal relationships. It is not necessary to wait for a "breakthrough" or a discovery of new methods or techniques in psychotherapy or human relations. We already have, in essence, the answer—the answer that has been reached through thousands of years of human experience and recognized by the great philosophers of various times and cultures.

The therapist is not a technician, operating objectively on the client. He cannot be detached or disengaged but must be involved in a personal, human encounter. If the therapist is to help the client, he must feel for him, love him in the sense of agape. It is perhaps a basic fact of human relationships that you can't really help a person without becoming involved with him, without caring for him or liking him. Arthur Burton notes that "after all research on psychotherapy is accounted for, psychotherapy still resolves itself into a relationship best subsumed by the word 'love'."[29] As the popular song puts it, "You're nobody until somebody loves you." Then you can become a self-actualizing person.

It is relevant to recall here the discussion in Chapter 3 on the self-actualizing person and society. There it was pointed out that self-actualizing persons are necessary for the survival of society. The conditions we have been discussing are characteristics of self-actualizing persons and thus are the conditions necessary for the survival of society. They are not limited to a single culture. They are characteristics of self-actualizing persons in all cultures, and the conditions for the development of self-actualizing persons in all cultures. Love is not culture-specific or culture-bound.

Psychotherapy is a human relationship involving two unique individuals. Thus, each relationship is unique. Since this is so, the nature or outcome of the relationship cannot be predicted in detail. But it is not necessary to predict the specifics of the relationship. The therapist need only begin, enter the encounter, without concern about its exact nature or outcome. He must commit himself to the client and to the relationship without knowing just what will develop or just what it will mean.

If the therapist must have assurance about what will happen and how the relationship will go, he will be unable to commit himself. If he can't trust himself in the relationship, he can't help the client. The relationship must be free to develop spontaneously. If the therapist has preconceived notions about its nature, he will control and restrict the relationship. The need for control, for predictability of the specifics, represents a lack of tolerance for ambiguity and is an indication that the individual is unsuitable for the practice of psychotherapy. The therapist must have confidence in himself as a person. Too many counseling students are seeking for *something to do to their clients,* rather than being concerned about how *to be somebody with them.*

This does not mean that the therapy process is unpredictable in its general nature and ultimate outcome. Not at all. *If the conditions for therapeutic personality change are present in the therapist as a person, then* a relationship will develop that will lead to the client becoming a more self-actualizing person and, in the process and/or as a result, changing in specific ways or achieving those specific goals that he desires and that are aspects of or by-products of a self-actualizing process.

IS LOVE CONDITIONAL?

There has been considerable discussion about the conditionality of the therapeutic conditions. Rogers used the term "unconditional positive regard." Yet, an analysis of a therapy interview conducted by Rogers indicated that Rogers' responses were not noncontingent but varied with the statements of the client.[30] Thus, the level of the conditions varies during therapy and in relationship to the behavior of the client.

Yet love, it would probably be generally agreed, is unconditional. It is given without demanding something in return. It is bestowed on a person not for *what* he is but for *who* he is.

The solution to the problem would appear to relate to distinguishing between the client as a person—the who—and the client's behavior—the what. The client is unconditionally accepted and respected as a person. The therapist manifests a basic respect, concern, and warmth regardless of *what* he is or of his behavior in or out of the therapy relationship. This basic, minimum level of love, of respect and warmth, is unconditional.

But one who loves and respects another is, of course, affected by the behavior of the other. He is pleased by some things and displeased by others, satisfied by some characteristics and behaviors and dissatisfied by others. In addition, love has great expectations. Real love expects—in a sense, "demands"—the best in others. The therapist who cares deeply about his client is affected by the client's behavior, both in and out of therapy. He is pleased or disappointed, happy or sad, approving or disapproving, depending on how the client behaves. The therapist is more interested in some things the client talks about than in others. And he expresses these feelings, whether he is aware of it or intends to or not. As we note in our discussion of relevance (Chapter 6), the therapist responds to what he thinks is relevant and does not respond to what he thinks is irrelevant. The therapist's responses are contingent upon the client's behavior.

But throughout all his differential responsiveness, there is a basic respect, concern, caring or love, for the client as a person. Without it he could not help the client. The client would not continue the relationship. Without it the therapist would not be a significant person to the client, and if he were not a significant person, his responses would not be meaningful or important to the client and would have no effect on him.

But when one really cares about another, he wants to help the other to be a better person and to prevent him from making mistakes. Thus, there is the temptation to intervene actively in the life of the other. If one loves another, he cannot allow the other to make a mistake, to fail, to do something that clearly seems to be bad or wrong. Or can he? Doesn't a real love, a greater love, respect the right of the other to make his own decisions, even to make mistakes, or to fail? And how is one to know what is a mistake or what actions will lead to failure, what is good or bad, right or wrong, for another? And even where certain actions are clearly wrong, or bad, can or should one, even on the basis of love, intervene, thus indicating his lack of faith in the other? Possibly so, in extreme instances where irreparable damage seems sure to be done. But it might be maintained that under the conditions of real love, which include faith and confidence in the other person, the other will not choose to act in a way that is clearly bad, wrong, or harmful to himself or others. The question perhaps revolves around the extent of the love or caring one has for the other, the respect one has for his integrity, the faith one has in the other and the relationship he is providing for the other .

Love must allow the loved one to make his own choices and, in the extreme case, must leave open the possibility that death rather than life may be chosen because it has such confidence that the power of love will lead to the choice of life. But the risk that death might be chosen must be taken because love requires that the loved one have the freedom of choice.

THE CONDITIONS AND THE GOAL

It will be apparent to the reader that there is a particular kind of relationship between the ultimate goal of counseling and the conditions of the therapeutic relationship—or for the development of self-actualizing persons. The description of the self-actualizing person (Chapter 3) , includes acceptance of and respect for others, openness, honesty and genuineness, and the capacity for deep interpersonal relations with others. The conditions are thus aspects of the goal; the goal includes the conditions. *The condition for self-actualizing persons is an environment of other self-actualizing persons.* The therapist, then, must be a self-actualizing person.

There is a final aspect of the conditions—or of love—that is significant for the problem of control. In reinforcement terms, the most potent reinforcer of human behavior is a good human relationship. The conditions—or love—are not effective, in the long run, unless they are real or genuine. When it is real and genuine, love prevents one from using or exploiting another for one's own purposes. It would thus appear that there is an inbuilt protection in the conditions against excessive control or manipulation.

Yet this does not appear to eliminate the possibility of control by "misguided" persons of good intentions. Possessive love, as is well known, can be harmful. Is there then no protection against influence by those who can offer love and understanding? It appears that brainwashing is most effective where there is real belief in what is being imposed and where there is real concern for the person being influenced—a desire to "save his soul," so to speak. In Orwell's *1984*, Winston, even though tortured by his inquisitor, O'Brien, felt love for him because O'Brien understood him.[31]

It has been pointed out that we should take comfort "in the knowledge that the behavior of those who exercise control is generally governed more by the behavior of those controlled than by anything else."[32] But is it? History, and *Walden Two*,[33] do not demonstrate this. It is only true on the assumption that behavior is mainly controlled by automatic reinforcement.

Perhaps here is the key, as Skinner himself has suggested. When there is awareness that one is being controlled—even by the loving and understanding of another—then one is not in the position of responding automatically to reinforcement. Looking at it in another way, if respect is not a part of love, it is not real love. Or, if respect as well as empathic understanding and genuineness is not present, the individual responds differently. And if respect is present, then there is no attempt to control in a manipulative sense, or in terms of what the controller thinks is best. It is man's ability to be aware of being controlled that is his protection. Respect for another prevents the controller from manipulating another, and the awareness of lack of respect prevents the other from being manipulated by a possessive love and understanding.

OTHER CONDITIONS

Are the conditions described in Chapters 4 and 5 the only conditions included in the psychotherapy relationship? We don't know. These conditions account for only part of the variance in therapy outcomes.

But it must be remembered that neither the conditions nor the outcomes are measured with a high degree of reliability, so that any measured relationship would be attenuated. And there are, of course, conditions in the client that affect outcome (Chapter 6).

There may be other important therapist variables. For example, there is good reason to believe that the expectations of the therapist exert a great influence upon the client's behavior.[34] All therapists expect their clients to change; otherwise they would not be engaged in psychotherapy. Furthermore, they believe that they and/or their methods are instruments of such change. The degree of confidence in themselves and their methods may vary, but it would appear that some such confidence must exist or therapists would leave the profession or change to other methods. The minimum level of confidence for some effectiveness may be relatively low, however; I have had students who were skeptical about the efficacy of the core conditions, but who found, somewhat to their surprise, that their clients did improve, or change. On the other hand, the confidence in a method may be so strong that therapists can be successful with any method in which they believe. This, of course, makes it difficult, if not impossible, to evaluate methods apart from therapist confidence in the method. We face the paradox that no method can be successful unless the therapist has confidence in it, yet a method may be successful only because the therapist (and the client) has confidence in it.

These factors have been given little attention in research. Most research comparing different methods of counseling or psychotherapy has not controlled for the therapists' belief in or confidence in themselves and their methods. Research that attempts to control for therapist personality differences by having the same therapists utilize different methods fails to control for the factor of relative belief in or confidence in the different methods (and also for different levels of experience and competence in different methods.)[35]

SUMMARY

In this chapter we continue the consideration of the conditions for the development of self-actualizing persons, or for the therapeutic process. Several conditions other than the core facilitative dimensions discussed in Chapter 4 have been identified or described and rating scales developed for their measurement. The three that are considered in this chapter are designated by Carkhuff as action-oriented or initiative conditions, as distinguished from the understanding or responsive conditions. These three conditions or dimensions are confrontation, therapist self-disclosure, and immediacy of the relationship.

It is emphasized that no sharp line can be drawn separating the two types of conditions. The understanding conditions lead to, and may be sufficient for, client action, while the initiative conditions facilitate understanding and client insight. It is suggested that the action-oriented conditions may be considered extensions of the responsive conditions or may represent high levels of these conditions.

The essence of the conditions, it is suggested, is love or agape. Whether love, or the conditions, are conditional or unconditional is discussed. It is concluded that a basic level of respect, warmth, and caring, or love for the client as a person is unconditional. But since the therapist does care for the client, the client's behavior does make a difference to him, and he responds positively or negatively. From the client's standpoint, unless he feels the basic unconditional respect and concern of the therapist for him, he will not be affected by the therapist's differential responding. Thus, both unconditional and conditional elements are present and necessary for the therapist to have any influence upon the client.

NOTES

[1] R. R. Carkhuff and B. G. Berenson. *Beyond counseling and therapy*. New York: Holt, Rinehart & Winston, 1967, chap. 9.

[2] R. R. Carkhuff. *Helping and human relations*. Vol. I, *Selection and training*. Vol. II, *Practice and research*. New York: Holt, Rinehart & Winston, 1969, Vol. I, p. 191.

[3] *Ibid.*, Vol. II, p. 93.

[4] *Ibid.*, Vol. I, p. 211.

[5] *Ibid.*, Vol. II, p. 93.

[6] Carkhuff and Berenson, *Beyond counseling*, p. 178. In the later published report of this study, it appears that there was no average difference in type of confrontation, but low-functioning therapists confronted clients with their limitations in both early (first) and later (fourth) interviews, while high-functioning therapists confronted clients with their assets more often in the earlier interviews, and reversed this in the later interviews. (S. Anderson. Effects of confrontation by high- and low-functioning therapists on high- and low-functioning clients. *Journal of Counseling Psychology*, 1969, **16**, 299–302.

[7] Carkhuff, *Helping*, Vol. II, pp. 324–325.

[8] Carkhuff and Berenson, *Beyond counseling*, pp. 176–177.

[9] *Ibid.*, p. 173.

[10] *Ibid.*, p. 174.

[11] G. T. Barrett-Lennard. Dimensions of therapist response as causal factors in therapeutic change. *Psychological Monographs*, 1962, **76** (43, Whole No. 562).

[12] W. A. Dickenson. Therapist self-disclosure as a variable in psychotherapeutic process and outcome. Unpublished doctoral dissertation, University of Kentucky, 1965.

[13] Carkhuff, *Helping*, Vol. I, pp. 208, 209.

[14] *Ibid.*, Vol. II, pp. 321–322.

15 *Ibid.*, p. 110.

16 F. S. Perls. *Gestalt therapy verbatim.* Moab, Utah: Real People Press, 1969.

17 B. L. Kell and W. J. Mueller. *Impact and change: A study of counseling relationships.* New York: Appleton-Century-Crofts, 1966.

18 M. R. Cudney. The use of immediacy in counseling. In J. C. Heston and W. B. Frick (Eds.). *Counseling for the liberal arts campus.* Yellow Springs, Ohio: Antioch Press, 1968, pp. 135, 136.

19 Carkhuff, *Helping*, Vol. I, p. 192.

20 *Ibid.*, p. 194.

21 *Ibid.*, p. 212.

22 *Ibid.*, p. 192.

23 R. Mitchell and K. M. Mitchell. The therapist immediate relationship scale. Unpublished research scale, Michigan State University, 1966; L. Leitner and B. G. Berenson. Immediate relationship scale: A revision. Unpublished research scale, State University of New York at Buffalo, 1967.

24 Carkhuff, *Helping*, Vol. II, pp. 326–327.

25 Carkhuff and Berenson, *Beyond counseling*, p. 149.

26 *Ibid.*, p. 189.

27 *Ibid.*, pp. 139, 229.

28 Carkhuff, *Helping*, Vol. I, p. 218.

29 A. Burton. *Modern humanistic psychotherapy.* San Francisco: Jossey-Bass, 1967, pp. 102–103.

30 C. B. Truax. Reinforcement and non-reinforcement in Rogerian psychotherapy. *Journal of Abnormal and Social Psychology,* 1966, **71,** 1–9.

31 G. Orwell. *1984.* New York: Harcourt Brace Jovanovich, 1949.

32 W. F. Day. Review of B. F. Skinner, *Beyond freedom and dignity. Contemporary Psychology,* 1972, **17,** 465–469.

33 B. F. Skinner. *Walden two.* New York: Macmillan, 1948.

34 R. Rosenthal. *Experimenter effects in behavioral research.* New York: Appleton-Century-Crofts, 1966.

35 E.g., G. Paul. *Insight versus desensitization in psychotherapy.* Stanford: Stanford University Press, 1966.

Chapter 6

Implementing the Conditions: The Counselor in the Therapy Process

The immediate goal of counseling or psychotherapy is the initiation and continuation of the therapeutic process. This is achieved, on the part of the counselor, by providing the basic core conditions. The client also has a contribution to the process, which is not one-sided but a relationship. In this chapter we consider the implementation of the conditions by the counselor and in the next chapter we view the process from the client's standpoint.

The conditions of a good therapeutic relationship are not techniques. They are often referred to as skills, which is a somewhat better term, though still not adequate. They are attitudes, but they are more than attitudes. They involve behavior, especially verbal behavior. But behind the words are the attitudes and feelings of the therapist. The expression of the attitudes and feelings is not, for the beginning counseling student, natural or spontaneous. It is therefore desirable, if not necessary, to offer some suggestions to the student about the implementation of the conditions. As the student gains experience, he becomes less aware of his implementing the conditions or of different ways of responding to the client. His behavior becomes spontaneous.

It is essential that the counselor first recognize the basic attitude or frame of reference from which he must operate if he is to understand his clients. This is the internal frame of reference of the client. It is not too much to say that if the student does not or cannot assume or adopt the internal frame of reference, he can never understand his clients and thus can never become a counselor or therapist. Yet, I have seen students who have not achieved this at the end of their practicum experience. In many cases it may be that this requirement was never pointed out to them by their instructors—who themselves may not operate on this basis—since it is my experience that students who are made aware of this requirement can learn to operate from the client's internal frame of reference during practicum.

THE THERAPIST'S RESPONSIBILITY

The beginning counselor may enter the practice of counseling or psychotherapy with unrealistic expectations or with dreams of quickly achieving far-reaching, even miraculous, changes in his clients. He may anticipate the glowing satisfaction from grateful clients attributing their new lives to the counselor.

This is an unrealistic expectation. The counselor who holds such an expectation is doomed to disappointment and frustration, as well as anxiety, which will interfere with his effectiveness as a counselor. Counseling or psychotherapy is no profession for anyone who is dependent upon spectacular results for the satisfaction of a need for accomplishment. It is no place for the impatient person, who must see immediate results, or the person dependent upon rapid, steady, and easily observable progress in his clients for his own professional satisfaction and self-esteem.

It is only reasonable not to expect sudden, miraculous changes in psychotherapy. The client has behind him years of living and experience, usually of unhappy, disturbed living under aversive conditions and detrimental interpersonal relationships. Attitudes and habits built up and practiced during this long period of time do not usually change easily or quickly. Counseling or psychotherapy, for an hour a week, or at most several hours, constitutes but a small part of the client's life. Freud was well aware of the difficulties and limitations of psychotherapy and cautioned against unrealistic expectations; he expected therapy to take several years. It was only when psychoanalysis came to America that brief psychoanalytic therapy was developed, under the pressure in

America to speed things up, to become more efficient (without always being more effective). But Wyatt notes that "it does not make biological sense that an organism molded into a certain pattern under innumerable influences over many years, should be changed profoundly through an influence within a few months. A therapist who insists on the rebirth of his patients may have missed his calling."[1] Therapy involves the development of a relationship, which takes time. The counselor must avoid impatience with the client for taking time to enter the relationship and for his slowness in trusting the therapist. There is no such thing as instant intimacy. As the popular song puts it, "You can't hurry love."

Few therapists have claimed much more than 50 percent success in their cases. The claims of Ellis, Wolpe, and others of up to 90 percent success are of doubtful validity. Few therapists would maintain that complete cures are possible for all emotionally disturbed persons. Studies of clients seldom find more than two thirds of them improved. Indeed, the discouraging early research on the outcomes of psychotherapy suggests no evidence that psychotherapy results in better than chance improvement or is better than no therapy.[2]

Actually, the results of psychotherapy are both better and worse than the early surveys indicated. Although on the average, clients may not appear to be any better off following therapy (at least on our inadequate and imperfect criterion measures), analysis of the data has shown that some clients improve considerably, while others get worse. Psychotherapy may be for the better or for worse.[3] In addition, there is evidence that people improve "spontaneously," that is, without psychotherapy. Since improvement cannot actually be spontaneous (that is, without some influence or cause), it appears that people who are not treated by professional counselors or psychotherapists receive help from other persons in their environment. Again, this is both encouraging and discouraging. It is encouraging in that it indicates that the conditions for therapeutic change are present in many nonprofessional people. It is discouraging in that it indicates that, on the average, psychotherapists apparently possess no greater degree of these conditions than does the population in general. It also suggests that all the special methods and techniques in which therapists engage, beyond the basic relationship, add little if anything to the outcome of the therapeutic relationship.

But recent research does show that positive change and improvement is possible and that this improvement is related to the existence of high levels of the basic core conditions. Thus, the counselor or therapist, while being patient and reasonable, should not be pessimistic. Positive change can and does occur, occasionally dramatically. And each therapist has a great responsibility to be among those therapists who help their clients rather than make them worse. By not expecting quick and extensive changes or expecting that every one of his clients will improve, the counselor is relieved of one source of anxiety that can impair his functioning. On the other hand, since at least some of the variables or conditions leading to therapeutic change are now known, *the counselor cannot evade the responsibility for providing at least minimal necessary levels of these conditions to his clients.* While this is an awesome responsibility, the fact that we know what these conditions are and that they can be learned or acquired, means that the counselor or psychotherapist can do something to meet this responsibility. This knowledge also means that the educator of counselors and the trainer of psychotherapists have the responsibility and obligation of teaching their students about these conditions. This is not always done success-fully—as should be obvious from research indicating that many ex-perienced, practicing therapists have clients who become worse.[4]

While no book or didactic instruction alone can teach counseling or psychotherapy, they can contribute to such teaching. The student needs to know what he should do before he can be expected to do it. In the preceding chapters we discuss the nature of the conditions for therapeutic personality change. Here we attempt to assist the student in applying or implementing these conditions. It should be emphasized that this is only a beginning, an orientation, and that it is only through supervised practicum training and then continuing experience in the practice of counseling or psychotherapy, that high levels of the condi-tions can be achieved and maintained. It is important also for the stu-dent to recognize that the facilitative or understanding conditions come first and that it is only in the context of these conditions that the initiative or action conditions are helpful or therapeutic.

COUNSELOR IMPLEMENTATION

Listening

If the therapist is to reach any understanding of the client, he must allow the client to present himself. Only the client can tell the therapist how he feels, what he thinks, how he sees himself and the world. Only by listening to the client can the therapist enter his world and see things as he does. The first rule of therapy is to listen to the client.

It should be obvious that one cannot listen if one is talking. Yet beginning counselors seem to find it extremely difficult not to talk. Perhaps they have been trained to initiate conversation in social situations. Many of them have had experience in teaching or preaching, where they have assumed the initiative and have taken responsibility for directing or guiding conversations or discussions, so that they are unable to relinquish the initiative to another. Or perhaps they have read something somewhere about the necessity for the counselor to establish rapport by finding some common experience, acquaintance, or activity with the client. At any rate, the problem is so common that I begin students in the counseling practicum with a simple, concrete rule: Keep your mouth shut. This is an objective, easily observed criterion for the instructor and the counseling student to evaluate in a tape recording. Someone has suggested that with beginning counselors adhesive tape might be more useful than recording tape.

The difficulty created by a counselor taking the initiative in the early part of counseling is that he imposes his frame of reference on the client. Rather than presenting himself from his own frame of reference, the client presents himself as he thinks the counselor wants him to. There are those who feel that if the counselor is to understand the client, he needs certain kinds of information about him, which should be obtained in the initial interview. But such an approach does two things: (a) it sets the structure of counseling as one in which the counselor leads and the client follows; and (b) it may lead to knowledge *about* or understanding *about* the client, but not to an empathic understanding from the client's frame of reference. Such an approach meets the counselor's needs, such as inability to tolerate ambiguity and the fear of an unstructured encounter, rather than being helpful to the client or to the progress of therapy.

Listening to another person, allowing him freedom to present himself freely without forcing him into one's own frame of reference, is a difficult thing to do. One must really be interested in the other person and what he has to say. In most social conversation, listening is only the necessary waiting for one's turn to speak and rather than the listener focusing attention on what another is saying, he is thinking about what he is going to say when his turn comes. Too many counselors engage in this kind of listening. Real listening is difficult. The listener must not be preoccupied with himself. Real listening is not a passive but an active process. The listener's complete attention must be given to the speaker. While he is listening to the client—indeed during the entire therapy process—the therapist must be totally committed to the client. Real listening is hard work. Some years ago I saw a cartoon in which two psychiatrists were in an elevator. One was impeccably neat and fresh; the other looked bedraggled, with tie askew and suit rumpled. The second psychiatrist asked the first: "How can you listen to people's problems all day and still look so fresh?" To which the other replied: "Who listens?"

Frieda Fromm-Reichmann writes:

What then are the basic requirements as to the personality and professional abilities of a psychiatrist? If I were asked to answer this question in one sentence, I would reply, "the psychotherapist must be able to listen." This does not appear to be a startling statement, but it is intended to be just that. To be able to listen to another person in this other person's own right, without reacting along the lines of one's own problems or experiences, of which one may be reminded, perhaps in a disturbing way, is an act of interpersonal exchange which few people are able to practice without special training. To be in command of this act is by no means tantamount to actually being a good psychiatrist, but it is a prerequisite of all intensive psychotherapy.[5]

The therapist in listening must not only suspend thinking about his own experiences and problems but must also suspend all evaluation and judgment of the client. The suspension of concern for his own experiences and problems does not mean, however, that the therapist represses all the feelings that arise in response to what the client is saying. These feelings and associations are useful in understanding what the client is saying.

Listening to another is a manifestation of respect to him. We all like those who really listen to us. It is not uncommon for someone to remark upon what a nice person and good conversationalist another person is, when observation would indicate that the other person is a good listener and seldom dominates the conversation. Listening is a potent reinforcer. It reinforces verbal productiveness in the client, and without such verbal productiveness therapy could not progress.

Structuring

Many clients do not know how to act or what to do in psychotherapy. They may have misconceptions about the nature of psychotherapy and its practice. The counselor or psychotherapist is a professional person, and people often have certain conceptions of their relationships with professional persons. Professional persons are experts and authorities. Therefore, one listens to them and is passive or subordinate in the relationship. Students often identify counselors with teachers. Thus, they often remain silent, waiting for permission to speak, or expect the counselor to interrogate them. Adults often equate the psychotherapist with the physician. Thus they may begin by stating their complaints or problems. But then they wait for the therapist to question them. They expect the therapist to give them advice or solutions to their problems.

Structuring is the orientation of the client to his role and responsibility in the relationship and to the role and responsibility of the therapist. Overt or verbal structuring may not be necessary. If the client enters the relationship by taking the responsibility for presenting himself and his problems and concerns, it is not necessary for the therapist to engage in formal structuring. He informs the client of his own role by his behavior, by modeling rather than by verbal discussion. Formal verbal structuring is necessary only where (a) the client has no idea about what he is expected to do or what the therapist's role is; and (b) the client has a misconception of what he is expected to do or what the therapist's role is.

In the early period of client-centered therapy, structuring was often routinely practiced by many counselors, and many instructors taught their students to structure routinely. Structuring was probably necessary in most cases since the approach was new and different from that used by most counselors. Now, the educated public knows what to expect. Popular magazines have carried articles on how to behave when seeing a psychotherapist. They have indicated that the client is expected to do the talking, that the therapist listens—and probably will not even ask many questions. However, many segments of the public, and many clients, including perhaps most students, at least below the college level, do not know what psychotherapy is really like.

Thus, the therapist should be prepared to structure when necessary. One of the problems regarding the practice of client-centered therapy has occurred here. There are those who have claimed that the client-centered approach is not appropriate for counseling in the public schools because students are dependent and not able to take responsibility for themselves in the counseling process. This opinion has arisen in part, at least, from a misconception on the part of many would-be client-centered counselors about the client-centered approach. In this misconception, to be client-centered is to be passive. Thus, when a student comes to see the counselor, he waits for permission to speak or, not knowing what he should do, he remains silent. The counselor does not structure. As a result, no relationship is established, and the student leaves, does not return, and is not helped. And the blame is placed on "client-centered counseling." The counselor may conclude that client-centered counseling is not appropriate for students, abandons all its principles, and becomes directive in his approach. But all that may be necessary is to give the student permission to speak and to define counseling as different from the classroom situation. Simply saying "Can you tell me why you are here?" may be sufficient to enable the student to enter a relationship.

Where structuring is necessary, it should be provided only to the extent necessary. It is undesirable and unnecessary for the counselor to go into a long lecture on the nature of his approach—probably saying that he is not going to do much of the talking or to dominate the relationship, at the same time as he is doing exactly that! Structuring should be brief, given only to the extent necessary at the moment, and provided more explicitly later as needed. As the relationship gets started, the behavior of the therapist provides the necessary structure.

To engage in structuring when it is not necessary, after the client has engaged in the appropriate behavior of talking about himself, can disrupt the process, at least temporarily. The following dialogue illustrates this. The client had begun talking about himself, but at a pause, the counselor, a practicum student who had been taught in a prepracticum course to structure routinely, did so.

THERAPIST: You see, you have an hour, your appointment, and of course we can give you the tests, but, you know if you want to talk more, I'll be glad to listen, you know, so I can help you. So feel free, and relax . . . it's your time and just use it as you want to.

CLIENT: Well, I don't know what to say, exactly . . . ah . . . Well . . . do you think it would help if I tell you a lot about my background and things like that?

One can easily imagine the thoughts of the client, who had been doing what he thought he was supposed to do but now must feel that what he was doing was not right. Rather than facilitating the process, structuring interfered with the client's progress in expressing himself spontaneously.

Responding

The function of the therapist, at least in the beginning of therapy (and, essentially, throughout the process), is to respond to the client. Interviews in which the client is responding to the therapist are not therapy interviews but interrogations, usually. A simple rule for beginning students in counseling that avoids the development of a situation where the client is responding to the counselor is: Never ask a question —except when you don't understand what the client is saying. Again, this provides a very simple, objective criterion for the beginning student. It is very easy to determine from a tape recording who is responding to whom.

If the client is responding to the counselor, it is clearly the counselor's interview. He is leading and guiding the talk of the client, usually along his own preconceived lines of what is important, relevant, or interesting to him. He is placing his own structure and frame of reference on the client. He is not likely to be able to enter the client's frame of reference and develop an empathic understanding of him.

A question that always arises in discussions of therapist listening and responding is what to do with a silent or inarticulate client. Can one listen to or respond to silence? To some extent one can. A sensitive therapist can sometimes feel or intuit what a client is thinking or can sometimes hazard a guess. He can then respond, perhaps in a tentative way. The client may display or communicate discomfort, uncertainty, hesitation, or confusion. The counselor may respond with "You don't know where to start" or "You find it hard to decide what to say first" or "You find it hard to talk" or "You don't know what you are supposed to do?" If the client is completely inarticulate, or says he is, the counselor is in a dilemma. Presumably he wants the client to take responsibility for his therapy and wants to avoid a relationship in which the client is responding to him. Even though the client is dependent at the beginning, the counselor presumably wants him to move toward independence and does not want to reinforce dependent behavior.

There is a possible way out of this dilemma. If it is necessary for the counselor to initiate the interaction, he can do so in a way that will insure that *at least fifty percent of the time he will be responding to the client*. He can do this by simply responding to every response he elicits from the client, before going on, if necessary, with another initiating action. Fifty percent reinforcement is perhaps not effective, but with most clients it will be greater than this, and the client is taught that the counselor responds to him. If the counselor assumes and continues the initiative, he is reinforcing the client in responding and makes it difficult if not impossible for a therapy relationship to develop.

Another question is what to do when the client engages in irrelevant talk. Here we must first ask: What is irrelevant talk? How does the therapist know what is relevant or irrelevant? What are the criteria for irrelevance?

In one respect, everything the client says is relevant, in some way, to the counseling interaction. That is, there is a reason for everything he says. The counselor can never be sure that what the client is saying is irrelevant, from his point of view. Fromm-Reichmann refutes the claim that therapists who fall asleep during the therapy hour only fall asleep when the client is producing irrelevant material and wake up as soon as his talk becomes pertinent.[6] Some things, of course, are more relevant than others, and the counselor has some feeling for relative relevance. In fact, he is always acting upon, or responding on the basis of, his perception of what is relevant, or most relevant.

There are several reasons why the client may engage in irrelevant talk. First, he may be encouraged to do so by the therapist's misconceived attempts to develop rapport. Second, he may not yet trust the therapist. Third, he may not be ready to move into emotionally significant or threatening material. Fourth, he may be "taking a rest" before attacking his problems again. In any case, for the therapist to charge the client with being irrelevant and to insist that he move into more relevant material does not help the situation; because it may be threatening, it leads to resistance and delays the client's return to relevant talk.

When the counselor does feel that the client is engaging in irrelevant talk, he simply does not respond but remains quiet, ready to respond when the client moves into relevant material. His lack of response withholds encouragement. In effect, by not responding he tends to extinguish the client's talk. This is an important point to recognize in relation to those who recommend that the counselor engage the client in "small talk" or social talk at the opening of the interview, particularly the first interview, supposedly to put the client at ease or to establish rapport. Such talk is a waste of time. If the client has come voluntarily, he does not come to discuss the weather or some other irrelevant material. And if the client has not come voluntarily, he knows damn well he was not referred to discuss the weather. Counseling is not a social conversation and for the counselor to begin it as such is misleading in terms of structuring and reinforces such an approach by the client. A study of therapeutic interviews found that the shift from conventional pleasantries to the work of therapy hindered the therapeutic process. The investigators concluded that "the absence of such pleasantries, with an immediate approach to the work of the interview, in itself seems to indicate a more conjunctive integration of therapist and patient."[7] The comments of Fromm-Reichmann are relevant here:

> I strongly advise against any attempt on the part of the psychiatrist to make things seemingly easier for the patient by pretending that the professional doctor-patient relationship is a social one. Deep down in his mind, no patient wants a nonprofessional relationship with his therapist, regardless of the fact that he may express himself to the contrary. . . . Moreover, the psychiatrist who enters into a social relationship with his patient may easily become sufficiently involved himself in the nonprofessional aspects of the relationship to be rendered incapable of keeping control over the professional aspect of the doctor-patient relationship.[8]

I have seen this happen with counseling students and their clients.

The counselor thus influences the client's verbalizations by his responsiveness or lack of responsiveness. Whatever he responds to is reinforced. The counselor selects from the client's productions those (or elements of those) he feels are most relevant and responds to them, ignoring others. One of the functions of the therapist's responses, then, is to influence the content and manner of the client's talk.

There is an aspect of the counseling process that fits in here, though it may be considered as a part of structuring. This is the tendency—nay, the need—of many counselors to make of counseling a logical problem-analysis and problem-solving process. This is an occupational handicap of therapists who have been trained in a program that emphasizes logic and research. Counselors working in college or university settings often seem to suffer from this problem-solving tendency.

But counseling or psychotherapy—as life—is a psychological, not a logical, process. To try to force the client to be logical is to lead him to intellectualize and to ignore his feelings—or to talk *about* his feelings rather than to express them. The counselor's insistence that the client talk about various aspects of his life, usually in an order determined by the counselor, is a manifestation of this tendency toward logical analysis. The chronological approach also imposes a structure on the client's thinking and talking.

Counseling or psychotherapy must take the client where he is and deal with his logic or apparent lack of logic. It must allow him to deal with his problems and his life as he sees them, in the order that is psychologically relevant to him.

TYPES OF RESPONSES

Another basic function of the therapist's responses, at least in the early phases of therapy, is to communicate to the client his understanding of what the client is saying or trying to say. There are a number of ways in which the counselor can respond to the client to communicate his understanding, as well as his interest in and concern about what the client is saying.

Acceptance Responses

These responses tell the client that the therapist is there, listening, with him, following him. They are simple indications of understanding: "Uh huh," "Yes," "I see," "I understand," "I follow you." Silence may also convey acceptance.

Reflection Responses

Reflection responses go somewhat beyond simple acceptance responses. Reflection of content, or restating what the client is saying in different words, lets the client know that the therapist is hearing what he is saying and that he understands the content, if not what is behind it. Reflections of feelings go beyond or behind the content. They are responses to the more obvious or clear feelings that the client has about the content. They let the client know that the counselor recognizes and is aware of what he is feeling. Simple acceptance and reflection of content responses need not represent empathic understanding. The therapist can emit such responses as a technique. They are easily faked. But reflection of feeling is more difficult to fake and requires some real, or empathic, understanding. Beginning students often find it difficult to respond to feelings rather than simply to content. I have sometimes suggested to a student that he begin a response, to himself if not overtly, with the words "You feel . . ." to help him focus on just what the client is feeling.

Clarification

The client's verbalizations, especially when he is disturbed and feeling deeply, are not always clear and obvious. They may be confused, jumbled, hesitant, incomplete, disordered, or fragmentary. In his clarification responses, the counselor attempts to put together what the client is saying or trying to say, to put into words vague ideas or feelings that are implicit if not explicit in the client's talking. What is confused to the client may not be clear to the therapist either, so that clarification responses are not easy to formulate, and the therapist often is not sure of their accuracy. This kind of response, therefore, is often tentative or phrased in the form of a question.

Specificity or Concreteness

The counselor attempts to make concrete and specific what may be general and abstract in the client's verbalizations. Concrete and specific responses help the client become more specific, help him move from vagueness to clarity and focus upon reality, upon the practical; thus he is helped to move from feeling to action.

Specificity, by avoiding abstractions and generalizations, helps the client analyze his problem in detail. Generalizations and abstractions give him the feeling that his problems are resolved because he can give them names and labels. Labeling has often been advocated to help the client discriminate and avoid overgeneralization. This may be true if the labeling is specific and discriminating in nature. But much labeling is general, often overgeneralized. It consists of assigning a specific problem to a higher category or concept. The effect of such labeling or generalization on the client is to discourage further discussion or exploration of the problem.

In Chapter 5, an example of lack of concreteness was discussed. A client talks about his early relationships with, and feelings about, his parents. The counselor, who has some familiarity with psychoanalytic theory, has an "insight"—the client has an Oedipus complex. He is unable to refrain from communicating his insight to the client, so he tells the client: "You seem to have an Oedipus complex." The client, who also has some familiarity with psychoanalytic theory, agrees: "You're right. I guess I do have an Oedipus complex." Then he discontinues his discussion of his relationship with his parents. What point is there in continuing? The problem is solved—it has been labeled. Thus, generalization discourages further client activity in analyzing his problems.

Silence

Silence on the part of the therapist has varying effects, depending upon how it is perceived by the client. To a vocal client, silence on the part of the therapist may be welcome—as long as he knows the counselor is listening. But silence can be ambiguous. Silence on the part of the psychoanalyst is probably one of the bases for transference, encouraging the client to project onto the therapist. Therapists are sometimes warned about the dangers of catharsis in the beginning of therapy. While I have never observed the dire results that are sometimes predicted, it is possible that clients who do not return after a first interview in which they have disclosed themselves with little if any response from the therapist may fail to return because of uncertainty about whether the therapist really was listening, was interested, or understood them. Fear that the therapist did not understand or accept them, because of their exposure of undesirable thoughts or behavior, may lead them not to return. Therefore, it is desirable that the therapist respond to let the client know he is heard, understood, and accepted, even if this means breaking in occasionally.

When the client pauses in his talk, he usually (though not always) expects and desires a response from the therapist. Not to receive a response may be perceived by the client as rejection. Or, at least, it may be seen as an indication that the client was not talking about what he should be talking about. Silence on the part of the counselor, it will be recalled, is a method of extinguishing irrelevant talk. But it can also extinguish talking by the client in general. Responsiveness on the part of the therapist facilitates deeper exploration on the part of the client, avoiding a one-way recital.

Thus, therapist silence has different effects, and the therapist must be aware of the possible effects and allow or break silence depending upon his sensitivity to how the client perceives the silence. Therapy can occur during long silences. But long silences in the first interview should usually be avoided.

Interpretation

Clarification responses deal with what is explicitly or implicitly in the client's behavior, verbal and/or nonverbal. Interpretations go beyond this, involving a contribution by the therapist. In interpretation, the therapist adds to what the client is saying, going beyond the client's verbalizations and putting in something of his own.

The line between clarification and interpretation is a fine one. They would appear to be on a continuum. There will often be disagreement on whether a therapist's response is a clarification or an interpretation. Whether it is classified as one or the other will depend, in part, on the sensitivity of the observer. What is clarification to a highly sensitive observer (or therapist) may appear to be interpretation to one who is less sensitive to what is implicit in what the client is saying. The highest level of empathy (level 5) may appear to be interpretation. Carkhuff talks about the "additive" element of the counselor beyond level 3. Carkhuff and Berenson state that the therapist who is functioning at level 3

> does not provide the level of empathic communication in which one person anticipates another. He does not facilitate the client's movement to a deeper level except insofar as he has understood the previous level. . . . In order for the therapy process to move effectively, the therapist must add something to the client's responses, and we might add, something which the client at his present level of development can use constructively. This brings us into the area of what we term depth reflections or moderate interpretations all of which, if accurate, enable the client to go a level deeper in his explorations.[9]

Yet a reading of the definition of level 5 makes it clear that the therapist is responding to what he senses is there, behind or below the words of the client. Rogers writes: "When the client's world is clear to the counselor and he can move about in it freely, then he can communicate his understanding of what is vaguely known to the client and he can also voice meanings in the client's experience of which the client is scarcely aware."[10] Martin states: "The therapist's task is to hear *what is implicit in the client's current experiencing*—what the client is trying to say and can't quite say."[11]

The counselor who thoroughly enters into the client's frame of reference, who perceives as the client does, can often speak *for* the client when the client is not able to speak adequately for himself. "The whole therapist can see the world through the eyes of his client, *sometimes better than the client who is functioning at low levels. . . .*"[12] But it is important to emphasize that the counselor is operating *in the client's frame of reference.* It would perhaps be as well to make the distinction between reflective and empathic responses on the one hand, and interpretive responses on the other, on this basis. Interpretation is based on the counselor's frame of reference, or an external frame of reference. The counselor views the client from the outside and attempts to fit him into a system, theory, or structure. In addition to the classification—or neglecting the uniqueness of the client—and generalization, or higher-order labeling, that may be involved, interpretative responses depart from the client's frame of reference and are thus less meaningful and helpful to the client.

A reading of the literature on so-called interpretative psychotherapies, including psychoanalysis, makes it clear that in most cases interpretation is actually clarification. It is one of the misconceptions of psychoanalysis that the analyst interprets from the beginning of therapy. The orthodox analyst usually doesn't venture what he calls interpretation until well along in therapy—often only after months of listening to the client—and then his interpretations are tentative. In fact, such interpretations are usually clarifications. Interpretations that go beyond clarification are called "wild interpretations." Yet the student who wants to become a psychoanalytically oriented counselor can hardly wait to interpret, often beginning early in the first interview, before he can possibly have any real understanding of the client. If an interpretive therapy is to be used, it is necessary for the therapist to thoroughly understand his client first.

E. H. Porter makes an interesting distinction between reflection and interpretation.

> The difference is not in what the therapist says. The difference is in the therapist's *purpose* when he says it. . . . When the therapist utters some words which are a construing of what the client or patient has expressed and it is the therapist's purpose to be asking of the client or patient whether or not the construction put on the client's expression was the meaning intended—that's a reflection.
>
> When the therapist utters some words which are a construing of what the client or patient has expressed and it is the therapist's purpose to be informing the patient what meaning his expression holds regardless of his, the patient's, intended meaning—that's an interpretation.[13]

Interpretations, that is, responses that go beyond what is explicit or implicit in the client's behavior, retard therapy rather than facilitate it. Interpretations are threatening and often lead to resistance. They give the client the impression that the therapist knows more about him than he does about himself and thus lead to less client talk and analysis of himself. And interpretations that are abstractions or generalizations, as suggested in the discussion of specificity, lead to the inhibition of client activity and exploration.

Immediacy

Immediacy is probably an aspect of empathy, involving the here-and-now behavior of the client. It sometimes involves confrontation, which is an aspect of empathic understanding. Therapist *self-disclosure,* as suggested in Chapter 5, is probably an aspect of genuineness, or a way of immediately implementing openness and genuineness.

Questioning

Little has been said so far about questioning as a technique (except in regard to the silent client), although textbooks on counseling and psychotherapy often give extensive space to the discussion of this topic. The reason is simple—questioning by the therapist has little place in counseling or psychotherapy. The topic would be omitted here except that counseling students must be explicitly warned against the use of questioning because so many of them fall into the trap of engaging in question and answer sessions with their clients. I have heard tapes of students nearing the end of an intensive practicum that are nothing but question and answer sessions.

Interviews in which the client does little but respond to questions by the therapist are not therapy interviews. They are more like interrogations. Counseling should not be modeled after Sgt. Friday or Perry Mason interviews. Questioning and probing are counterindicated for at least two reasons—they may be threatening to the client, and they lead to or set up the interview as an externally oriented process, rather than one in which the therapist is assuming the internal frame of reference of the client. In addition, they often lead to an intellectually or cognitively oriented process. The result is that the client does not take the initiative and is discouraged or prevented from engaging in the process of exploration.

Ornston and his associates found that beginning therapists ask more questions than experienced therapists.[14] Friel, Berenson and Mitchell in a study of high-functioning and low-functioning counselors found one major factor for the low-functioning group. Carkhuff refers to it as the "stupid question" factor.[15]

It is relatively easy to get counseling students to avoid this non-therapeutic activity by simply instructing them not to ask questions. My statement to beginning practicum students includes three simple rules: (a) Keep your mouth shut—you can't listen to the client when you are talking; (b) Never ask a question, except when you do not understand what the client is saying, or when you have a silent client; and (c) Respond to the client—don't have him responding to you.

TWO PROCESSES OR ONE?

Carkhuff and Berenson have suggested that there are two rather distinct phases of counseling, indeed, different enough to be considered as two separate processes. The first is characterized by such terms as facilitative, understanding, passive, nondirective, and responding, while the second is characterized by such terms as action, active, directive, assertive, and initiating.

In the first phase, characterized by Carkhuff and Berenson as the downward and inward phase, the counselor is relatively passive, concentrating on gaining an understanding of the client and assisting the client to gain an understanding of himself, or to achieve insight. In this phase, the therapist conditions of empathic understanding, respect or warmth, concreteness, and genuineness are most important. The emphasis is on the minimal condition level (level 3 on the 5-point scales). Empathic understanding does not move greatly beyond the client's clear or obvious communication. Respect is unconditional. The emphasis in genuineness is on not being phoney or inauthentic, rather than on the therapist's openness or expressiveness. Concreteness is directed toward helping the client become more specific in his communications.

But the achievement of insight by the client is not enough; Carkhuff and Berenson criticize traditional therapies because they do not go beyond insight. They say that "most therapists conclude therapy where we conclude the first phase."[16]

The second phase, the upward and outward phase, or "the period of emergent directionality"[17] moves from the facilitative conditions to the action conditions. Genuineness continues, but as an open sharing. Therapist self-disclosure enters into the relationship, though it diminishes as the process proceeds. The therapist "actively interprets with immediacy his experience of the helpee's motives and attitudes toward the helper that present obstacles to progress, both in terms of internal understanding and external action" (levels 4 and 5 on the immediacy scale).[18] Confrontation is used to present the client with discrepancies and inconsistencies in his behavior. Concreteness is directed toward specific alternatives in problem solution and action. Empathy must still be present but is now subordinated to the action dimensions, serving to keep the therapist's understanding current. The therapist acts upon the understanding achieved in the first phase to encourage and guide or direct the client toward action. Respect, or unconditional positive regard, becomes conditional.

Carkhuff and Berenson recognize that there can be no sharply divided phases. There is no specific point at which the therapist moves from one phase to another. The facilitative conditions continue throughout the second, or action, phase. In some cases the action conditions may precede the facilitative conditions: "Frequently, . . . it is necessary for the person to act in the absence of understanding. . . . the helper directs the activities of those who cannot initiate either meaningful communication or action on their own."[19] However, these instances involve clients—or individuals—at such a low level of functioning that they are unable to enter a relationship, and the helping process would not be called psychotherapy.

While it may be useful to think in terms of stages or phases in the total therapeutic process, there is a danger that the phases or stages will be considered as separate and discrete steps, particularly by counseling students and beginning counselors. It is probably better to think in terms of a single, but developing, process. In the case of the phases described by Carkhuff and Berenson, it would appear that they reflect a single continuing, developing process, or a growing, deepening relationship between the therapist and the client. The process is a natural development of an interpersonal relationship. In beginning such a relationship, it is natural and necessary that the therapist, or helper, be more responsive—listening, following the client, providing a warm atmosphere—in order to get to know and understand the client. As the relationship develops and the therapist increases his understanding, he can respond at higher levels of empathy—levels that may appear to be more active, even interpretative. With this increased understanding, he can respond to the client's behavior in the interview in the ways that are encompassed under the concept of immediacy. His greater understanding also enables him to make statements or responses that we define as confrontations. The therapist also becomes more relaxed, at ease, and spontaneous, so that he becomes more open, honest, and genuine, engaging in higher-level therapeutic genuineness and self-disclosure. Carkhuff himself notes that "the dimension of self-disclosure is one facet of genuineness. . . ."[20]

In fact, then, it appears that the action conditions are essentially high levels of the facilitative or understanding conditions. The difference is perhaps one of degree or depth of response, of specificity, clarity, certainty, strength, and openness of the therapist's responses.

A second question can be raised regarding the two phases described by Carkhuff and Berenson. Their second, or action phase, seems to be based on the assumption that the client, under the influence of the facilitative relationship and on the basis of his self-understanding and insight, is unable to determine and undertake appropriate action on his own. Rather, he must be directed or guided by the therapist. Yet clients of traditional, or client-centered, therapists have made decisions and engaged in actions without such direction and guidance, under the influence of only (although at high levels) the facilitative conditions. Perhaps the assumption that clients on their own can move into action needs to be tested, with each client, before the therapist enters with direction and guidance. No client should be deprived of the satisfaction of acting on his own if he is capable, even if it may take longer. The reluctance to wait for the client, or the abandonment of the assumption that he can do it on his own, may be an indication of lack of patience on the part of the therapist or lack of confidence in the client rather than inability of the client to move into action on his own.

If the development of autonomy or independence is one of the goals of psychotherapy, then active direction or guidance by the therapist is inconsistent with this goal. Every effort should be made to allow the client to initiate his own actions. To the extent that he does so he becomes independent; moreover, the satisfaction involved in doing it himself reinforces independence and thus increases the probability of continuing independence.

Carkhuff recognizes that some clients are able to act upon their discriminations and insights. These are apparently clients functioning at level 3. Carkhuff and Berenson state that

> The level 3 client, having established that the counselor is functioning at minimally facilitative levels, continues with his self-exploration and problem expression independent of the counselor. . . .
>
> Once the high-level functioning client is aware that his counselor is functioning at high levels and is genuinely sensitive and respectful, the client can continue on his own independently, whether or not the counselor continues to function at high levels.[21]

And again, they suggest that during the second phase the therapist must be guided by the client; "indeed he may discern the client's readiness and ability to determine his own direction."[22] Perhaps more clients would be able to act upon their discriminations and insights if permitted to do so by a patient, discerning therapist who had confidence in the client's ability. Carkhuff's statement is important here: "The helper does not commit too much of himself in the interest of offering the helpee as much opportunity as possible to develop himself as fully as possible."[23]

SUMMARY

In this chapter we consider how the counselor implements the facilitative conditions and the initiative or action conditions in the therapy process. The responsibility of the therapist for providing at least minimal conditions is emphasized, since counseling or psychotherapy can be for better or worse, depending on whether the counselor provides high or low levels of the conditions.

Although, for purposes of discussion, the conditions have been divided into two phases, the usefulness, or the existence, of such a division is questioned. It is probably better to think in terms of a single process, which develops as the relationship between the therapist and the client grows and becomes more intimate and intense. Thus, the therapist, as he comes to know and deeply understand the client, becomes more involved and more active in the sense that he is more genuine and spontaneous and responds more in the way indicated by the so-called action conditions of self-disclosure, immediacy, and confrontation. It is suggested that these conditions are essentially high levels of the so-called facilitative or understanding conditions.

It is suggested that the therapist should act on the assumption that most clients, under these high level conditions, can and will make their own choices and decisions and translate their self-understanding and insights into action without specific direction or guidance by the therapist.

While this chapter may appear to emphasize technique, it is emphasized that we are concerned not with the impersonal application of techniques as a means of manipulating the client's behavior. We are concerned with the implementation of the basic attitudes or conditions of psychotherapy. Therapy is more dependent on who the therapist is than on what he does. Counselors must be more concerned about *being someone* with the client than in *doing something to him*. Methods or techniques cannot be separated from their user or his personality. And the user cannot be separated from his theories, his beliefs, and his values and attitudes. Relationship therapy is, as Burton notes of existential therapy, the technique of no technique.[24] It is the therapist's attitudes "rather than the therapist's technical knowledge and skill, which are primarily responsible for therapeutic change."[25]

NOTES

[1] F. Wyatt. The self-experience of the psychotherapist. *Journal of Consulting Psychology*, 1948, **12**, 83–87.

[2] H. J. Eysenck. The effects of psychotherapy: An evaluation. *Journal of Consulting Psychology*, 1952, **16**, 319–334; E. E. Levitt. The results of psychotherapy with children. *Journal of Consulting Psychology*, 1957, **21**, 189–196.

[3] C. B. Truax and R. R. Carkhuff. For better or for worse: the process of psychotherapeutic personality change. In Academic Assembly on Clinical Psychology (Ed.), *Recent advances in the study of behaviour change*. Montreal: McGill University, 1963, chap. 8. See also A. E. Bergin. The effects of psychotherapy: Negative results revisited. *Journal of Counseling Psychology*, 1963, **10**, 244–250; A. E. Bergin. Some implications of psychotherapy research for therapeutic practice. *Journal of Abnormal and Social Psychology*, 1966, **71**, 235–246; A. E. Bergin. An empirical analysis of therapeutic issues. In D. Arbuckle (Ed.). *Counseling and psychotherapy: An overview*. New York: McGraw-Hill, 1967, pp. 175–208; A. E. Bergin. Further comments on psychotherapy research and therapeutic practice. *International Journal of Psychiatry*, 1967, **3**, 317–323; A. E. Bergin. The evaluation of therapeutic outcomes. In A. E. Bergin and S. L. Garfield (Eds.), *Handbook of psychotherapy and behavior change: An empirical analysis*. New York: Wiley, 1971, pp. 217–270.

[4] R. R. Carkhuff and B. G. Berenson. *Beyond counseling and psychotherapy*. New York: Holt, Rinehart & Winston, 1967, chap. 1.

[5] Frieda Fromm-Reichmann. *Principles of intensive psychotherapy*. Chicago: University of Chicago Press, 1950, p. 7.

[6] *Ibid.*, p. 10. She is apparently referring to Ferenczi's statement: "The danger of the doctor's falling asleep. . . . need not be regarded as grave because we awake at the first occurrence of any importance for the treatment." (S. Ferenczi. Missbrauch der Assoziansfreiheit. In *Bausteine zur Psychoanalysis*, II. Vienna: International Psychoanalysis, Verlag, 1927, p. 41. (Quoted by H. Racker. The meaning and uses of countertransference. *Psychoanalysis*, 1957, **26**, 303–357.)

[7] S. H. Eldred *et al.* A procedure for the systematic analysis of psychotherapeutic interviews. *Psychiatry*, 1954, **17**, 337–346.

[8] Fromm-Reichmann, *Principles*, p. 46.

[9] Carkhuff and Berenson, *Beyond counseling*, p. 136.

[10] C. R. Rogers. The interpersonal relationship: The core of guidance. *Harvard Educational Review*, 1962, **32**, 416–429.

[11] D. G. Martin. *Learning-based client-centered therapy*. Monterey, California: Brooks/Cole, 1972, p. 81.

[12] Carkhuff and Berenson, *Beyond counseling*, p. 184.

[13] E. H. Porter. In S. W. Standal and R. J. Corsini (Eds.). *Critical incidents in psychotherapy*. Englewood Cliffs, N.J.: Prentice-Hall, 1959, p. 57. Carl Rogers, independently commenting on the same incident, suggests that what was labeled an interpretation by the therapist was actually not an interpretation since its intent was to be empathic (p. 58).

[14] P. S. Ornston, D. V. Cuchetti, J. Levine and L. B. Fierman. Some parameters of verbal behavior that reliably differentiate novice from experienced psychotherapists. *Journal of Abnormal Psychology*, 1968, **73**, 240–244.

[15] T. Friel, B. G. Berenson and K. M. Mitchell. Factor analysis of therapeutic conditions for high and low-functioning therapists. *Journal of Clinical Psychology*, 1971, **27**, 291–293. R. R. Carkhuff. *Helping and human relations*. Vol. II, *Practice and research*. New York: Holt, Rinehart & Winston, 1969, Vol. II, p. 32.

[16] Carkhuff and Berenson, *Beyond counseling*, p. 135.

[17] *Ibid.*, p. 141.

[18] Carkhuff, *Helping*, Vol. II, p. 99.

[19] *Ibid.*, pp. 37, 44.

[20] *Ibid.*, Vol. I, p. 208.

[21] Carkhuff and Berenson, *Beyond counseling*, pp. 57, 138.

[22] *Ibid.*, p. 142.

[23] Carkhuff, *Helping*, Vol. II, p. 97.

[24] A. Burton. *Modern humanistic psychotherapy*. San Francisco: Jossey-Bass, 1967, p. 6.

[25] C. R. Rogers. *On becoming a person*. Boston: Houghton Mifflin, 1961, p. 63.

Chapter 7

The Client
in the Process

In Chapter 6 we consider the counselor's or therapist's contribution to the therapy process. Therapy is a relationship that involves the client. The client is not, or cannot be, a passive recipient. Change in attitudes and behavior—or learning—requires some activity on the part of the person who is being changed—the learner. In this chapter we consider the process from the standpoint of the client—the nature of his involvement or participation in the process. First, however, it is necessary to view the client as he presents himself for help.

CLIENT CHARACTERISTICS

There has been considerable discussion about whether it is necessary that clients come voluntarily to counseling or psychotherapy to be helped. There has been some confusion regarding the use of the words voluntary and involuntary. There is general agreement that psychotherapy is not, and cannot be, imposed upon an unwilling client. Counseling or psychotherapy is concerned with voluntary change in the client. Of course it is possible to change a person's behavior without his consent or voluntary involvement. This can be achieved through the use of drugs and psychosurgery, through coercion or threats or through physical force, and to some extent through conditioning. But these methods of change are not counseling or psychotherapy.

People may be compelled to submit themselves to an exposure to the counselor or therapist, but they cannot be forced to become involved in the therapy relationship. Many counselors or psychotherapists will accept persons who are referred to them but who are unwilling to come, as in the case of a person required to "have psychotherapy" by the courts. These referrals sometimes become clients through voluntarily entering into a therapy relationship when it is offered by the therapist. They are not, then, involuntary clients.

Thus, one of the requirements of therapy is that the client voluntarily enters a relationship that he expects will lead to some kind of change in himself. He wants to change, expects to change, and believes that the therapist and the therapy relationship will effect that change.

Why do people want to change, and seek psychotherapy? Such people are often labelled mentally ill, neurotic, or emotionally disturbed. But these labels tell us little, even though clients may accept them as applying to themselves. From their own point of view, however, clients present themselves for psychotherapy because they "hurt" or suffer in some way, to a greater or lesser degree. They are unhappy, discouraged, depressed, anxious, dissatisfied. They have feelings of inadequacy and of failure, they have unfulfilled desires and aspirations, their lives lack meaning, goals, or a sense of direction. They want to be different, and they realize that they are not what they want to be or what they can be. They recognize the discrepancy between what they could be and what they are, a discrepancy between their self-concept and their ideal self-concept. In short, whether they think of it in these terms or not, *they are not self-actualizing persons* or not as highly self-actualizing as they want to be or could be. The drive for self-actualization is frustrated or not satisfied, and this motivates them to want to change.

Not all persons who are not self-actualizing persons can benefit from psychotherapy or are open to the possibility of benefitting from psychotherapy. Some persons are functioning at such a low level that they are no longer open to the establishment of the interpersonal relationship of psychotherapy. This is the case with many of the regressed patients in mental hospitals. Perhaps they are "unmotivated"; that is, they have given up hope. They may have been hurt so much that the drive for self-actualization has been repressed or even killed; all that is left is the minimal drive for physical self-preservation. Sometimes even that is lost in patients who refuse to eat. These persons are inaccessible to psychotherapy, and other methods are used to try to help them, including shock treatment, which for unknown reasons sometimes makes them accessible to interpersonal relationships, including psychotherapy. Behavior modification techniques may also reach these otherwise unreachable patients. Persistent offering of a human or therapeutic relationship also may succeed with some of them.[1] Perhaps anything that succeeds in getting such patients to realize or recognize that someone is genuinely and sincerely concerned about them, interested in them, and desperately wants to help them, can be successful in arousing them from their regression. This may be the explanation for the success of any new and different treatments applied with enthusiasm and hope by a committed hospital staff.

The importance of the recognition by the client of the interest and concern of the therapist must be recognized in relation to the conditions offered by the therapist. *The offering or providing of the conditions by the therapist is not sufficient; they must be recognized or perceived by the client.* Rogers, in his necessary and sufficient conditions for therapeutic personality change, includes the condition that "the communication to the client of the therapist's empathic understanding and unconditional positive regard is to a minimal degree achieved."[2]

There is another characteristic necessary for initiation of therapy. The client must be able, in some way and at least to some degree, to communicate his feelings, attitudes, and experiences to the therapist. The most empathic therapist cannot understand the client or enter his frame of reference unless the client lets him in and in some way communicates how he sees himself and the world. The most common and the most effective way is, of course, through verbalization. The therapist's listening is ineffective unless the client talks. There are other ways of communicating in addition to verbalization, and the therapist must be sensitive to these; for example, sometimes the client's writing or such other expressive activities as art may communicate.[3] These, while helpful in addition to verbalization, are usually not adequate by themselves.

Thus, the client presents himself to the counselor or psychotherapist as a person who is motivated to change, at least to the extent that he is ready to commit time and, often, money to achieve this change. He has faith and confidence in the therapist and his methods, so that he trusts himself to the relationship. And he is able to perceive, at least to a minimal degree, the therapist's respect, interest, concern, and understanding. These are the conditions in the client that make possible the beginning of therapy. While it would appear that some motivation to seek help is a necessary condition for psychotherapy, belief in the therapist and his methods, while desirable, may not be necessary. That this is so is suggested by the fact that some people get help and improve their relationships when working with nonprofessional "therapists" where no strong belief or faith is present (so-called "spontaneous" remission—see Chapter 8) .

STRUCTURING THE CLIENT'S WORK

The client who presents himself to the therapist begins with some uncertainty, doubts, hesitations, anxiety, and even fear connected with the therapy situation and the therapist. He may not know what to expect, or he may have misconceptions about the process, about what the therapist will do and about what he is expected to do. Where this is the case, the therapist clarifies the situation by structuring.

Part of the structuring consists of explaining to the client the nature of the client's work, which is essentially to talk about himself, his feelings, attitudes, and experiences. Even though the client recognizes and accepts this task, it is often not easy for him to do it. He may begin in a perfunctory way, or he may only be able to give a general, superficial statement of his problem and then wait, depending upon the therapist for help. The prospect of revealing himself openly to another is threatening. He may not yet trust the therapist, or he may see the therapist as a cold surgeon who is going to open him up without concern for how much it will hurt.

If the client is to engage in his work, he must not feel threatened. The facilitative conditions provided by the therapist minimize threat. Love—real love—is challenging but not threatening. Learning, it is recognized, does not occur under conditions of threat. Behavior becomes restricted and narrowed rather than variable and exploratory, as is necessary for problem-solving. It is important that the therapist communicate these conditions, and that the client perceive them. It is only when the client feels accepted, respected, understood, safe, and secure with the therapist that he can begin to make progress. With an anxious, fearful, threatened, and hesitant client, it is difficult to communicate the conditions and to establish a nonthreatening atmosphere. Prolonged silence on the part of the therapist can be highly threatening. On the other hand, profuse verbalization and reassurance can be inhibiting to the client. The process may be slow in beginning. The therapist must have patience and not impose himself too forcefully upon the client. The therapy relationship, like any other human relationship, takes time to develop. There is and can be no such thing as instant intimacy.

CLIENT SELF-EXPLORATION

There have been many discussions of the counseling process in terms of client involvement. But it appears that the basic activity of the client is to engage in a process of self-exploration or intrapersonal exploration. In every approach to psychotherapy, the client talks about himself, about his beliefs, attitudes, feelings, experiences, thoughts, and actions. Considerable research supports the existence of a relationship between client self-exploration and successful therapy or favorable outcomes.[4] There is also considerable research indicating that the level of client self-exploration is related to and influenced by the level of facilitative conditions provided by the therapist. However, there are differences among clients in their levels of self-exploration that are not related to therapist levels of the conditions.[5]

The process of self-exploration is a complex one, involving several aspects or (perhaps) stages.

Self-Disclosure

Before the client can explore himself, he must disclose or reveal himself. In the beginning of counseling, this is most often the disclosure of negative aspects of himself—his problems, failures, inadequacies, and so on. Since these constitute the bases of his dissatisfaction and unhappiness, they are the reasons he has sought counseling. But since they are negative—indicating a low or negative self-concept, they are difficult for him to express. Self-disclosure at this level represents self-exposure.

The question often arises among students about the desirability of accepting, or listening with acceptance to, extensive disclosures of negative feelings and emotions, self-negation and self-criticism, the expression of feelings of worthlessness, discouragement, depression— even suicide. Isn't this likely to reinforce these feelings and make the client worse? Shouldn't the counselor reassure the client that things aren't as bad as he thinks they are, that he isn't as bad as he thinks he is?

The therapist must remember that the client has come just because he has problems, negative feelings, and a negative self-concept. His low opinion of himself is not (usually) simply a misperception or unrealistic—it has some basis in reality. He is failing to be his best self, to be a self-actualizing person. To deny this or his feelings that this is the case (even when it is not so bad as he feels it is), is not to help the client but to prevent him from going on to a recognition of the positive aspects of himself and his situation. The process of reaching the positive cannot be short-circuited. If the client is to reach a positive self-concept, he must be allowed to express his negative feelings. And the counselor must be willing and able to go with him to the depths and face the worst with him; the counselor must not allow his own anxiety, fears, and discomfort to prevent this descent. It is only when he has plumbed the depths and seen himself at his worst, that the client can rise again and, knowing the worst, build a new and positive self.

The assumption is that there is some good in every client, something positive in every situation, but that the client can only recognize this if he is allowed to express the worst:

CLIENT: Things look pretty discouraging.
THERAPIST: It's pretty grim.
CLIENT: It's worst than that—it's hopeless.
THERAPIST: There's just *no* hope.
CLIENT: No—none at all. There's no way out.
THERAPIST: It's the end—a dead end—completely black, without a ray of light or hope.
CLIENT: (Pause)   Well—maybe not completely. I'm not ready to give up completely yet.

If the client can see no hope and does give up, it is possible that he is right—that it is the end. And reassurance by or optimism on the part of the counselor isn't likely to help him.

The client who is able to disclose himself is already at stage 4 of Rogers' Scale of Process in Psychotherapy, as illustrated by his example of a client at this stage: "I'm not living up to what I am. I really should be doing more than I am. . . ."[6] Rogers notes that successful cases begin at a higher level on the process scale than do unsuccessful cases. At stage 4, the client has perceived that the therapist understands him and is able to engage in self-disclosure. It is the difficulty of reaching this level with seriously disturbed clients that is responsible for many drop-outs from therapy and thus the failures with the more severely disturbed.

Rates of Self-Exploration

Once the client has disclosed himself, or has put himself out and on view to himself and the therapist, he is able to look at himself and to engage in the process of exploring what and who he is. He is "free to explore, experience, and experiment with himself. . . ."[7] He can *be himself* in a way he can't in ordinary interpersonal relationships; he can be open, real, and honest with himself as well as with the therapist. He is able to face himself as he is.

The process of self-exploration does not proceed simultaneously and at equivalent levels in all areas of the client's life, with all of his problems, or in all aspects of his difficulties. Progress may occur to some extent in one area and then be blocked or slow down. The client shifts to another area only to reach a level beyond which he is not ready or able to go. This may repeat itself in still other areas. Eventually the client returns to the first area and to each of the other areas, to progress further. Exploration in each area makes it possible to explore the other areas more deeply. It is not useful or possible to insist that the client stick to one area or problem until it is thoroughly explored before moving on to another. The total process is not a logical one, but a psychological process in which the areas or problems are interrelated and cannot be explored completely as independent problems.

The client begins where he is able to and usually in areas where he is most conscious of a problem. He moves to other relevant areas and problems when he is ready and able to do so in the nonthreatening relationship. To attempt to push the client or to direct him toward other areas the therapist considers important is to introduce threat and to risk retarding rather than facilitating the client's self-exploration. Attempting to introduce the action conditions (confronting, particularly) as the client is beginning the exploration of new areas or problems can be inhibiting because it is threatening. Even moving to high levels of the facilitative conditions

> may have harmful effects at this stage of helping. The minimally facilitative conditions enable the helpee to know that someone can understand him on his terms in addition to providing him with the feedback necessary for later reformulations. The minimally facilitative conditions are sufficient in and of themselves to elicit a depth of self-exploration in all relevant areas.[8]

In 1963, Truax developed a nine-point Depth of Self-Exploration Scale.[9] Carkhuff revised this into a five-level scale for measuring client self-exploration.

HELPEE SELF-EXPLORATION IN INTERPERSONAL PROCESSES[10]

Level 1

The second person does not discuss personally relevant material, either because he has had no opportunity to do such or because he is actively evading the discussion even when it is introduced by the first person.

EXAMPLE: The second person avoids any self-descriptions or self-exploration or direct expression of feelings that would lead him to reveal himself to the first person.

In summary, for a variety of possible reasons the second person does not give any evidence of self-exploration.

Level 2

The second person responds with discussion to the introduction of personally relevant material by the first person but does so in a mechanical manner and without the demonstration of emotional feelings.

EXAMPLE: The second person simply discusses the material without exploring the significance or the meaning of the material or attempting further exploration of that feeling in an effort to uncover related feelings or material.

In summary, the second person responds mechanically and remotely to the introduction of personally relevant material by the first person.

Level 3

The second person voluntarily introduces discussions of personally relevant material but does so in a mechanical manner and without the demonstration of emotional feeling.

EXAMPLE: The emotional remoteness and mechanical manner of the discussion give the discussion a quality of being rehearsed.

In summary, the second person introduces personally relevant material but does so without spontaneity or emotional proximity and without an inward probing to discover new feelings and experiences.

Level 4

The second person voluntarily introduces discussions of personally relevant material with both spontaneity and emotional proximity.

EXAMPLE: The voice quality and other characteristics of the second person are very much "with" the feelings and other personal materials that are being verbalized.

In summary, the second person introduces personally relevant discussions with spontaneity and emotional proximity but without a distinct tendency toward inward probing to discover new feelings and experiences.

Level 5

The second person actively and spontaneously engages in an inward probing to discover new feelings and experiences about himself and his world.

EXAMPLE: The second person is searching to discover new feelings concerning himself and his world even though at the moment he may perhaps be doing so fearfully and tentatively.

In summary, the second person is fully and actively focusing upon himself and exploring himself and his world.

Level 1 (which corresponds to points 0 and 1 on the Truax scale) is illustrated by the following dialogue:

THERAPIST: As though you're just feeling kind of down about these things . . .
CLIENT: Tired.
THERAPIST: What?
CLIENT: Tired.
THERAPIST: Tired . . . kind of worn out?
CLIENT: Couldn't sleep last night. (Pause)
THERAPIST: You're just feeling kind of worn out.
(Client does not respond—silence to end of tape.) [11]

An example of the highest level is the following dialogue:

CLIENT: (She is relating experiences in Germany during World War II)   I don't want to exaggerate but, why, you could have killed for some things! And the pendulum was always swinging. You never knew. You'd steal carrots to eat because you were always so dreadfully hungry. There was no clothing, no fuel . . . and the cold . . . (Voice soft, reflects a great deal of concentration) They had . . . they always announced the dead, those who had been killed in the war. And one always went and read the lists. I don't recall exactly where they were . . . (Pause) It was conducive to think that life was . . .
THERAPIST: Unendurable, and getting used to the, that way of living.
CLIENT: Yes, yes, uh hum, I had no . . . I was not . . . I have a very close girlfriend who shared my things, but I was not kind and tender with my brothers. I remember one thing that really shames me still. I was to watch out for them, and my younger brother fell and bruised his head one day, and I just pulled his cap over that. Really, really, but . . . but my excuse I think I can say was that nobody ever treated me lovingly. At least I think that.
THERAPIST: It was a hard life and you have to be hard. This is what you knew.
CLIENT: I think I was harder than I really had to be but I was just, ah, hard . . .
THERAPIST: Because you hadn't been taught to be soft and loving.
CLIENT: Yes, ah, yes. I don't know whether you teach somebody to be, to be . . . do you?

THERAPIST: Well, you haven't experienced it?

CLIENT: I feel that way now, toward my family, my husband and children . . . I can . . . love them.[12]

CLIENT AWARENESS OF HIS BASIC SELF

The process of self-exploration leads to self-discovery, self-understanding, and self-awareness, among other things. This is more than what is commonly meant by insight, which is usually an intellectualized statement of a problem in terms of its origins or etiology. Self-understanding is not limited to intrapersonal processes but includes an understanding of the impact the client has on other people, or the nature of his functioning in interpersonal relationships. He begins to see himself, at least to some exent, as others see him.

Self-exploration reveals inconsistencies and contradictions. Attitudes and feelings that have been experienced but denied to awareness are discovered. Experiences inconsistent with the self-concept, or self-image, previously denied or distorted, become symbolized in awareness. The client becomes more open to his experiences.

With increasing self-awareness, the client's self-concept becomes clearer. And with a clear self-concept his vague dissatisfactions with himself become more specific. He begins to see in what specific respects he is failing to actualize himself, and in just what ways he fails to measure up to his self-ideal. He begins to reorganize his self-concept to assimilate all his experiences of himself; his self-concept becomes more congruent with his experiences and thus more realistic. In turn, his perception of his ideal self becomes more realistic and more attainable, and his self becomes more congruent with his ideal self. With these changes in the self and his self-concept, the client becomes more accepting of himself and feels more confident and self-directing. He experiences more acceptance from others, both because he perceives more realistically and accurately and because his changed self elicits more positive reactions from others. He becomes a fully functioning person, a more self-actualizing person.[13] His feelings of adequacy and of self-esteem increase. In the process of developing self-understanding and self-awareness, both positive and negative attitudes about himself arise. Not all that the client discovers about himself is negative or bad. Experiences that at first do not seem to belong to, and cannot be integrated into, the self, become accepted as the self; "the client discovers that he can *be* his experience, with all of its variety and surface contradiction. . . ."[14] As the process continues, negative attitudes toward the self decrease and positive attitudes increase. "The client not only accepts himself—a phase which may carry the connotation of a grudging and reluctant acceptance of the inevitable—he actually comes to *like* himself."[15] The self that emerges—the deep, basic nature of the client—is not bad, antisocial, or destructive. The core of the self "is not bad, nor terribly wrong, but something positive. Underneath the layer of controlled surface behavior, underneath the bitterness, underneath the hurt, is a self that is positive, that is without hate."[16]

In a very significant way, then, therapy does not necessarily require the changing of the basic self. It involves the discovery of the positive core of the self, and its freeing so that the client can be his real, basic self. The conditions of therapy provide a nonthreatening environment in which the client does not have to respond negatively, aggressively, or defensively, but can be the self that he really is or is capable of being. Therapy is, then, a situation in which the client can be himself—his best self, the potential self that has been covered up, or not allowed to develop, by the absence of the conditions of good interpersonal relationships. In terms of the relation of the self-concept and the self-ideal, the discrepancy may be reduced by change in the self-ideal as much, if not more than, change in the self-concept. Or, perhaps more accurately, changes in the self-concept may occur without changes in the basic self.

It is important that the process of self-exploration not be confused with client talk *about* himself. This is often a problem with students beginning practicum. By continued questioning, they get the client to make statements about himself and mistake this for client self-exploration. But in such talk the client (as well as the counselor) is viewing himself as an object and is not actually expressing or disclosing himself. His talk is externally oriented, abstract, generalized—an intellectual or rational discourse about himself as an object.

INSIGHT AND ACTION

Insight, it has been frequently stated, is not enough. Self-understanding is not acceptable as a goal of counseling or psychotherapy. There must be action or changes in client behavior, or therapy cannot be considered successful. We have noted that Carkhuff and Berenson have claimed that traditional therapies stop at self-understanding and insight. They have suggested that the core or facilitative conditions lead to insight but not to action, and that new conditions, the action conditions, must be introduced in a second phase of psychotherapy to move the client beyond understanding to action.

In our consideration of the implementation of the conditions by the counselor (Chapter 6), we indicate that we prefer to think in terms of a single process rather than two processes, or a continuous process rather than two phases. We question whether the so-called action conditions are actually new or different conditions but suggest that they can be incorporated into the facilitative conditions, representing essentially high levels of these conditions. And we do not include a separate action phase in our discussion of the client's work in the process but end with the development of self-awareness in the client.

The position we take is that action by the client or changes in his behavior accompany or follow the development of self-awareness as a natural consequence. In fact, as has been noted by many writers, action or changes in behavior may precede insight, or a clear verbalizable understanding, or self-awareness. Action and understanding are interacting or reciprocal processes. Carkhuff notes that "in healthy people understanding is simultaneous with action. . . ."[17] He suggests, however, that low-level functioning persons, including the majority of clients, are unable to act upon their self-understanding and need to be pushed by the therapist. If, in the process of therapy, low-level functioning clients develop self-understanding and begin to function in the therapy relationship at a higher level, why cannot they then act upon their understanding? It is possible that the problem is one of time, with an impatient therapist being unable or reluctant to wait for the client to begin acting and changing his behaviors.

For it is apparent that *the client's behavior does change in the therapy relationship itself*. He discloses himself and engages in productive self-exploration, which he was not able to do before. He develops and expresses self-awareness. He becomes more accepting of himself. He becomes more accepting of others, including the therapist. He becomes more open, honest, and genuine. In other words, he becomes more like the therapist; he manifests the conditions of a good interpersonal relationship—empathic understanding, respect and warmth, genuineness, concreteness, and self-disclosure. He becomes, within the therapy relationship, a more self-actualizing person.

The result of therapy, then, is that the client becomes a more self-actualizing person. The characteristics of the self-actualizing person include the facilitative conditions of a good human relationship. The client, in becoming more like the therapist, manifests the conditions to which he is exposed. If, as has been indicated earlier (Chapter 5), the essence of these conditions is love, then the client learns to love as a result of therapy. To love others, then, is an aspect of being self-actualizing. Glasser states that one of the two basic psychological needs of man is to receive love and to give love. "At all times in our lives we must have at least one person who cares about us and whom we care for ourselves. . . . To either love or allow ourselves to be loved is not enough; we must do both."[18]

Now there is no question that the generalization of these changes outside the therapy relationship is a difficult and slow process. But it does occur, and it is facilitated by the fact that, through the principle of reciprocal affect, the persons with whom the client relates become more accepting, understanding, and genuine.

Furthermore, in terms of more specific or more concrete changes in behavior, the client's basic drive toward self-actualization, freed from its frustration by lack of facilitative interpersonal relationships, produces changes in the client. The motivation is there, the self-understanding is present, and, to the extent possible in his external environment, the client's behavior changes. In perceptual or phenomenological terms, his perceptions have changed, and his behavior changes accordingly. With a change in the self-concept, behavior then changes to become consistent with the self-concept, which is a basic determiner of behavior. Specific behavior changes occur as a by-product of self-actualization.

A LEARNING VIEW OF THE THERAPEUTIC RELATIONSHIP

If learning is defined as those changes in behavior that are not due to native response tendencies, maturation, or temporary states of the organism (as a result of fatigue or drugs, for example),[19] then counseling or psychotherapy must involve learning. But there are different views of the nature of learning, differing descriptions of the learning process, and different theories of learning. When we referred to perceptual or phenomenological changes leading to behavior changes, we were speaking in terms of one theory of learning. The detailed considerations of the therapy process by Carl Rogers are formulated, essentially, in terms of a perceptual theory of learning and behavior.[20] Perceptual theory is not currently popular or influential in psychology, however. The prevailing orientation in the field of learning is toward behavior theory, and discussions of a learning approach to counseling or psychotherapy usually assume this orientation.

To a certain extent at least, behavioral change, or learning, can be described by, or cast into, various theoretical orientations. Each orientation is to some extent a different way of viewing the same phenomena. One orientation may be more restricted or limited than another, but even a restricted viewpoint can be expanded or extended to encompass, at least in a general way, a wide variety of phenomena. In this respect, reinforcement, a basic concept of the behavioral approach to learning and behavior, can be extended to apply to the therapy process, as can other concepts as well. We shall therefore describe the process of counseling or psychotherapy that has been developed in this and the two preceding chapters in terms of a behavioral approach to learning.[21]

The way in which the therapist conditions operate can be described—or "explained"— in terms of learning theory concepts. Truax and Carkhuff suggest that there are four learning modalities or channels by which the basic facilitative conditions operate in psychotherapy.[22]

Reinforcement of Human Relating

Clients are characterized by difficulties in interpersonal relations. Thus, interpersonal relations are sources of anxiety and fear. Their interpersonal relations have been associated with painful experiences— rejection, lack of understanding, hostility, threat, and so on, from others. As a result, they are hesitant to approach others and are threatened by the prospect of relating to others. Yet they come for therapy because the pain or disturbance is so great that they will do almost anything to seek help. They approach the therapist, though at the same time they have strong avoidance responses. They suffer from the approach-avoidance conflict described by Miller.[23]

The therapist responds to the client with warmth, respect, concern, and understanding. These constitute, then, rewards for the approach responses of the client. The therapist presents a nonthreatening relationship. It is more than a situation in which the process of extinction operates, where the client finds that the therapist does not act toward him in the negative ways in which others have acted or continue to act toward him. He is actually rewarded for his efforts to relate to another.

The therapist must begin with the behavior that the client is able to express. Even slight, tentative, or hesitant relating behaviors are met with warmth and empathy, with positive responses. Truax and Carkhuff state that, for most effective results:

> The therapist would tend to offer relatively high levels of warmth and empathy to any and all verbalizations by the patient (random continuous reinforcement) and also, on a selective basis, provide higher levels of warmth more frequently to the patient's attempts toward human relating. Thus the effective therapist might respond with empathy and warmth 40 percent of the time to definite attempts at human relating. As in all learning situations, for "shaping" to be effective, the reinforcement must begin with the responses currently available in the patient. Thus, responses with even the slightest resemblance to attempts at human relating

would immediately be followed by a relative increase in empathy and warmth. With some patients this would particularly mean that even negative or hostile reactions to the therapist would be met by heightened expressions of warmth and accurate empathy. Over time, as the patient consequently begins to relate more frequently, more closely and more effectively, the therapist should become more selective in his offering of warmth and empathy. The criterion for reinforcement is gradually raised as the patient is better able to relate. This suggests that the therapist, to be more effective, would offer high levels of warmth and empathy more and more selectively across time in therapy.[24]

This passage suggests that while the therapist begins by being unconditional (providing continuous reinforcement for any client responses), he moves toward discrimination, or conditional reinforcement. The implication is that the therapist consciously and deliberately delivers reinforcements on a contingency basis—or that he should do so. However, attempts to do this in research, either in interview situations or counseling analogue studies, indicate that it is not possible for therapists to discriminate and respond to, or to recognize and reinforce, predetermined classes of behavior with accuracy and consistency. Skinner has noted that "the contingencies of reinforcement which are most efficient in controlling the organism cannot be arranged through . . . personal mediation. . . . Mechanical and electrical devices must be used. Personal arrangement and personal observation of results are unthinkable."[25] He is referring to teaching in a class of children, but the same can be said for the individual personal situation. Thus, conscious, deliberate attempts to reinforce specific client responses are not very effective, since to be effective every (or almost every) response must be reinforced, and this is not humanly possible. Moreover, the conscious and deliberate dispensing of predetermined rewards or reinforcements leads to an unnaturalness and lack of spontaneity or genuineness that can dilute or destroy their effectiveness as the client becomes aware of their artificial nature.

However, the therapist is not unconditional in his responses, even in the beginning of therapy. He is more concerned about some of the client's verbalizations than about others; he is more interested in some topics than others. It is well known that what clients talk about is related to the theoretical orientation of the therapist. If the therapist values dreams, clients dream and report their dreams. If the therapist is interested in sex, clients talk about sex. If the therapist deals with phobias or fears, clients present these to the therapist.

The presence of minimal levels of the facilitative conditions provides a nonthreatening atmosphere in which the client can begin to relate to another person. If the client is to remain in the therapy situation, the lack of threat must continue. Thus, it would appear that minimal levels of the core conditions must continue throughout therapy. In fact, contrary to the implication in the quotation from Truax and Carkhuff that the more effective therapist would be highly conditional, Truax later found that the overall level of facilitative conditions in group therapy was independent of the degree to which the conditions were offered differentially as reinforcers.[26]

While there are those who maintain that an "optimum" level of anxiety (which is never defined) is necessary to keep the client working on his problems, it is suggested that there is sufficient anxiety present within the client, without the therapist adding to it. The therapist

> must discriminate between those anxiety changes evoked by the patient's self-exploration and those evoked by his own threatening or inept attempts at interpretation or empathic responses. If the therapist fails to make this discrimination it is unlikely that he will prove helpful. It may be best to assume that whenever the patient shows an increase in anxiety and *withdrawal,* the therapist's response (or lack of response) is the source of the anxiety arousal."[27]

Reinforcement of Self-Exploration

The therapist does respond, intuitively, to some activities or verbalizations of the client and not to others. After the relationship begins, and after the opening remarks of the interview sessions, the therapist does not respond to social conversation by the client. As indicated in Chapter 6, such material is considered irrelevant. The therapist does respond to self-talk, since this is assumed to be relevant. At the beginning of therapy, such self-talk is usually of a negative character. The therapist thus is reinforcing negative self-references. But negative self-references are only one subcategory of the self-reference category. So when, as normally happens, positive self-references begin to occur, these also are reinforced. But self-references are themselves only a subcategory of a broader kind of client statements—self-exploratory statements. The therapist, in responding to the several categories of self-exploratory statement, participates in a process known as shaping. In this process, in the absence of the desired behavior (here self-exploration), behaviors that approximate this response (here spontaneous verbalization) are reinforced; when behavior that is closer to the desired behavior occurs (such as self-talk), it is reinforced. Eventually, the client engages in self-exploration, which is then reinforced by the therapist, leading to self-exploration at deeper and deeper levels.

Self-exploration is often a painful or anxiety-arousing process. Thus, even though it is reinforced by specific therapist responses of interest, acceptance, and understanding, the client may become anxious or threatened by the nature of the material he is exploring. The therapist must be careful that his responses do not increase threat. Probing questions and interpretations are likely to do this. They cause the client to retreat—to resist, the phenomenon noted by interpretative therapists. It is desirable that the client be helped to explore as deeply as he can at the moment. The context of the facilitative conditions maintains a safe nonthreatening atmosphere for this. This atmosphere can be considered "a counterconditioning agent, a pleasant stimulus to be paired with the mildly anxiety-provoking cues associated with the leading edge of the conflict region," or the self-exploratory process.[28] In this respect, the nonthreatening therapy relationship is similar to the inducement of relaxation by behavior therapists. In fact, "it seems probable that eliciting warmth and comfort as responses incompatible with anxiety and fear and avoidance produces more potent and adaptive counter-conditioning than deep muscle relaxation."[29]

The warm, accepting, nonthreatening therapy environment would appear to be a more relevant condition for reducing or extinguishing anxieties related to social or interpersonal processes than physical relaxation. However, as Truax and Carkhuff suggest, clients may have developed conditioned anxiety responses to "human warmth" (probably phoney or manipulative in nature), so that the therapist should be cautious about offering strong, overwhelming warmth at the beginning of therapy.

The client, then, engages in the process of self-exploration in a warm, relaxing, nonthreatening atmosphere. Nevertheless, the process arouses anxiety as he progresses; he stops, retreats, "rests," takes a breather by moving into irrelevant, or less relevant, areas. Self-exploration is a step-by-step process, or a two-step forward and one backward process—an approach-avoidance situation. If the therapist, by his specific responses (including concreteness and confrontation), helps the client explore himself in the presence of the facilitative conditions, the client progresses. The therapist's accepting, warm, empathic responses are rewarding. The client feels a satisfaction in his achievement. His anxiety related to the topic which he is exploring is reduced.

Behavior therapists emphasize that they are systematic in their rewards or reinforcements and, while recognizing that other therapists utilize reinforcement, insist that it is unsystematic.[30] But it has already been suggested that it is extremely difficult, if not impossible, to really be systematic in dispensing rewards in the ongoing complex process of psychotherapy. (The process of systematic desensitization *is* systematic, but this is a process of extinction not of positive conditioning.) It is suggested that the relationship therapist, intuitively and spontaneously, is more systematic in his reinforcements than it is possible to be by taking thought and attempting to provide reinforcements on a conscious, mechanical basis.

Martin describes this intuitive reinforcement process when he says:

> the client is progressing through an "anxiety hierarchy" as he moves to more and more anxiety-provoking cues, and the nature of the hierarchy continually changes as more and more cues become available to increase his understanding. A consequence of this is that an anxiety hierarchy established at any point in therapy will necessarily be at least partially incorrect. The process of therapy I am describing permits the therapist and client to modify continuously the nature of the hierarchy, as correction of it becomes necessary with new knowledge. Clients do indeed progress in therapy along an anxiety hierarchy, but it is a hierarchy that the client and therapist discover together during the therapy process. The client will attempt to take the next step on his hierarchy. The therapist's job is to hear this attempt and to facilitate it by responding to the leading edge of what the client is trying to deal with.[31]

The therapist's empathic responses facilitate self-exploration. Being understood is rewarding. The therapist's empathic responses are conditional. But they vary not by the intent or design of the therapist. They are contingent on the client's success in clarifying his self-exploration. While minimal levels of warmth, accetpance, and concern maintain the client in his self-exploration, highly empathic responses reward especially successful or clear self-exploratory efforts. The therapist cannot be highly empathic if the client is extremely vague and confused. He can only respond to, or reward, the effort. But when the client engages in clear, specific, highly insightful self-exploration, the therapist is able to respond with high levels of accurate empathy, which is highly reinforcing to the client.

The recognition of the influence of reinforcement provides the counselor with a way of meeting the problem of responding to the silent or highly nonverbal client. Counselor responses of attention, interest, concern, and understanding to the verbalizations of the client are rewarding and encourage the client to continue self-talk and self-exploration. Continuous questioning by the counselor will not accomplish this. In fact, it will teach the client to be responsive to the counselor and to wait for the counselor to continue questioning or initiating the interchange.

Recognizing the principle of reinforcement also suggests that the questions of the counselor should be directed toward eliciting self-talk by the client rather than factual information or personal history material. It is not necessary—or perhaps even desirable—that the questions be of the type frequently recommended by instructors in counseling; that is, questions directed at past or present feelings (e.g., "How do you feel about that?" or "How did that make you feel?"). Contrary to the assumption that these questions lead to the expression of real or basic feelings, it is more likely that they will lead to the expression of considered or intellectualized feelings. The direct focusing upon feelings by the client, rather than the unconsidered spontaneous expression of feelings, introduces a cognitive element that leads to talk *about* feelings rather than the *expression of* feelings.

The objection has been raised that encouraging client self-talk and self-exploration would, by generalization, lead to the client imposing such talk on those he interacts with outside therapy. However, a moment's thought should lead to the recognition that, if such talk were not responded to positively, it would be extinguished, and the client would learn to discriminate regarding with whom he could engage in such talk. In this regard also, it would be anticipated that the generalization of his other learnings in therapy—understanding, respect, warmth and acceptance, and openness, honesty and genuineness—would be responded to positively by others in his environment and thus be reinforced. Since such characteristics are responded to by the development of the same characteristics in those who are exposed to them, the client would experience an increase in these conditions in his everyday environment, which would enhance the therapy.

Eliminating Specific Anxieties and Fears

If the client has learned specific anxieties or fears in the area of human relating, these may be removed through desensitization or adaptation, reactive inhibition or internal inhibition, and counterconditioning. These processes occur in the traditional psychotherapies, as a result of the nonspecific or general nature of the nonthreatening, accepting therapy relationship. The shaping process for progress in self-exploration would appear to fall under this learning modality of Truax and Carkhuff, at least insofar as specific anxieties and fears are dealt with. Where the client's problem appears to be an isolated specific fear or anxiety, the use of techniques of behavior modification, such as systematic desensitization, would appear to be appropriate.

Reinforcement of Positive Self-Concepts and Self-Valuations

As the client progresses in therapy, his responses become more positive in regard to himself or his self-concept. These responses are welcomed by the therapist. He sees them as desirable, as indications of progress. He is thus pleased with the client, and indications of this pleasure and approval are communicated to the client. It is important to emphasize here that such positive client responses come late in therapy, as a result of the process of self-exploration. It is not desirable —or possible—to short-circuit the process by extinguishing negative self-references and reinforcing positive self-references from the beginning of therapy. It might be possible to condition clients to emit positive self-references in a relatively short period of time. However, this would simply be the conditioning of verbal behavior. Efforts to do this, with "normal" subjects in analogue studies, have not always been successful. Whether this is related to a social set to be self-critical rather than self-praising, or to an innate resistance to glossing over negative feelings, is not known. The ignoring of negative self-references and the reinforcement of positive self-references prevents or inhibits the process of client self-exploration.

Modeling

In addition to the specific behavioral learning process operating in counseling or psychotherapy, a more general learning process occurs. This is the process called modeling. Modeling, of course, is not strictly a behavioristic technique. The behaviorists did not invent it or discover it, and it did not arise from laboratory research, as the behaviorists are so fond of claiming for other techniques. Modeling is a basic and pervasive method of learning and, in primitive societies, constitutes the educational process, or the process by which the young acquire the behaviors necessary for survival. Modeling as a method of teaching and learning has the advantage over reinforcement of specific behaviors, in that it makes possible the learning of complex wholes, the acquisition of patterns of behavior, rather than the piecemeal learning of wholes by the prior learning of parts, which must then be integrated. It also often leads to rapid learning, often one-trial learning, without practice being necessary.

Modeling involves the observation and imitation by the subject of another person. The process is a highly complex one, and its effects or results involve numerous factors, in the model, the subject, and the relationship between them.[32] It is not necessary, for modeling to occur, that the model intend to model; he becomes a model for others in the appropriate setting.

Thus, the therapist becomes a model for the client. The attitudes of the client toward him make him a model. Modeling has focused upon nonverbal behaviors. But most of the behaviors in which we are interested in psychotherapy, at least in relationship therapy, are interpersonal behaviors that are verbal, or verbally mediated. The verbal behavior of the therapist in the interpersonal relationship of psychotherapy is a model of interpersonal relationships. Bandura suggests that, since change agents model certain attitudes and social behaviors, these activities should be analyzed in terms of the behavior being modeled, or its functional value for clients. He then criticizes "conventional interview therapists" because they "mainly exemplify silence and interpretive behaviors that have limited functional value for clients. To the extent that clients emulate these behaviors in their everyday behavior they become pests or bores."[33] This may be the case in psychoanalysis; I have experienced this in groups of persons undergoing analysis. But if we substitute listening for silence and empathic understanding for interpretation, the criticism is inappropriate. Listening to and understanding others are useful and facilitative conditions for all interpersonal relationships. The relationship therapist is modeling the facilitative conditions for good human relationships.

Relationship therapy is thus not a therapy in which the client only talks about his problems—"verbal substitutes," as Bandura calls it—but one in which he deals directly with problem behavior, with difficulties in interpersonal relationships. He is thus actually doing what Bandura says social-learning behavior therapists do—"devoting the major portion of their time to altering the conditions governing deviant behaviors rather than conversing about them."[34] It would appear that relationship therapy fits at least the first part of Bandura's description: ". . . a powerful form of treatment is one in which therapeutic agents themselves model the desired behavior and arrange optimal conditions for clients to engage in similar activities until they can perform the behavior skilfully and fearlessly."[35]

It may be questioned whether, if self-disclosure on the part of the client is desired, the therapist shouldn't model this at the beginning of therapy. The answer, I think, is that this would be inconsistent with other objectives of the therapist—respecting the client, listening to and understanding the client, and not imposing himself on the client. Therapy is for the client, not for the therapist. In his approach to groups, Mowrer does engage in self-disclosure as a model to the group members.[36] Whether this is helpful in individual therapy (it is apparently not necessary) is not known, although Dickenson has reported positive effects.[37]

It may be helpful or facilitative for the client to have some pretherapy orientation or training in preparation for entering a therapy relationship, and this could include modeling of self-disclosure. Truax and Carkhuff have found that such "vicarious therapy pretraining" did facilitate therapy to some extent and resulted in greater improvement.[38] Hoehn-Saric *et al.* developed a Role Induction Interview to influence clients' expectations about psychotherapy (including the behavior expected of the client and the therapist) and to prepare him for certain developments, such as resistance and the expectation that improvement would occur in four months. The interview appeared to be effective to some extent, including greater likelihood of the client continuing in therapy.[39]

Modeling is a complex process, and although it no doubt incorporates elements of conditioning, it is not explainable simply in conditioning terms. While vicarious conditioning (observation of the model being rewarded) may be an element, modeling is effective without this. Cognitive elements are certainly present. Truax and Carkhuff discuss the principle of reciprocal affect, referring to the fact that people respond with affect similar to that to which they are exposed. This would appear to be modeling. But the principle is descriptive, not explanatory.

In summary, it is possible to describe the therapy process developed in this book in behavioral learning terms. Conditioning, both classical and operant, is involved in the process. Whether this description is explanatory or sufficient to understand the total process perhaps depends on the point of view of the reader, or the breadth of his concept or theory of learning. At any rate, the description given here is incomplete. The process of psychotherapy is complex and cannot be reduced to simple stimulus-response components. Behavior therapists no longer attempt to do this; the inclusion of modeling is an expansion of the earlier, restricted behavioristic approach. Learning is a complex process involving more than stimulus-response elements or conditioning. "Research has begun to make it increasingly clear that the learning in the behavioral therapies involves complex cognitive, emotional and motivational changes operating within a social context."[40]

If the facilitative conditions can be described in behavioral terms, behavior therapy techniques can be described in terms of the facilitative conditions. Thus, Truax has indicated that recent (unpublished) studies show that "the level of empathy, etc., of the therapist is the crucial factor in traditional desensitization therapy."[41] This, of course, does not show, or imply, that the process is not a learning process. It is only to say that facilitative conditions are part of the learning or behavior changes that occur in behavior therapy. Certainly, psychotherapy is not a simple conditioning process. The fact that behavior changes follow a reward does not mean that the therapeutic relationship is an automatic sequence of conditioning without awareness on the part of the client. It must be recognized that the extension of the concept of reinforcement beyond the simple conditioning that occurs in the laboratory leads to the introduction of other variables that influence and change the nature of the process. In complex situations what is labeled reinforcement may actually be described in other terms. What is termed a reinforcement may operate on a cognitive basis, such as providing information regarding the consequences of behavior.

Learning, it is being increasingly recognized, is a complex process, and a strict behavioristic interpretation is limited. The extension of the concept of reinforcement as a universal factor in learning appears to be impressive, but it must be remembered that such usage extends the term beyond its origins in laboratory situations. "No one will dispute that reinforcement is important. As Michael Polanyi once pointed out, since it includes anything that can change behavior, it must be."[42]

But this is only one way of describing behavior change, and it is not explanatory. There are different kinds or different levels of learning. Razran describes four evolutionary levels—reactive (nonassociative or reflexive) ; connective (conditioning); integrative (perceiving) ; and symbolic (thinking) .[43] The importance of the last two, or the cognitive aspects of learning, has been neglected by the behaviorists until recently.

There is a useful way of looking at the relationship between the core or facilitative conditions and the techniques of behavior modification (such as reinforcement, desensitization, extinction, and modeling) . Rather than viewing them as separate or independent, or as different approaches or techniques, they can be incorporated in a single approach, in which the behavioristic techniques are seen as modes of operation of the conditions. Then it becomes clear that there is no necessary or inherent contradiction or inconsistency. The influence of the core conditions is mediated, at least in part, through the behavioristic conditions. On the other hand, as is being increasingly recognized, the behavioristic techniques operate in the context of a relationship, and, in fact, their effectiveness depends to a great extent on the nature and quality of the relationship.

SUMMARY

In this chapter we consider the client's role and activities in the therapy process. Client characteristics related to client involvement and progress in psychotherapy are suggested, including desire to change and confidence in the therapist as an agent in inducing change. The basic motivation to change is the drive toward self-actualization. While the facilitative conditions must be present in the therapist for therapy to occur, this is not sufficient. They must be perceived by the client. The client who will not or cannot perceive the conditions cannot be helped.

The work of the client consists essentially of self-exploration. This begins with self-disclosure and ends with self-awareness, self-understanding, or "insight." The problem of insight versus action is discussed, and it is concluded that action or behavior changes accompany or follow the development of self-awareness as a natural consequence of a change in perceptions, particularly change in perception of the self, or in the self-concept.

The chapter concludes with a section discussing the therapeutic process from a behavioristic learning point of view. It is recognized that the therapist's responses and behaviors act as reinforcers for the client's behavior. In fact, it is suggested that the relationship therapist naturally or intuitively provides more systematic reinforcement than could be provided by a conscious effort to do so. The facilitative conditions that the therapist provides are, in behavioristic terms, the most powerful reinforcers for client self-exploration and for the development of the conditions themselves in the client. This process may also be described as modeling.

Behavior therapists have rejected the medical or disease model of psychopathology and psychotherapy.[44] Traditional or psychodynamic psychotherapies, such as psychoanalysis, client-centered therapy, and existential analysis have been associated with the disease or medical model by many behavior therapists. But it should be clear that relationship therapy is not based upon the medical model. In fact, it could justifiably claim to be based upon the behavioral or environmental model, since the cause of emotional disturbance is seen as developing from the nature of the human environment, and its amelioration is the modification of the human environment. However, the description in behavioral or learning theory terms is not necessarily explanatory. Although psychotherapy is a learning process, it is not simply stimulus-response learning or conditioning. Learning is much more complex than these simple theories would imply, involving complex cognitive and affective elements and a social context that influences the process. The client in the process is more than a rat in a Skinner box being taught tricks by operant conditioning.

NOTES

1 E. T. Gendlin. Client-centered development in work with schizophrenics. *Journal of Counseling Psychology,* 1962, **9,** 205–211.

2 C. R. Rogers. The necessary and sufficient conditions of therapeutic personality change. *Journal of Consulting Psychology,* 1957, **21,** p. 96.

3 L. Pearson (Ed.). *The use of written productions in counseling and psychotherapy*. Springfield, Ill.: Thomas, 1965.

4 C. B. Truax and R. R. Carkhuff. *Toward effective counseling and psychotherapy*. Chicago: Aldine, 1967; R. R. Carkhuff and B. G. Berenson. *Beyond counseling and therapy*. New York: Holt, Rinehart & Winston, 1967; R. R. Carkhuff. *Helping and human relations*. Vol. I, *Selection and training*. Vol. II, *Practice and research*. New York: Holt, Rinehart & Winston, 1969.

5 Truax and Carkhuff, *Toward effective counseling*, p. 192.

6 C. R. Rogers. *On becoming a person*. Boston: Houghton Mifflin, 1961, p. 139.

7 Carkhuff and Berenson, *Beyond counseling*, p. 7.

8 Carkhuff, *Helping*, Vol. II, p. 41.

9 Truax and Carkhuff, *Toward effective counseling*, pp. 194–208.

10 Carkhuff, *Helping*, Vol. II, pp. 327–328.

11 Truax and Carkhuff, *Toward effective counseling*, p. 196.

12 *Ibid.*, p. 206.

13 Adapted from C. R. Rogers. A theory of therapy, personality, and interpersonal relationships. In S. Koch (Ed.). *Psychology: A study of science*. Vol. III, *Formulations of the person and the social context*. New York: McGraw-Hill, 1959, pp. 218–219.

14 Rogers, *On becoming a person*, p. 80.

15 *Ibid.*, p. 87.

16 *Ibid.*, p. 101.

17 Carkhuff, *Helping*, Vol. II, p. 35.

18 W. Glasser. *Reality therapy*. New York: Harper & Row, 1965, pp. 7, 10.

19 E. R. Hilgard and G. H. Bower. *Theories of learning* (3rd ed.). New York: Appleton-Century-Crofts, 1966, p. 2.

20 See A. W. Combs and D. W. Snygg. *Individual behavior* (Rev. ed.). New York: Harper & Row, 1959.

21 The relevant literature goes back some twenty-five years and is extensive. See, for example, the following: F. J. Shaw. A stimulus response analysis of repression and insight in psychotherapy. *Psychological Review*, 1946, 53, 36–42; L. F. Shaffer. The problem of psychotherapy. *American Psychologist*, 1947, 2, 459–467; E. J. Shoben, Jr. A learning theory interpretation of psychotherapy. *Harvard Educational Review*, 1948, 18, 129–145; E. J. Shoben, Jr. Psychotherapy as a problem in learning theory. *Psychological Bulletin*, 1949, 46, 366–392; E. J. Shoben, Jr. Some observations on psychotherapy and the learning process. In O. H. Mowrer (Ed.). *Psychotherapy: Theory and research*. New York: Ronald, 1953; Ann Magaret. Generalization in psychotherapy. *Journal of Consulting Psychology*, 1950, 14, 64–70; J. Dollard and N. E. Miller. *Personality and psychotherapy*. New York: McGraw-Hill, 1950; F. H. Kanfer. Comments on learning in psychotherapy. *Psychological Reports*, 1961, 9, 681–699; A. Bandura. Psychotherapy as a learning process. *Psychological Bulletin*, 1961, 58, 143–149; C. B. Truax. Some implications of behavior therapy for psychotherapy. *Journal of Counseling Psychology*, 1966, 13, 160–170 (also as chap. 4 in C. B. Truax and R. R. Carkhuff. *Toward effective counseling and psychotherapy*. Chicago: Aldine, 1967); C. H. Patterson. Some notes on behavior theory, behavior therapy and behavioral counseling. *The Counseling Psychologist*, 1969, 1 (4), 44–56; D. G. Martin. *Learning-based client-centered therapy*. Monterey, Calif.: Brooks/Cole, 1972.

22 Truax and Carkhuff, *Toward effective counseling*, pp. 151–161.

23 Dollard and Miller, *Personality and psychotherapy*.

24 Truax and Carkhuff, *Toward effective counseling*, pp. 152–153.

25 B. F. Skinner. *The technology of teaching.* New York: Appleton-Century-Crofts, 1968, p. 29.

26 C. B. Truax. Therapist interpersonal reinforcement of client self-exploration and therapeutic outcome in group psychotherapy. *Journal of Counseling Psychology,* 1968, **15,** 225–231.

27 Truax and Carkhuff, *Toward effective counseling,* p. 155.

28 Martin, *Learning-based client-centered therapy,* p. 67.

29 Truax and Carkhuff, *Toward effective counseling,* p. 155.

30 L. P. Ullmann and L. Krasner (Eds.) . *Case studies in behavior modification.* New York: Holt, Rinehart & Winston, 1965, p. 37.

31 Martin, *Learning-based client-centered therapy,* pp. 69–70.

32 A. Bandura. *Principles of behavior modification.* New York: Holt, Rinehart & Winston, 1969; A. Bandura. Psychotherapy based upon modeling principles. In A. E. Bergin and S. L. Garfield (Eds.) . *Handbook of psychotherapy and behavior change: An empirical analysis.* New York: Wiley, 1971, pp. 653–708.

33 Bandura, Psychotherapy based upon modeling principles.

34 *Ibid.*

35 *Ibid.*

36 O. H. Mowrer. *The new group therapy.* Princeton, N.J.: Van Nostrand Reinhold, 1964.

37 W. A. Dickenson. Therapist self-disclosure as a variable in psychotherapeutic process and outcome. Unpublished doctoral dissertation, University of Kentucky, 1965. In an experimental interview situation, Powell found that interviewer self-disclosure statements were more effective than approval-supportive statements or reflections in increasing subject self-references, both positive and negative. (W. J. Powell. Differential effectiveness of interviewer interventions in an experimental interview. *Journal of Consulting and Clinical Psychology,* 1968, **32,** 210–215.)

38 Truax and Carkhuff, *Toward effective counseling,* pp. 153, 362–363. See also: G. A. Marlatt, E. A. Jacobsen, S. L. Johnson and D. J. Morrice. Effect of exposure to a model receiving evaluative feedback upon consequent behavior in an interview. *Journal of Clinical and Consulting Psychology,* 1970, **34,** 104–112.

39 R. Hoehn-Saric, J. W. Frank, S. D. Imber, E. H. Nash, A. R. Stone and C. L. Battle. Systematic preparation of patients for psychotherapy. I. Effects on therapy behavior and outcome. *Journal of Psychiatric Research,* 1964, **2,** 267–281.

40 E. J. Murray and L. I. Jacobson. The nature of learning in traditional and behavioral psychotherapy. In Bergin and Garfield, *Handbook of psychotherapy,* p. 723. See also F. H. Kanfer and J. S. Phillips. *Learning foundations of behavior therapy.* New York: Wiley, 1970.

41 C. B. Truax. Personal communication October 26, 1972. Relevant here is the study by Vitalo, in which it was found that verbal conditioning occurred only with experimenters who were high on the core conditions. R. Vitalo. The effects of interpersonal functioning in a conditioning paradigm. *Journal of Counseling Psychology,* 1970, **17,** 141–144. See also A. Sapolsky. Effect of interpersonal relationships upon verbal conditioning. *Journal of Abnormal and Social Psychology,* 1960, **60,** 241–246; D. J. Mickelson and R. R. Stevic. Differential effects of facilitative and non-facilitative behavioral counselors. *Journal of Counseling Psychology,* 1971, **18,** 314–319. Krasner emphasizes the importance of the therapist-client relationship in all forms of behavior therapy (L. Krasner. The operant approach in behavior therapy. In Bergin and Garfield, *Handbook of psychotherapy,* pp. 612–652) .

[42] Quoted by W. R. Thompson. Review of J. P. Scott and S. F. Scott (Eds.). *Social control and social change. Contemporary Psychology*, 1972, **17**, 524–525.

[43] G. Razran. *Mind in evolution: An East-West synthesis of learned behavior and cognition*. Boston: Houghton Mifflin, 1971.

[44] L. P. Ullmann and L. Krasner. *A psychological approach to abnormal behavior*. Englewood Cliffs, N.J.: Prentice-Hall, 1969.

Chapter 8

The Relationship: Placebo, Friendship, or More?

In this chapter we are concerned with two major questions: Is the therapy relationship anything more than a nonspecific placebo? and Is therapy any different than a good friendship?

THE PLACEBO EFFECT

Shapiro, who has probably engaged in more intensive study of placebos than anyone else, gives the following definitions:

> A *placebo* is defined as any therapy, or that component of any therapy, that is deliberately used for its nonspecific, psychologic, or psychophysiologic, effect, or that is used for its presumed specific effect on a patient, symptom, or illness, but which, unknown to patient and therapist, is without specific activity for the condition being treated.
>
> The *placebo effect* is defined as the nonspecific, psychologic, or physiologic effect produced with placebos.
>
> A *placebo*, when used as a control in experimental studies, is

defined as a substance or procedure that is without specific activity for the condition being evaluated.[1]

In medicine, it is relatively easy to study the placebo effect, or the effect of psychological factors. Although all medical procedures and substances involve placebo effects in their ordinary use (by physicians), so that specific (pharmacological or other) effects are confounded with the nonspecific (placebo) effects, the nonspecific effects can be established by a double-blind experiment in which a nonspecific or inert substance (for example, sugar pills) is prescribed without either the physician or the patient being aware of the substitution.

In psychotherapy, the problem is different. Wolpe has claimed that the total psychological relationship between the therapist and the patient is nonspecific and thus a placebo,[2] and that only particular techniques are specific. It would appear that Wolpe assumes a strict, and invalid, analogy with medicine, in that he implies that there are specific nonpsychological (or nonrelationship) treatments for emotional disturbances. However, it would appear to be reasonable to argue that the specific treatment for a psychological disturbance would be itself psychological in nature. Thus, the relationship itself, or certain aspects of it, is potentially a specific treatment and not, as in medicine, a placebo.

This appears to be a source of confusion, even in the writing of Shapiro. Shapiro discusses the various variables included in the placebo effect. These include patient variables, such as the patient's belief and faith in the therapist and his methods; his expectations and hopes for cure or change; his suggestibility, submissiveness, dependence, and compliance; and his anxiety. Therapist variables include the therapist's prestige and status; his confidence and belief in himself and his methods; his optimism, expectations and enthusiasm; and his interest in his methods and approach. In addition, variables such as suggestion, hypnosis, persuasion, and reassurance are aspects of the placebo effect. And beyond these, the therapist's attitudes and behavior toward the client—his interest, concern, attention, warmth and empathy—are all included in the placebo effect. Thus, it would appear that the placebo effect includes all the psychological factors in psychotherapy. Therefore, psychotherapy is nothing but a placebo treatment. Or, if it is not, then there must be some other, nonpsychological, factors that are the specific methods of treatment. It is, of course, true that drugs and physical methods of treatment are used with some emotionally disturbed persons, but it is doubtful that these can be considered as psychotherapy or that they are accepted as examples of kinds of specific treatments that would eventually become available for treating all emotionally disturbed persons.

The question may be raised as to whether it is possible to provide any psychological treatment outside of or devoid of some psychological relationship. For example, is it possible to evaluate the effects of the techniques of behavior modification without some relationship being present? In perhaps the most elaborate attempt to do so, Lang and his associates developed a Device for Automatic Desensitization (DAD), which desensitizes a subject by means of a programmed audiotape.[3] However, the human factor is not entirely eliminated. The subjects are introduced to the apparatus by a person, and the voice on the tape is that of a human being. Given the propensity of human beings to anthropomorphize, it can be assumed, or at least conjectured, that the subjects enter into a personal or a psychological relationship in the situation.

If it be accepted that the psychotherapy process is psychological, then it might be argued that the concept of placebo has no relevance for psychotherapy. Krasner and Ullmann appear to say this:

> Whereas the problem had previously been conceptualized in terms of eliminating the "placebo effects," it would seem desirable to maximize placebo effects in the treatment situation to increase the likelihood of client change. The evidence is growing that "placebo effect" is a euphemism for examiner influence variables.[4]

However, Shapiro's definition includes the notion that a placebo "is without specific activity for the condition being treated." The problem, then, is one of separating the nonspecific from the specific aspects of the psychotherapy relationship. Shapiro notes that the therapist's characteristics have specific as well as nonspecific effects. Although the placebo is universal, "it does not preclude concomitant specific effects, however. . . . It may function as a prerequisite or catalyst for therapies that involve psychological factors or interpersonal relationships."[5]

How can we differentiate specific from nonspecific effects in psychotherapy? It might be argued that all psychological factors are specific in terms of their effects, so that there is no such thing as a placebo in psychotherapy. Nevertheless, attempts have been made to study aspects of the psychotherapy relationship to distinguish between more specific or less specific effects, particularly in relation to more or less specific conditions, or outcomes.

The therapy relationship is exceedingly complex and involves, or can involve, many factors. Some of these factors are probably nonspecific. But the question of specificity or nonspecificity cannot be considered except in terms of outcomes or criteria. The lack of agreement on criteria in psychotherapy, or, at least, the wide variety of outcomes toward which different psychotherapists work, makes it exceedingly difficult to determine what variables are specific and what are non-specific. The problem of immediate versus long-term results is important here also. In addition, the matter of additional, or "side" effects, beyond those specifically sought for, must be considered. All psychological conditions or variables may be considered specific for some effects.

Thus, there are a number of psychological factors entering the psychotherapy relationship that may or may not be considered desirable, depending upon acceptance or rejection of their specific results. A number of these factors may be grouped under the term authority, for want of a better word. They include the status and prestige of the therapist, which may be made clear to the client in varying degrees, including ostentatious and luxurious office furnishings and decorations, equipment, professional books and journals, the display of diplomas and certificates, and even the wearing of a white coat. The use of hypnosis and suggestion would also be included, as would persuasion, reassurance, advice, and direction. Many, if not most, of these factors are not considered desirable or even useful by most therapists or schools of therapy. Frequently, this is because they are not effective, particularly in terms of long-term results. Yet they do exert an influence on the client. This influence is most apparent in suggestible, dependent, submissive, compliant clients. But in all clients, such psychological factors may lead to the development or increase of these dependency characteristics as side effects. Thus, the manipulation of these psychological factors is rejected by those whose goals in psychotherapy include the avoidance of the development of dependency and submissiveness and by those who wish to foster the characteristics of autonomy, independence, initiative, and assertiveness.

It is difficult, however, and perhaps impossible, to eliminate all authority from the therapy relationship. An authoritative role is usually assigned to the therapist by the client. The imputing of status or prestige is perhaps helpful or desirable if the therapist is to be a model for the client. Nevertheless, the degree of authority may vary tremendously, and it can be maximized or minimized in the relationship; it may be exploited or its explicit use may be avoided. Burton believes that

> Of course, it is necessary to maintain a position of authority or prestige with patients. . . . [But] Nevertheless there is an increasing acceptance of the philosophy which says that a true encounter can only take place when patient and psychotherapist meet each other on an I-Thou basis. In such a relationship there is no basis for privilege.[6]

Whether authority is viewed as a placebo or as a method of specific treatment depends on the outcomes or goals the therapist accepts or desires. If it is accepted as a specific treatment, it should be maximized; if it is regarded as a placebo, it should be minimized. Therapists who minimize authority, prestige, and status and who attempt to achieve a more nearly equal relationship with their clients, do influence their clients or achieve results. The current trend in psychotherapy, as Burton notes, appears to be in this direction.

Another set of factors may be involved in the placebo effect. These consist of the therapist's belief and confidence in himself and his approach and his interest, not simply in his clients, but in his work, in applying his methods, in obtaining results. These factors appear to be identical to what Orne has called the "demand characteristics" in psychological experiments.[7] Rosenthal, among others, has demonstrated the influence of the experimenter's beliefs, expectations, and desires upon the outcome of psychological experiments both in and outside the laboratory.[8] Thus, psychological experiments are subject to unwanted, or placebo, effects.

The question whether these expectancy factors function as a placebo or are specific variables again depends upon how we view their outcome, that is, whether the results are necessary and desirable. The methods of the therapist and his belief in his methods are apparently inextricable. If a therapist did not believe in his methods, he would use some other methods. If he did not have confidence in himself or interest in his work, he probably would not continue for long in it. And it appears that when a method that the therapist does not believe in or have confidence in is used, it is not likely to be effective. (It would appear, however, that a *strong* conviction or belief is not necessary. Students who have been skeptical of client-centered or relationship therapy but who nevertheless have tried it, have, to their surprise, found it effective.) We face the dilemma from a research point of view, of not being able to apply a fair test of the effectiveness of a method apart from its application by a therapist who believes in the method. From the standpoint of practice, however, it appears that such belief is necessary.

If we look at the situation in terms of outcomes, we find that the therapist's belief, confidence, and interest in his work have specific effects on the client that are necessary for his progress. The client responds to the therapist's beliefs by maintaining his attitudes of belief and confidence in the therapist. He perceives the therapist's interest in his work as interest in him. He thus enters and continues in the therapy process rather than giving up and leaving.

The client's attitudes, beliefs, and expectations can be viewed in the same way. Their specific effects are to keep him in the therapy process. They are thus necessary for the achievement of any final outcomes of psychotherapy. In Chapter 7, it was suggested that the client's belief or faith in the therapist and his methods, while helpful, is not necessary. But apparently client belief or faith can be a very powerful factor in some kinds of behavior change. It seems to be a major source of the changes—or "cures"—in faith healing and nostrums. Thus, there seems to be reason to consider client belief—at least strong (unreasonable?) belief—to be a placebo factor.

So far we have been discussing aspects of the therapy relationship that are necessary but not sufficient conditions for successful outcomes. The conditions we have emphasized in this book are proposed as the necessary and sufficient (and thus the specific) conditions for a particular objective—the facilitation of the process of self-actualization in persons whose self-actualization is prevented by the lack of facilitative interpersonal relationships. The conditions are the elements of a facilitative interpersonal relationship. They are therefore the specific treatment for a specific condition.

The evidence for the specific effects of the facilitative conditions has been accumulating. Although much research has indicated that the conditions lead to a wide variety of desirable behavior changes, research now beginning to accumulate indicates that the conditions lead to the development of the conditions themselves in clients. Whereas for the development of many kinds of behavior change (including changes which may be considered subgoals of the ultimate goal of self-actualization), the conditions may be necessary but not sufficient, they are necessary and sufficient for the development of the conditions themselves, which are basic characteristics of the self-actualizing person. They also lead to the development of other characteristics of the self-actualizing person. The variety of other (often specific) changes in behavior that have been found to be related to high levels of the core conditions in therapy may be considered to be by-products of self-actualizing behavior (see Chapter 9).

It can be concluded that the conditions of a facilitative interpersonal relationship are specific conditions with specific desired effects. They do not constitute a placebo.

PSYCHOTHERAPY AS A GOOD HUMAN RELATIONSHIP

In 1950, Fiedler published the results of a study in which 18 experienced and inexperienced therapists with client-centered, psychoanalytic, and Adlerian orientations and three laymen sorted statements descriptive of client-therapist relationships, using the Q technique. Fac-

tor analysis yielded one common factor, which Fiedler called g
of therapeutic relationships. The ideal relationship, as describe
statements most highly rated by the expert therapists, included the following:

1. The therapist is able to participate completely in the patient's
   communications.
2. The therapist's comments are always right in line with what
   the patient is trying to convey.
3. The therapist is well able to understand the patient's feelings.
4. The therapist really tries to understand the patient's feelings.
5. The therapist always follows the patient's line of thought.

These statements clearly relate to empathic understanding; other
highly rated statements relate to respect and to genuineness. The lay
raters described the ideal therapeutic relationship in a manner similar
to the way the therapists described it, leading Fiedler to conclude that
"a good therapeutic relationship is very much like any good interpersonal relationship."[9]

Since Fiedler's study, it has become generally accepted that the
conditions of empathic understanding, respect and warmth, and genuineness are characteristics of all good interpersonal relationships. This
being the case, it is relevant to ask if counseling or psychotherapy is
simply an ideal friendship.[10] If counseling or psychotherapy is essentially the providing of a good human relationship, is psychotherapy a
profession? If the conditions of the psychotherapy relationship are effective with disturbed people, wouldn't they be helpful to other, more
"normal" people? What are the implications of the recognition that
psychotherapy is a good human relationship for prevention of emotional disturbances?

Another question students often ask is whether everyone needs
psychotherapy in order to become a self-actualizing person. The answer
I usually give is that everyone needs the conditions of a therapeutic
relationship to become a self-actualizing person. But many, if not most,
people receive minimal or adequate levels of these conditions from
some person in their lives. Those who need psychotherapy, as has been
emphasized throughout this book, are those who have not received
and/or do not receive adequate levels of these conditions from others.

Some people who apply for therapy but do not receive it (for
whatever reason) are known to improve so that later, when therapy is
available or offered, they do not need it or want it. This has been called
spontaneous remission. But of course there is actually no such thing

as spontaneous remission. Something happened to change these people. It has been suggested that they have been influenced therapeutically by nonprofessionals—they have sought and obtained a relationship that includes the core conditions from other persons in their lives. Such therapy may not be as effective, on the average, as professional therapy (though professional therapy appears not to be highly effective, on the average). But it is important to note that the core conditions are naturally effective, even in people with no professional preparation operating on an informal, casual basis, and even *without any other specialized methods or techniques.*

That this (so-called) spontaneous remission occurs and that there are so many persons who do not require psychotherapy, suggests that the conditions of a therapeutic relationship are widespread in our society. Looked at in another light, it suggests that there are many people who are potential professional therapists. On the other hand, the high (and apparently increasing) incidence of persons in need of psychotherapy in our society raises questions about the extent and level of these conditions. Studies by Carkhuff and his associates indicate that the levels of these conditions are low in a variety of groups, including the general public, lay helpers, college students, and even in counselors and psychotherapists.[11] It is a sad commentary on our society that good human relationships are so scarce that many people must seek professional help and pay for, if not friendship, a good interpersonal relationship with another person. Society has reached a low level when the providing of a good human relationship is designated as psychotherapy. It is paradoxical that we must prepare people, through programs of education and training, to provide such a relationship to others. In effect, we must teach people to be good human beings.

The development of psychotherapy as a means of meeting the need of large numbers of people for a good human relationship institutionalizes the process as a profession. Thus, although the nature of the relationship offered by psychotherapists is basically the same as the relationship offered by a close or ideal friend, or the good or ideal parent, when offered on a professional basis to persons who are disturbed and suffering from its lack, the therapeutic relationship differs from the relationship offered by a friend or a good parent. These differences relate to the formalizing of the procedure for the sake of efficiency and to the interests of the therapist as a person as well as a professional.

In order to help the maximum number of people, the therapy relationship is restricted in comparison with a friendship. The therapist could help only a limited number of people if he became a close friend in the usual sense of the word, since close friendships are demanding in time and thus are limited in number. They are demanding in other ways. Orthodox psychoanalysis required (and in some instances still does) daily appointments, six days a week. The analyst could treat only a very limited number of clients (usually 5 or 6). The potentially close personal relationship that develops between the therapist and the client even on the basis of six-hours contact a week can be a drain on the therapist. It was perhaps to avoid or prevent this, as much as for theoretical or technical professional reasons, that the therapist rendered the relationship relatively impersonal by placing himself outside the line of vision of the client and by prohibiting social relationships outside of therapy.

Conceivably, therapy as a good interpersonal relationship could be offered in a variety of settings, particularly in the home. In fact, there are those who now question the standard procedure of counselors remaining in their offices and having clients come to them. It is not clear just where and how counselors would function outside their offices. But the desirability and efficiency of counselors or therapists traveling about to visit their clients is a matter for consideration. The cartoon of a man walking down the street carrying a couch over his head, with the caption "Psychiatrist making a house call," strikes us as incongruous. Physicians, in the interest of efficient use of their time, now rarely make house calls, except in emergencies.

Counseling or psychotherapy, in the interest of efficient use of the therapist's time and to protect his personal life and privacy, is conducted in an office and on an appointment basis; friendships do not operate with this restriction. In a friendship, there is a sharing of much time in pursuing common interests. The therapy relationship is restricted to the therapy hour. The therapist has a personal, nonprofessional life, in which his friends are other than his clients. Although he may to some extent select his clients, he does so on a different basis than he selects his friends. One can, if necessary, contact a friend for help in an emergency any hour of the day or night. But therapists, though they are usually available in emergencies, do not encourage their clients to contact them between appointments.

The limiting of social contacts with the client is of value in another way. The nature of ordinary social relationships, with their customs, conventions, and restrictions (or prohibitions), is quite different from the therapy relationship. Ordinary everyday social relationships could introduce many other variables and complexities into the therapy relationship that could detract from or interfere with its concentration and purity.

Friendships differ from psychotherapy in another respect. Although, in some friendships, one person may be more dependent on the other, or one may be more helpful than the other, the relationship normally is one of equals. One is not usually consistently a helper and the other a helpee. One is not usually in much greater need of help. In psychotherapy, on the other hand, one (hopefully the therapist) is the helper, and the other (the client) is the helpee throughout the relationship. One is a person who is not in (great) need of help, while the other is. One is a (relatively) self-actualizing person, while the other is (relatively at least) not. Despite the trend toward equality in psychotherapy, there still remains, and will remain, the differentiation in terms of the giving and receiving of help.

With the limiting of therapy contacts in time and the helper-helpee distinction, therapy differs from a friendship in the structuring of the relationship when the therapist and the client do meet. Time is limited and must be used most effectively in relation to the purpose of the relationship. While friends may engage in conversations about the interests and experiences of each—whether shared or not—the therapist and client restrict their conversation. Because the client lacks relationships characterized by core conditions and is thus in more or less dire need of them, the therapist attempts to provide them in the purest and most concentrated forms of which he is capable. It is essentially this requirement of the therapist that leads to the need for intensive preparation for the practice of psychotherapy, or the offering of a good human relationship on a professional basis.

Thus, while there are similarities between a good friendship and psychotherapy, there are differences. A good friendship is therapeutic but is not therapy in the sense that it is structured and conducted for the specific purpose of providing help for one of the participants. In the interests of effectiveness and efficiency, as well as to preserve the personal life of the therapist, it appears undesirable for therapy to be offered on a casual, unstructured, completely informal basis. While counselors or therapists roaming about college campuses (as it has been suggested they do) or society, offering therapy to passersby with worried looks on their faces may be helpful, it is not a very effective or efficient way of providing therapy to those who need it.

IS PSYCHOTHERAPY A PROFESSION?

But is this requirement—providing the core conditions in a pure and concentrated form—a sufficient basis for establishing psychotherapy as a profession? One of the basic requirements of a profession is a command of specialized knowledge and skills not possessed by those who are not members of the profession, knowledge and skills acquired by long and arduous education and training. But psychotherapy requires no esoteric knowledges and skills, acquired through a long period of graduate study. On the contrary, it has been demonstrated that persons can be prepared to offer a psychotherapeutic relationship without having had a college education, without extensive knowledge of psychology, and in a relatively short period of time. It is possible to produce lay therapists, not simply in Freud's meaning of not possessing a medical degree, but in the sense of not requiring any academic degree. *Neither the M.D., Ph.D., M.A., or B.A. is required for the offering of a therapeutic relationship. Psychotherapy, the providing of a good human relationship, though requiring preparation and training, is not a profession.* The providing of good human relationships should not be limited to those currently designated as psychotherapists. The practicing of facilitative human relationships should not be restricted to a few people with higher degrees, most of whose education is unnecessary and irrelevant for the practice.

> For most purposes and most problems, . . . lay people can learn to help as effectively and often more effectively than professional helpers, that is, teachers, guidance counselors, psychologists, psychiatrists and social workers. For one thing professional helpers do not have a monopoly on understanding and action. Lay persons can learn to understand others as well as or better than professionals and they can learn to act upon this understanding as well as or better than professionals.[12]

There are some areas of counseling that do have professional status. The most obvious—possibly the only one—is vocational counseling. Here the counselor must be trained to use tests and measurements if he is to function adequately in helping the client with problems involving vocational planning and decisions. Whether psychometrists and computers can take over this function is questionable, since a counselor must be knowledgeable about aptitude, ability, and interest measurement to discuss the data provided by the computer with the client.

The tremendous effort that has been made to gain professional recognition and status for the practice of counseling or psychotherapy will, of course, mean that the resistance to the recognition that psychotherapy is not a profession will be great. It will be a long time before this is accepted and its implications developed in terms of our social system and its institutions, including education at all levels.

One of these implications is the extension of the principles, or conditions, of psychotherapy beyond the therapy relationship to all areas of life. We can teach these principles or conditions to anyone and everyone. Thus, we can prepare not only counselors or psychotherapists to provide therapeutic or good human relationships, but we can teach these principles to parents, teachers, mental hospital attendants, prison guards, police, and so on. We can teach them to children in our schools.[13] We have now reached the point where it is possible to look forward to the extinction of psychotherapy as a specialized human relationship, when it will be unnecessary because everyone will have been prepared to provide an environment of good human relationships to others. Emotional disturbance resulting from the lack of or the inadequacy of good human relationships will no longer exist. There will, of course, continue to be psychological disturbances resulting from organic or physiological causes.

We are back where we started. If the conditions of a facilitative human relationship are present in the environment of all people, we will have a society of self-actualizing persons and will have no need for counseling or psychotherapy as it has been defined in this book.

THE PLACE OF PROFESSIONALS

However, as long as we need counselors or psychotherapists—which will certainly be for a very long time to come—we will need professionals. But professionals will not be needed to provide the actual counseling or psychotherapy, except perhaps in the most serious or difficult cases; they will be needed for other purposes. First, of course, is the training or preparation of lay therapists. Training is necessary, whether in a formal educational setting or in other settings. But training will become less and less a function of graduate education and move first, perhaps, to undergraduate education, then perhaps to two-year post–high school educational institutions, and finally to other social or community agencies, perhaps special training institutes or workshops offered by institutions of higher education. Adequate preparation will not simply be technique oriented or of a how-to-do-it type. It must include some theory and principles. The counselor or therapist must have some understanding of the why as well as of the what. He will need some understanding of the nature of human behavior and its change. But rather than being required to study a variety of theories of personality or learning, he will study a distillation of principles from an integrated theory of human behavior.

In addition to educating and training therapists, professionals will be involved in the education of other groups in human relations, both directly, as in the education of teachers and other professionals in the area of human relations, and indirectly through the preparation of human relations educators and the providing of curriculums and methods of human relations training.

Psychological education, particularly in the schools, would appear to be the place where psychologists interested in behavior change and social change should focus their activities. One of the most significant findings in recent research, in my opinion, is the effectiveness of teaching interpersonal relationships to clients or patients.[14] Truax has stated that, on the basis of his (unpublished) research, "training clients or patients in interpersonal skills is, in fact, more effective than traditional counseling and psychotherapy or behavior therapy."[15]

Professionals will also be involved in training significant persons in the client's life in the core conditions.[16] This is similar to the training by behaviorists of persons in the client's environment in the application of behavior modification principles.[17] Such training currently emphasizes efforts to eliminate, or reduce, specific deviant behaviors rather than providing the conditions for facilitating general personal development, or self-actualization.

In connection with both the functioning of therapists in various settings and the education of other professionals, the professional person will be involved as a consultant to those agencies and institutions utilizing therapists or engaged in programs of human relations education.

The professional will also be required to supervise the lay therapists. Although the latter will be competent in providing a therapeutic relationship, they will not be prepared to make decisions regarding the appropriateness of counseling or psychotherapy for particular applicants for help. Some will require other kinds of helping relationships or other kinds of assistance, such as medical treatment. Some will require referral for neurological evaluation. Supervision during the therapy process will be necessary to detect needs for referral for other kinds of help or treatment that were not evident or recognized at the beginning of therapy.

Finally, of course, there is the need for professionals to conduct continuing research into the selection and training of therapists and on the therapy process.

THE SOCIAL RESPONSIBILITY OF THE PROFESSIONAL

There has been increasing concern about the social responsibility of psychologists, particularly those in the applied areas of clinical and counseling psychology. It has been stated, justifiably, that there are not enough counselors or psychotherapists to meet the needs of people who are disturbed or unhappy. Many recognize that the source of much unhappiness and disturbance lies not within the individual but in society.[18] They are therefore calling for social action or political action, to change the institutions or social conditions which foster psychological disturbance.

But most of those who are calling for social action by psychologists do not seem to be very clear about their programs or goals, or just what it is that should be done, or done better, by psychologists as psychologists, in distinction to psychologists as citizens or human beings. It is certainly true that the socioeconomic conditions under which many people are ill-fed, ill-clothed, and ill-housed should be changed. And psychologists as human beings and as citizens should be concerned about these conditions and work to change them. But, though these conditions have psychological effects, they are not psychological in nature, and psychologists have no special expertise in relation to them; economists, sociologists, political scientists, statesmen, and politicians have more expertise.

The remedying of these conditions would of course reduce psychological suffering. But they are not the only or, indeed, the main source of psychological disturbance. The thesis of this book is that a major source of such disturbance is the lack of or inadequate levels of good human relationships. This is an area where psychologists do have some expertise, which can and should be used not only, as in counseling or psychotherapy, remedially but also preventively.

Human relationships always come down to an individual or one-to-one relationship. There is no way to influence or change the level of human relationships on a mass basis, acting upon large numbers of people at one time. There seems to be no short-cut, as some appear to be hoping to find, to change the level of human relationships in society. It must be done by the relatively slow process of changing individuals. It is not necessary, however, that it be on the one-to-one basis of psychotherapy. It can be done in small groups, through the educational process.

The professional who engages in teaching therapists, teachers, parents, and children, or who contributes to their education in human relationships through supervising, writing, or preparing teaching materials, and through consulting, is making his professional contribution to changing the detrimental influence of society on human beings. Society and its institutions are changed always and only through people and the way they treat other people. The solution is certainly not to abandon psychotherapy for those who now need it, but to extend the conditions of psychotherapy through teaching its principles to everyone in our society.

SUMMARY

This chapter deals with two objections about relationship therapy. The first is whether the therapeutic relationship is nothing more than a placebo. While there are probably some aspects of the relationship, particularly those associated with authority and prestige, that partake of a placebo, it is concluded that the essence of the relationship, the core or facilitative conditions, provide the specific treatment for the condition toward which relationship therapy is directed, namely, the lack of or inadequate levels of these conditions in the lives of clients.

The second question is whether the therapy relationship, as simply a good human relationship, is nothing more than a good friendship. The answer is that while there are some similarities, there are some basic differences between psychotherapy and a good friendship. A related question is considered: Is psychotherapy a profession? The conclusion reached, somewhat reluctantly because of the efforts that have been invested in professionalizing counseling, is that providing a good human relationship is not a professional activity. However, the education and training of counselors or lay therapists, their supervision, and research and consulting in therapy and human relations are professional activities.

A further responsibility of professionals is in the area of psychological education. Psychotherapy, even when provided by so-called lay therapists, cannot reach all who need it. Furthermore, we must be concerned with the prevention of emotional disturbance. This means that we must become involved in widespread education in good human relationships, beginning in the preschool years and continuing throughout the educational process. It is only in this way that we can eventually develop a world in which people can live together in peace as self-actualizing persons.

NOTES

1 A. K. Shapiro. Placebo effects in medicine, psychotherapy, and psychoanalysis. In A. E. Bergin and S. L. Garfield (Eds.). *Handbook of psychotherapy and behavior change: An empirical analysis.* New York: Wiley, 1971, pp. 439–473.

2 J. Wolpe. *Psychotherapy by reciprocal inhibition.* Stanford: Stanford University Press, 1958; J. Wolpe. *The practice of behavior therapy.* New York: Pergamon, 1969.

3 B. Malamed and P. J. Lang. Study of the automated desensitization of fear. Paper presented at the Midwestern Psychological Association Convention, Chicago, 1967.

4 L. Krasner and L. P. Ullmann (Eds.). *Research in behavior modification.* New York: Holt, Rinehart & Winston, 1965, p. 230.

5 Shapiro, Placebo effects, p. 463.

6 A. Burton. *Modern humanistic psychotherapy*. San Francisco: Jossey-Bass, 1967, p. 122.

7 M. E. Orne. On the social psychology of the psychological experiment; with particular reference to demand characteristics and their implications. *American Psychologist*, 1962, **17**, 776–783.

8 R. Rosenthal. *Experimenter effects in behavioral research*. New York: Appleton-Century-Crofts, 1966.

9 F. E. Fiedler. The concept of an ideal therapeutic relationship. *Journal of Consulting Psychology*, 1950, **14**, 239–245.

10 Cf. W. Schofield. *Psychotherapy: The purchase of friendship*. Englewood Cliffs, N.J.: Prentice-Hall, 1964.

11 R. R. Carkhuff and B. G. Berenson. *Beyond counseling and therapy*. New York: Holt, Rinehart & Winston, 1967, p. 9.

12 R. R. Carkhuff. *The development of human resources*. New York: Holt, Rinehart & Winston, 1971, p. 168.

13 C. H. Patterson. *Humanistic education*. Englewood Cliffs, N.J.: Prentice-Hall, 1973.

14 R. M. Pierce and J. Drasgow. Teaching facilitative interpersonal functioning to psychiatric inpatients. *Journal of Counseling Psychology*, 1969, **16**, 295–298.

15 C. B. Truax. Personal communication, October 26, 1972.

16 R. R. Carkhuff and R. Bierman. Training as a preferred mode of treatment of parents of emotionally disturbed children. *Journal of Counseling Psychology*, 1970, **17**, 157–161.

17 For a review of this area, see G. R. Patterson. Behavioral intervention procedures in the classroom and in the home. In Bergin and Garfield, *Handbook*, pp. 751–755.

18 See, for example, S. L. Halleck. *The politics of therapy*. New York: Science House, 1971.

Chapter 9

Diagnosis

Emphasis upon diagnosis in psychiatry has waxed and waned throughout the history of psychotherapy. Psychiatry, accepting the medical model, has assumed that differential diagnosis followed by differential treatment is its necessary goal. As a result, a tremendous amount of time and effort has been devoted to the development of diagnostic classifications for psychiatric and psychological disturbances. In the field of medicine, the discovery of different etiologies in terms of foreign agents—chemical, bacteriological, or viral—has led to the development of specific differential treatments. By analogy, it is assumed that the discovery of different causes for emotional disorders can lead to differential specific treatments. The classical paradigm is the discovery that the spirochete of syphyllis led to the development of paresis; this model has stimulated the hope that etiological agents (whether biological or psychological) will be discovered for other discrete conditions.

So far, no progress has been made. Yet the attempts to develop classification systems continue. It is recognized that existing systems, which are not based upon different etiologies but upon symptoms or syndromes are not adequate, but efforts to find a system of classification are continuing. Perhaps the most elaborate diagnostic classification developed to date is Thorne's.[1]

At present, concern with diagnosis in psychiatry is relatively quiescent. But diagnosis in psychology is experiencing a revival. Ford and Urban note the resurgence of interest in diagnosis and classification of clients and problems in their chapter in the 1967 *Annual Review of Psychology*. They point out that both Eysenck and Rachman, and Ban "are pursuing the notion that differential problems require differential treatment"; referring to Angyal's *Neurosis and Treatment,* they note that he "finds one element, 'universal ambiguity,' at the core of all neurosis. . . . Such oversimplification of the problem seems anachronistic."[2] Ford and Urban discuss the objectives of psychotherapy in the following terms:

> Most of the theories which have guided psychotherapy during the last half century have characterized all behavior disorder as resulting from a common nucleus, whether it was an oedipus complex (Freud), a conflict between strivings for independence and dependence (Rank), strivings to overcome inferiority (Adler), or conflicts between learned and organismic evaluations (Rogers), to name only a few. If the cause of all disorder is basically the same, it follows that one psychotherapeutic approach will suffice for all. *The trend now is clearly to reject this view.* There is growing evidence that disorders may differ in the patterns of behavior which become involved, the antecedents which elicit these patterns, and the consequents to which they lead.[3]

In a later publication, they write that the task of the therapy field is "to articulate the conditions under which specific tactics are appropriate for particularized sets of problems . . . the discovery of which set of procedures is effective for what set of purposes when applied to what kinds of patients with which sets of problems and practiced by which sorts of people."[4]

This theme has been echoed by other writers. Paul writes: "In all its complexity, the question toward which all outcome research should ultimately be directed is the following: *what* treatment, by *whom,* is most effective for *this* individual with *that* specific problem, and under *which* set of circumstances."[5] Blocher writes: "The old question of, 'Is counseling effective?' or 'Which counseling theory is correct?' are seen as largely rhetorical. They give way to questions of 'What treatment in the hands of which counselors can offer what benefit to particular clients?' "[6]

Strupp and Bergin, following their review of research in counseling and psychotherapy, make a similar statement:

> We have become convinced that the therapy of the future will consist of a set of specific techniques that can be applied under specifiable conditions to specific problems, symptoms or cases. . . . It has become increasingly clear that psychotherapy as cur-

rently practiced is not a unitary process and is not applied to a unitary problem. Consequently, the traditional problem "Is psychotherapy effective?" is no longer appropriate.

In the light of these observations, we feel that the problem of psychotherapy research in its most general terms, should be reformulated as a standard scientific question: what specific therapeutic interventions produce what specific changes in specific patients under specific conditions?[7]

In his introduction to a review of research in psychotherapy, Bergin writes:

We appear to be beyond the stage of asking the overly general and unanswerable question, 'Is psychotherapy effective?' Instead we are prepared to ask, 'Under what conditions will this type of client with these particular problems be changed in what ways by specific types of therapists?'[8]

And in a later review, Bergin states:

We feel quite strongly that researchers and therapists should begin to think more precisely in terms of *kinds of change* rather than in terms of a general multiform change;

and notes

the development of a general trend toward *specific* rather than global improvement indices.[9]

And Kiesler, who in 1966 wrote about the myths of the uniformity of clients and the uniformity of therapists, declares that "it takes different therapist behaviors to effect different changes for different kinds of patients."[10]

Although these phrases become repetitious, the arguments have a compelling logic. Yet the position which they represent has not been consistently held, perhaps because it has failed to be supported by any acceptable system of classification of clients or patients or of their problems or disturbances.

UNITARY THEORIES OF EMOTIONAL DISTURBANCE

Though subject to the charge of oversimplification and, currently, of anachronism (see the quote from Ford and Urban), unitary theories of emotional disturbance have persisted. In fact, as Ford and Urban note, every major theory of or approach to psychotherapy, in its acceptance of a single method of treatment, has implicitly if not explicitly assumed that emotional disturbance is unitary in nature. The only exception is behavior therapy, whose development has been the stimulus for the recurrence of interest in diagnosis.

The failure to develop an acceptable diagnostic classification system after decades of effort may be an indication that emotional disturbances cannot be differentiated into meaningful categories. There seems to be no logical—or psychological—system of classification that is satisfying or generally acceptable, that leads to non-overlapping, discrete categories on the same level of abstraction, and that are related to differential methods of treatment. The failure to find such discrete categories may be because they do not exist. Perhaps we are attempting to break up something that is homogeneous. Perhaps the apparent differences, such as symptoms, are all accidental or irrelevant differences in terms of etiology and the essential nature of emotional disturbance. There may be no essential or fundamental differences among so-called functional emotional disorders that will allow us to distinguish classes of disorder.

Menninger and his associates began to write of a unitary concept of mental illness in 1958.[11] The concept later was incorporated in a book, in which they noted that many psychiatrists were coming to the conclusion that there is but one type of mental disturbance.[12] Menninger reports that he began to question diagnosis at the beginning of his career but remarks: "I am somewhat ashamed to admit that it has taken me a quarter of a century to realize that this formula (treating the patient according to his diagnosis) rarely works out this way in actual practice."[13]

Menninger and his associates did not drop the use of the word *diagnosis,* however. They used it to distinguish differing degrees of severity of disturbance. It is this difference in severity of disturbance that seems to be the basis for recommendations for differential treatment. It is the basis of the difference between disturbances that are labeled neurotic and those that are labeled psychotic, a differentiation that is not always easy to make.

Bergin, in his work on the studies on which Eysenck based his claim that psychotherapy is not effective, notes that the rate of success varies among different diagnostic categories. He suggests that diagnosis or the distinguishing of differences among clients or patients is necessary in evaluating the effects of psychotherapy.[14] However, it appears that the differences can be accounted for in terms of the degree of severity of the condition. A ranking of the diagnostic categories in terms of degree of disturbance, I suggest, would correlate perfectly with the success rates.

The extensive research upon the relation of client variables to continuance in psychotherapy or to outcome has not resulted in the discovery of any classification of clients in terms of diagnosis or personality.[15] Fulkerson and Barry, following their review on predicting outcome by the use of tests, concluded that "the variables which appear to have the strongest relationship to outcome have been nontest variables: severity and duration of illness, acuteness of onset, degree of precipitating stress, etc."[16]

The only client variables consistently related to continuation and/or outcome are client motivation, socioeconomic variables, and severity of the disturbance. Motivation is probably related to severity of disturbance; the most severely disturbed clients often do not recognize the nature or severity of their condition or their need for help. There is research evidence that the less severely disturbed clients persist in therapy and improve, which has led to the statement that those who need psychotherapy least are the ones who receive it. Motivation is essentially the recognition of the need for help and a desire to get help by seeking and persisting in psychotherapy. The relevant variable in the socioeconomic factors is probably what may be called psychological mindedness. This is a psychological sophistication about emotional disturbance, contrasting to the unsophisticated attitude or belief that disturbance is physical or physiological in nature. This attitude is related to or a part of motivation. Socioeconomic factors also relate to intelligence and ability to verbalize, particularly introspectively, both of which are facilitative for therapy. In addition, the problems of clients at the lower socioeconomic levels often involve situations not suitable for psychotherapy. That is, many people come to or are referred to counselors or psychotherapists with problems that are not essentially psychological, and it should not be expected that counseling or psychotherapy would be helpful. To summarize, the extensive research on client variables in psychotherapy has turned up little or no evidence upon which relevant classifications of clients could be constructed as a basis for differential treatment. The so-called myth of client homogeneity may not be a myth after all. To be sure there are differences among clients, but these are essentially irrelevant and, where relevant, are differences not in quality but in quantity, essentially in the degree of disturbance.

The notion of a common basic etiology for all functional emotional disturbance is not a new idea. It is implicit at least in all major methods of psychotherapy. Perhaps instead of continuing to act upon the assumption that there are different kinds of emotional disorder and persisting in attempts to discover what they are, we should operate upon the assumption that there is no basic essential difference and attempt to discover and understand the common etiology. The theory presented in this book is such an attempt.

A UNITARY THEORY OF PSYCHOTHERAPY

If there is a single basic cause for emotional disturbance, *then* it would follow that there should be a single method of treatment. This is the implicit premise of all major approaches to psychotherapy. As Urban and Ford note:

> It is more parsimonious to presume that all changes in behavior occur as a consequence of learning, and that all learning proceeds in essentially the same fashion, that is, that the same principles govern the modification of all behavior regardless of its type or the characteristics of the person in whom they are taking place. If all behaviors . . . follow essentially the same sets of laws, then the procedures effective with one category of behavior will be effective for all.[17]

But, it may be asked, if this is so, why are there so many obviously different theories and methods of psychotherapy, all of which are apparently equally successful? The answer is simple. While there may be obvious differences among the various approaches, there are basic common el ments, or a common basic element. Parallel to the concept of the unitary nature of emotional disturbance, there has developed the concept of the unitary nature of psychotherapy.

It is the common elements, rather than the obvious but superficial differences, that are responsible for the (equal) effectiveness of all approaches. The basic common element in all psychotherapies is the interpersonal relationship. The nature of this relationship, and its aspects, are now beginning to be understood.

In their 1967 book, Truax and Carkhuff present the results of their survey of some of the major approaches to counseling or psychotherapy.[18] They indicate that all theories either implicitly or explicitly recognize these basic ingredients or conditions: (a) empathic understanding, (b) nonpossessive warmth or respect, and (c) genuineness. There is now extensive evidence of the effectiveness of these conditions, enough so that it is not too soon to conclude that these conditions, perhaps with the addition of some others (see Chapter 5), are the effective elements in all methods of counseling or psychotherapy. The myth of the uniformity of conditions is, it appears, not entirely a myth.

The significant fact about these conditions is that they are effective with all kinds of clients with all kinds of problems—with children and adults, the poor and disadvantaged as well as the rich and the advantaged, and with educational, vocational, marital, and other so-called personal problems. Truax and Carkhuff, reviewing the research on the conditions, write:

These findings suggest that the person (whether a counselor, therapist or teacher) who is better able to communicate warmth, genuineness and accurate empathy is more effective in interpersonal relationships no matter what the goal of the interaction (better grades for college students, better interpersonal relationships for the counseling center outpatient, adequate personality functioning and integration for the seriously disturbed mental patient, socially acceptable behavior for the juvenile delinquent, or greater reading ability for the third-grade reading instruction student).[19]

Truax and Mitchell reviewed the research and discovered that the earlier findings

have been replicated, not only in several American studies, but also cross-culturally. Clearly these findings are true of all human relationships, regardless of age, sex, degree of disturbance, or even cultural and langue contexts. . . . [The findings] seem to hold with a wide variety of therapists and counselors, regardless of their training or theoretic orientation, and with a wide variety of clients or patients, including college underachievers, juvenile delinquents, hospitalized schizophrenics, college counselees, mild to severe outpatient neurotics, and the mixed variety of hospitalized patients.[20]

In short, these conditions lead in all kinds of clients to more self-actualizing persons, which, as noted in Chapter 1, leads to changes in more specific behaviors as by-products of becoming more self-actualizing. In other words, a relationship high in these conditions is the necessary and sufficient condition for a wide variety of specific changes in a wide variety of persons.

The essential variable in which the effectiveness of the therapists varies is the quality of the interpersonal relationship they provide. The low level of effectiveness of psychotherapy in general can be attributed to the fact that professionals have not been selected on the basis of their potential to provide a good interpersonal relationship. Their training has not focused upon fostering and developing this capacity. In fact, with the emphasis upon evaluation and diagnostic skills and upon cognitive or intellectual performance in academic subjects and research, those individuals who are high in interpersonal skills to begin with may leave or be dropped from training programs or, if they remain, may even show a drop in the level of their interpersonal relationship skills.

When the levels of the conditions offered by the therapist are high, other variables, including client variables, are less important. Truax and Mitchell concluded that the therapist, rather than the client, is the most important determiner of the conditions.[21] However, client psychological-mindedness, verbal expressive productivity, the severity of his condition, and his socioeducational level were found to be related to therapist conditions in the Wisconsin study of Rogers and his associates.[22] Clients who are not psychological-minded, who are less verbal, less introspective, and who are concerned about reality problems, are not responded to with as much interest, concern, liking, respect, acceptance, and so on by the therapist and are more difficult for the therapist to understand.

If there is a myth regarding the homogeneity of psychotherapists, it has been that all therapists of all theoretical orientations or using all techniques are equally good. There are, however, as we now know, good therapists and bad therapists. It was fashionable a short time ago to ridicule those who, like the author, insisted that there were some counselors, some methods, or some theories that were better than others. We were, it was said, playing the game of setting the men in the black hats against those in the white hats. But in therapy, as in all of life, there *are* black hats and white hats.

THE PLACE FOR DIAGNOSIS

It should not be concluded that there is no place for diagnosis in psychotherapy and, more broadly, in helping relationships. There is a place, in the model developed in this book.

It may be that the development of so-called behavior therapy, with its emphasis upon specific treatments for specific conditions, is related to the resurgence in interest in diagnosis. But it is also the extension of the terms psychotherapy and counseling (which is in part related to the rise of behavior therapy) that has led to an increased interest in specific treatments for specific conditions. For it is true as Kiesler notes, that psychotherapy is not homogeneous. Psychotherapy has come to encompass many things, or many kinds of helping relationships, including most if not all of the continuum described in Chapter 1. A major source of the confusion regarding diagnosis, as well as of the disagreements and contradictions in much of the research, is the inclusion of so many different things under the term psychotherapy. Urban and Ford recognize this problem:

> One can legitimately ask at this point whether there is a definable realm of psychotherapy any longer, and what the justification is in continuing to speak of it as a field. It has become increasingly

clear that these procedures which operate under the label of psychotherapy no longer represent an homogeneous grouping. Psychotherapy as currently practiced is not a unitary process, applied to unitary problems, by a set of professionals with a definable common background and training and a common set of criteria by which the fruits of their labor can be evaluated.[23]

If this is the case, then it would appear to be desirable to agree upon some definitions of terms to apply to the heterogeneous things that now go by the name of psychotherapy. Yet one encounters great resistance in attempting to do so. No one appears to want to limit the term, even though it is recognized that failure to do so is the source of much confusion. Attempts of the writer to delimit counseling or psychotherapy as has been done in this book have led to strong objections. Students often ask, what difference does it make what we call it? But the problem is that "it" is not an "it" but a number of quite different things.

The realm of behavior with which we are now concerned has widened, and we are involved with the whole continuum of helping relationships rather than with the treatment of neurotics or psychotics, the "mentally ill," or the emotionally disturbed. We are now being faced with a large number and variety of persons seeking a wide variety of specific behavior changes. Behavior modification is a term used to refer to the treatment of many of these specific problems. For some (or many, apparently) psychotherapy and behavior modification are interchangeable terms. Kiesler, for example, without any justification and apparently without recognizing the implications, states that psychotherapy "has been defined as the science of behavior modification."[24] While it should be apparent that the latter is a much more inclusive term and that the two cannot be equated, their juxtaposition does provide a suggestion for the resolution of the problem of diagnoses.

With the increasing variety and heterogeneity of methods of behavior modification and the increasing variety of persons who are called clients, the matter of distinguishing them and matching one to the other becomes more relevant.

The diagnostic question is not "What kind of emotional disturbance does this client have?", but (a) "Does this client have an emotional disturbance of psychological origin, or does the disturbance originate from an organic or physiological condition?" and (b) "If the client has a psychological problem, is it one for which counseling or psychotherapy (defined as a relationship consisting of the conditions dealt with in this book) is appropriate (necessary and sufficient), or is it one which requires another kind of helping relationship (the facilitative conditions plus other methods of helping) ?" The latter question involves placing the client on the continuum of helping relationships that is described in Chapter 1. Of course, it may be the case, as indicated there, that some if not many clients need or could benefit from more than one kind of helping relationship.

In the light of the research indicating that the conditions alone are sufficient for a wide variety of outcomes, it becomes difficult to determine when other kinds of help should be provided. It would be easy to conclude, on the basis of the effectiveness of behavior modification techniques with certain disturbances, that the relationship itself is not sufficient for solving many of the specific problems to which behavior modification techniques have been successfully applied. But there is evidence that the relationship is also effective, at least for some clients with such specific problems. For example, Paul found that systematic desensitization was more effective than "insight therapy" or "attention placebo" (probably a weak relationship therapy) in the treatment of fear of public speaking in college students. But both the insight and the attention placebo groups also improved (or, perhaps more accurately, though Paul did not ascertain this, some of the members improved) .[25]

It might be expected that children with reading problems would benefit more from remedial instruction than from relationship therapy or, if it be conceded that there are emotional factors involved, more from instruction and therapy than from either alone. But Bills, in an early study, found that retarded readers who participated in play therapy improved their reading significantly during the therapy period compared to control periods preceding and following the experimental period.[26] In a more recent study, Lawrence found, contrary to his expectation, that poor readers who were provided with both counseling and remedial instruction did not gain as much as those who were provided with counseling alone.[27] Truax's statement, that the effectiveness of behavior modification may be essentially due to the relationship, may be relevant in this study.

It is not clear just to what extent the conditions of relationship therapy are necessary and sufficient. When the conditions are successful in leading to a greater level of self-actualization, the self-actualizing client may then, on his own and as a by-product of the therapy, change many specific behaviors and/or seek specific kinds of help and assistance to achieve specific goals. But since not all clients do this, it is important to know how they differ from those who do, or how their therapists and/or their therapy differ in the implementation of the action conditions, particularly.

Relationship counseling or psychotherapy is the specific treatment for clients whose self-actualization is hindered by the lack or inadequacy of facilitative interpersonal relationships. This may appear to be an extremely narrow definition, limiting counseling or psychotherapy to only a small proportion of those who need or desire help. However, the evidence that the therapeutic relationship alone is effective with so many clients with so many apparently different problems suggests that the lack of good interpersonal relationships is widespread in our society and is the source of the major part of what we call emotional disturbance, or the failure of so many to become self-actualizing persons, capable of achieving—by themselves in many cases, providing the opportunities are present, or through the help of others—the many specific goals with which psychotherapy has been concerned.

SUMMARY

In this chapter we deal with the problem of diagnosis in counseling or psychotherapy. Emphasis on diagnosis has increased with the development of the techniques of behavior modification. Writers are calling for studies that will determine what specific techniques used by what kind of therapists are effective with what kinds of clients with what kinds of problems.

While this may appear to be an eminently logical and desirable approach, the necessary systems for classifying techniques, therapists, clients, and problems are not available. Research to date has not succeeded in identifying relevant variables that would form the basis for such classifications. The results of studies of clients to date indicate that client motivation, socioeconomic level, and degree of disturbance are the only variables significantly and consistently related to continuation in therapy and to successful outcomes.

In the area of therapies and therapist variables, research has supported consistently only the existence of a facilitative interpersonal relationship characterized by high levels of empathic understanding, warmth or respect, genuineness and concreteness. Therapy that provides high levels of these conditions is successful with a wide variety of clients presenting a wide variety of problems. Changes in many kinds of specific behaviors occur without the use of direct or specific modifying techniques such as are advocated by the behaviorists and the others quoted at the beginning of the chapter.

Thus, it appears that, despite the apparent logic of specific treatments for specific conditions, there is evidence for the unitary nature of emotional disturbance and for a single method of treatment. The human interpersonal relationship is the effective factor in all counseling or psychotherapy. There is no compelling evidence to support the doctrine of specific treatments for specific conditions. In fact, the evidence we have is against this.

Diagnosis does have a place in the practice of counseling or psychotherapy, however. In the first place, it is necessary to determine whether the client's emotional disturbance is of psychological origin or not. Psychotherapy is appropriate only for psychological problems. Second, it may be necessary or desirable to ascertain if the client's problem is one that can be helped by psychotherapy (defined as a facilitative interpersonal relationship) or whether he needs, or also needs, other kinds of help, involving a different kind of helping relationship.

NOTES

[1] F. C. Thorne. *Principles of psychological examining.* Brandon, Vt.: Clinical Psychology Publishing Co., 1955, pp. 96–106; F. C. Thorne. Diagnostic classification and nomenclature for psychological states. Monograph Supplement No. 17. *Journal of Clinical Psychology,* 1964 (also in F. C. Thorne. *Integrative psychology.* Brandon, Vt.: Clinical Psychology Publishing Co., 1967, pp. 86–157).

[2] D. H. Ford and H. B. Urban. Psychotherapy. *Annual Review of Psychology.* Palo Alto: Annual Reviews, 1967, p. 336.

[3] Ford and Urban, Psychotherapy, p. 340. Italics added.

[4] H. B. Urban and D. H. Ford. Some historical and conceptual perspectives on psychotherapy and behavior change. In A. E. Bergin and S. L. Garfield (Eds.). *Handbook of psychotherapy and behavior change: An empirical analysis.* New York: Wiley, 1971, p. 20.

[5] G. L. Paul. Strategy of outcome research in psychotherapy. *Journal of Consulting Psychology,* 1967, **31**, p. 111.

[6] D. Blocher. What can counseling offer clients? In J. M. Whiteley (Ed.). *Research in counseling.* Columbus, Ohio: Merrill, 1968, p. 16.

[7] H. H. Strupp and A. E. Bergin. Some empirical and conceptual bases for coordinated research in psychotherapy. *International Journal of Psychiatry,* 1969, **7**, pp. 68, 19–20.

[8] A. E. Bergin. Preface. In Bergin and Garfield, *Handbook,* pp. ix-xii.

[9] A. E. Bergin. The evaluation of therapeutic outcomes. In Bergin and Garfield, *Handbook,* p. 257.

[10] D. J. Kiesler. Experimental designs in psychotherapy research. In Bergin and Garfield, *Handbook,* pp. 36–74. For the earlier discussion of myths, see D. J. Kiesler. Some myths of psychotherapy research and the search for a paradigm. *Psychological Bulletin,* 1966, **65**, 110–136.

[11] K. Menninger, H. Ellenberger, P. Pruyser and M. Mayman. The unitary concept of mental illness. *Bulletin of the Menninger Clinic,* 1958, **22**, 4–12.

[12] K. Menninger, M. Mayman and P. Pruyser. *The vital balance.* New York: Viking, 1963.

[13] B. Hall (Ed.). *A psychiatrist's world: The selected papers of Karl Menninger.* New York: Viking, 1959.

[14] Bergin, *Evaluation of therapeutic outcomes.*

[15] S. L. Garfield. Research on client variables in psychotherapy. In Bergin and Garfield, *Handbook,* pp. 271–298.

[16] S. C. Fulkerson and J. R. Barry. Methodology of research on the prognostic use of psychological tests. *Psychological Bulletin*, 1961, **58**, 177–204.

[17] Urban and Ford, Some historical and conceptual perspectives, p. 17. They go on to say, however, that the evidence does not support this view.

[18] C. B. Truax and R. R. Carkhuff. *Toward effective counseling and psychotherapy.* Chicago: Aldine, 1967, chap. 2.

[19] *Ibid.*, pp. 116–117.

[20] C. B. Truax and K. M. Mitchell. Research in certain therapist skills in relation to process and outcome. In Bergin and Garfield, *Handbook*, pp. 330, 310.

[21] *Ibid.*

[22] C. R. Rogers, E. T. Gendlin, D. J. Kiesler and C. B. Truax. *The therapeutic relationship and its impact: A study of psychotherapy with schizophrenics.* Madison: University of Wisconsin Press, 1967.

[23] Urban and Ford, Some historical and conceptual perspectives, p. 5.

[24] Kiesler. Experimental designs in psychotherapy research.

[25] G. L. Paul. *Insight vs. desensitization in psychotherapy: An experiment in anxiety reduction.* Stanford, Calif.: Stanford University Press, 1966.

[26] R. E. Bills. Nondirective play therapy with retarded readers. *Journal of Consulting Psychology*, 1950, **14**, 140–149.

[27] D. Lawrence. The effects of counseling on retarded readers. *Educational Research*, 1971, **13**, 119–124; see also D. Lawrence. The counseling of retarded readers by non-professionals. *Educational Research*, 1972, **15**, 48–52.

Chapter 10

Relationship Group Counseling or Psychotherapy

We are entering the era of the group. To be sure, man has always lived in groups. This is a biological necessity, and society has developed its institutions, including the basic group—family—to meet this need. But society has increased in size and complexity, with a resulting increase in impersonality. The increase of formal groups that involve only limited aspects of the person or individual, coupled with the decline of groups that involve the total person—the primary or face-to-face groups —have created problems in human relationships.

A gap has developed in society's meeting of man's need for the close interpersonal relationships of small groups. A new social institution is arising to fill this gap. This is the group movement, represented by such diverse methodologies as those of the T-group or sensitivity group, the encounter group, and the personal growth group.

In view of the basic need for close interpersonal relationships and the fact that many if not most of the problems bringing people to counselors or therapists involve interpersonal relationships, group therapy is probably the preferred mode of treatment. It makes possible the practice of the principles of good interpersonal relationships as they are learned. It provides an opportunity for experiential learning.

KINDS OF GROUPS

For many years, group guidance has been a part of the counseling and guidance service in secondary schools. The term *group guidance* has been used to include such activities as homeroom programs, field trips, clubs, assemblies, college and career days, and the imparting of educational and occupational information and sometimes test scores to students in groups. Less frequently, group guidance has included discussions of social skills and social development, human relations, and adjustment or mental health.

Group guidance is not group counseling but group teaching or instruction and is differentiated from the usual classroom instruction in that it deals with content that is not considered part of the standard curriculum. The focus is upon content; the process is highly structured, with guided discussion; and the groups are of classroom size.

Recently there has been a proliferation of groups with varying designations—T-group, sensitivity group, and encounter group being most common. It has become difficult if not impossible to distinguish among these groups, since there is as much variability among groups having the same designation as among those with different designations. The *T* (for training) *group* was originally concerned with the teaching of skills in human relations, through a group experience that was analyzed in terms of what was happening in the group—group dynamics. There was no concern about personal development. However, T-groups have merged into *sensitivity groups* and become concerned with increasing an individual's sensitivity to his own and others' actions and reactions.

Encounter groups are concerned with the personal growth and development of their members but do not include analysis and didactic discussion of the process, as do T-groups. There is thus a continuum on the dimension of cognition-affect. Indeed, some groups prohibit any cognitive discussion, and some groups permit only nonverbal behavior.

There is also a continuum of structuring, which cuts across the group designations. T-groups can be quite unstructured, though they tend to be task-oriented, at least to some extent. Encounter groups are generally unstructured; however, there are encounter group leaders or facilitators who use a highly or completely structured approach, going through an ordered series of exercises or games.

Group psychotherapy is not a new or recent concept. Its orgin is generally attributed to a physician named Joseph H. Pratt, who in 1905 introduced group meetings for tuberculosis patients. However, this was not group therapy as it is recognized or practiced today. The meetings were lectures and discussion groups. In the 1920's, group methods were employed with psychiatric patients. They too were cognitively oriented, or instructional in nature. In the 1930's, psychoanalytically oriented group therapy developed. Client-centered principles were used in groups in the 1950's.

Group counseling as a term has been in use for about two decades. However, it has only been in the last few years that interest and attention has been given to group counseling in the preparation of counselors. The University of Illinois has had a course in group counseling, as distinguished from group guidance, since the early 1950's, first taught by W. M. Lifton and M. M. Ohlsen. It has only been in the last few years, however, that most counselor education programs have included such a course.

Just as there is no essential difference between individual counseling and individual psychotherapy, there is no essential difference between group counseling and group psychotherapy. Attempts to differentiate between them have been unsatisfactory, leading to artificial distinctions. Group therapy is what is practiced by psychiatrists, psychologists, and social workers in a medical setting. Group counseling is what is practiced by counselors (and to some extent social workers, clergymen, and others) in a nonmedical setting. The difference, as in the case of individual counseling, is in the degree of disturbance of the clients, not in terms of the process or the goal.

All groups, whether sensitivity groups, encounter groups, counseling groups or therapy groups, involve interpersonal relationships. Insofar as there are common ways of relating and general principles of interpersonal relationships, all groups are similar. This probably is strictly true only in free or unstructured groups. Groups that are controlled by the leader, facilitator, or counselor or therapist will differ according to the structure imposed upon them. As Yalom states it: "The psychotherapy group, provided its development is unhampered by severe structural restrictions, evolves into a social microcosm" of interpersonal relationships.[1]

THE GROUP RELATIONSHIP

It is often, if not usually, assumed that when one moves from the dyadic relationship to group relationships, one enters an entirely new realm involving new principles and new concepts. But groups are composed of individuals—they do not exist apart from their members. Thus, the group itself is not the focus of the therapist; his focus is the individuals in the group. Group therapy is not therapy of the group but of individuals *in* a group setting. It is necessary to point out here that the writer does not include as group therapy the kind of treatment of individuals *in the presence* of a group that is practiced by many Gestalt therapists as well as by those practicing transactional analysis. In group therapy as defined by the writer and most others there is interaction among the group members.

Groups consist of interrelationships among the individuals who compose them. One can interact with only one other individual at a time, even though it is in the context of previous interactions with other members of the group and with awareness of the presence of others. The interrelationships among members of groups are not qualitatively different from the interrelationship between two individuals. They are, of course, more complex. The group counselor is not relating to or responding to a group, but to individuals in a group. It is, of course, much more difficult to relate to a number of individuals in a group context, or in the context of the interrelationships among these individuals, than to one person at a time.

It may thus be questioned whether there is such a thing as "group dynamics," at least as something qualitatively different from or involving entirely new principles than interpersonal relationships on a dyadic basis. The acceptance of the concept of group dynamics tends to lead to a reification of the group and the group process as something apart from, above, or in addition to the individuals composing the group and their interrelationships. But there is no such thing as a "group mind." There is no group goal or group task, in group therapy, as there is in task-oriented groups. Yalom says the task of the group is "to achieve a group culture of intimacy, acceptance, introspection, understanding, and interpersonal honesty."[2] But this is not a group task—it is the task of the individual members, or, as Yalom goes on to note, an interpersonal, and thus a personal, task. The concept of group dynamics grew out of the T-group movement. Its principles or concepts represent the description and terms developed by a particular group of social psychologists. It is possible that other principles or concepts could be used to describe the same process. Perhaps the terms used in the field of group dynamics refer to the same things as other terms used by other psychologists in describing the group process, or the interrelationships of individuals in groups.

As an example, we can take the term group cohesion, a basic and perhaps the most important concept of group dynamics. Its importance is emphasized because there is evidence that group cohesiveness is related to successful outcomes in group counseling or psychotherapy.[3] If we look at the definitions given of this concept, and at the instruments used to measure it, we find the following terms: feelings of personal involvement in the group, including feelings of mutual warmth, respect, acceptance, concern, trust, empathy, and genuineness. These are terms we have met before. They are the characteristics of good human relationships as described in earlier chapters. Yalom equates cohesiveness in group therapy to the relationship in individual therapy.[4] Perhaps the basis for the concept of cohesiveness is the sense of "we-ness" or group attractiveness that develops in successful groups. But this is an outcome of the presence of good interpersonal relationships and occurs in dyadic relationships, including individual therapy or a good marriage. Perhaps it is important to note here that most of the research on groups is not relevant to group therapy, since it has usually involved task-oriented, structured, controlled, or artificial groups composed of "normal" individuals meeting in a nontherapy setting over a short period of time.

Relationship therapy, based upon the principles of good human relationships, extends naturally to group therapy. *The conditions for effective individual therapy are the conditions for effective group therapy.*

THE GROUP PROCESS

Most writers see the group as going through a number of stages. Yalom distinguishes three stages in the formation of the group.[5] The first is the initial stage—the stage of orientation, hesitant participation and search for meaning. There is a search for acceptance and approval, both from other members and the therapist. Members are puzzled, dependent, and are looking for structure. Behavior is socially stereotyped, with impersonal discussion of general topics, and rational discussion of external problems and solutions. Members search for commonalities. Mahler[6] refers to this first phase as the involvement stage. It includes getting acquainted, beginning accepting relationships, and beginning to discuss personal behaviors and feelings. Bonney and Foley call it the establishment stage.[7] This stage is of no specific duration. It may last for one or two or several sessions. Group members have many doubts, anxieties, even fears, about disclosing or exposing themselves to the group. Most ordinary social interaction is at a formal and superficial level, and it takes time to get down to basic feelings and genuine expression of them to others. Mintz refers to "the social masks which participants wear, which they gradually doff with apprehension and relief and finally delight. . . ."[8] The development of trust cannot be forced or accelerated by the therapist but must come at its own pace.

Yalom's second stage is the stage of conflict, dominance, and rebellion. Negative feelings are expressed to other group members and to the therapist, perhaps because of disappointment in his leadership or his lack of special interest in them or jealousy of his position. There is preoccupation with dominance, power, and control. Many negative comments and criticisms are offered, and moralistic advice-giving occurs. Scapegoating may appear. Mahler's second stage is called the transition stage, in which the group moves from a social orientation to a therapeutic orientation in which the members recognize that for progress to occur the content must become highly personal in nature. Bonney and Foley describe this stage succinctly:

> Early in this stage, they [the group members] realize that the purpose for their existence as a group is to develop a situation that will allow for therapeutic experiences. . . . There ensues a period characterized by lack of involvement on the part of group members for fear of violating the perceived social norms inhibiting the discussion of personal problems in groups. The incongruency is resolved through the acceptance of a new norm that demands the discussion of personal concerns.[9]

There is resistance and anxiety, which may be reduced by the therapist structuring the therapy group as different from the social group, as a place where the discussion of personal problems is not only permissible but necessary. The transition stage ends when the group members accept the need for self-disclosure.

Yalom's third stage involves the development of cohesiveness—group members develop trust, mutual acceptance, intimacy, and closeness. An in-group feeling develops—a sense of we-ness. Members engage in self-disclosure. Expressions of negative affect are suppressed. Mahler terms this the working stage in which the members of the group engage in the process of self-exploration and assist each other in the process.

Yalom's fourth stage is the longest stage by far, continuing from the three preliminary stages for the life of the group. In this stage, his working stage, the group is a fully developed, mature working group, engaging in the working-through process.

Mahler adds as a fourth stage the ending of the group. This is the process of divorce or disengagement from the close relationships that have been formed, and the movement toward independence from group members and the substitution of close relationships with persons outside the group.

These stages are, of course, not discrete or clear-cut. There are overlappings. Moreover, the group may move back and forth or in cycles as new material emerges. Also, the stages and their nature are influenced by the therapist, both his personality and his style or technique. A therapist who directs and gives clear-cut structure will find the group responding differently in its beginning or first stage than the therapist who provides little or no structure. The composition of the group will also influence its functioning and thus the nature of its development.

The description of the process in basic encounter groups by Carl Rogers is particularly relevant because the philosophical and theoretical bases of his approach are essentially those of relationship therapy as developed in this book. The following is in part an adaptation from Rogers.[10]

1. *Milling around.* When the group is initially given freedom, with little structure except that of a place where individuals can relate to each other and get to know each other, there is a period of confusion, silence, frustration, small-talk, lack of continuity. There is often a demand for the leader to "do something." In one group (conducted by the writer), after two sessions of this one member addressed me: "Why haven't you done something, why don't you do something?" Before I could respond, she said: "Well, I'm going to do something," and then she launched into a very personal expression of her problems.

2. *Resistance to personal expression or exploration.* Although one member may reveal something personal, there may be a hesitancy, reluctance, or refusal by the others to respond on a personal level. There may be an embarrassment in the others, who gloss over the personal statement. People don't disclose themselves in ordinary social situations, and it takes time for them to feel comfortable in doing so even when they have been, in effect, given permission to do so. A trust in the group must develop first.

3. *Description of past feeling.* Expressions of feelings begin with telling about past feelings. They are experienced in the past, not in the present. They do not involve members of the group.

4. *Expression of negative feelings.* The first current feelings to be expressed, about other members in the group, are negative. The feelings are often first directed at the counselor. Negative feelings are apt to be expressed first because of feelings of threat, anxiety, defensiveness, because we are not used to expressing positive feelings, and also because of a need to test the freedom and safety of the group.

5. *Expression and exploration of personally meaningful material.* The voicing of negative feelings is followed by someone revealing himself to the group. Rogers says that "the reason for this no doubt is that the individual member has come to realize that this is in part his group. He can help to make of it what he wishes." This is beautifully illustrated by the woman in the writer's group who took responsibility for her contribution to getting the group started. A climate of trust begins to develop. Members are willing to take the risk of disclosing themselves.

6. *Expression of immediate interpersonal feelings in the group.* Members become able to express their feelings and attitudes about each other, both positive and negative. The negative feelings are not critical, bitter attacks but simple statements of feelings and reactions. The result is not conflict but exploration in an atmosphere of trust.

7. *Development of a healing capacity in the group.* Members of the group begin to help each other. They begin to care for each other, to understand each other, to try to help, each in his own way.

8. *Self-acceptance and the beginning of change.* This is an awareness of what one is, an admission, even, of what one really is behind the facade. This recognition of what one is, is necessary before one can begin to change. One can then explore what one is. A growing sense of realness, genuineness, or authenticity develops. Members feel they can be themselves, both their strong and weak selves.

9. *Cracking of facades.* The growing recognition of oneself leads to the throwing off of defenses, the taking off of masks and facades. Each group member, apparently realizing the possibility of a deep relationship where everyone is real and open and honest, demands or requires that other members be themselves.

10. *The individual receives feedback.* As the group members become open and honest with each other, the members learn how they seem to others, how they affect others. Again, this can involve both positive and negative feelings, but the negative expressions take place in a concerned and caring environment. Feedback can lead to greater self-understanding. Feedback lets us see ourselves as others see us.

11. *Confrontation.* When one member reacts to another very strongly, usually in a negative manner, confrontation seems to be a better term to use than feedback. Sometimes people do feel strongly against others, and these feelings have to come out. But it is only when people have come to know each other well that these feelings can be meaningfully expressed with the possibility of constructive results.

12. *The helping relationship outside the group sessions.* Group members relate to each other outside the group in a more human way and often are very helpful to another member of the group who is going through the painful process of self-awareness and change.

13. *The basic encounter relationship.* Group members feel close to each other and highly empathic with each other. An extremely close personal relationship develops, a basic human encounter, an I-thou relationship.

14. *Expression of positive feelings and closeness.* The group becomes warm, trusting, with a sense of human togetherness and closeness. This and the preceding stage appear to constitute "cohesiveness."

15. *Behavior changes in the group.* Group members change and

become different right before one's eyes. They become more empathic and understanding, they become more accepting, respecting and warm, they become more honest, real and genuine—they act like self-actualizing persons! Interpersonal relationships change, personal problems are resolved. A member in one of the writer's groups, who had presented himself as needing to be strong and independent, to have people lean on him (at the age of 6, he had taken his younger brother on a train halfway across the country) began openly to ask for and accept help from others. A man who could not bear to be touched by a woman was unaware later when a woman touched him and when he touched her. There is considerable evidence that people are different following even a brief but intensive group experience. Too often, though, in the reality of the world outside the group, changes fade away. It is difficult to be really human in a world where there are so few really human beings —or where so few human beings are able to express their humanness.

THE THERAPIST IN THE PROCESS

The major function of the therapist is to create, set up, or "permit" a situation where group members can express themselves, can start out on and continue along the pattern described above. The therapist is not a controller, with his hand on the throttle, pushing and pulling to speed up or slow down the process by manipulating the behavior of group members, as if he were trying to reach a preconceived destination on a time schedule. The group is a real-life situation and should be allowed to develop naturally. The purpose of the therapist should be to help provide an atmosphere in which the members can interact more naturally, more realistically, more honestly, and more humanly than is possible in the so-called real, but actually artificial, social environment in which we live. How does the therapist do this?

The therapist is not a leader in the usual sense of the word. There is no specific goal for the group. The goal, as in individual therapy, is the development of self-actualizing persons. The purpose of the therapist is to create, or facilitate, the development of the conditions under which members of the group can become more self-actualizing persons.

As in individual relationship therapy, the therapist in a group tries to establish the core conditions.

1. *Structuring.* The amount of structuring necessary or desirable depends on the group and the situation. If the group has no idea of what is expected of them, some structuring is necessary. If the group, or some of its members, have some misconceptions about the group and how they are to function, then structuring is necessary. In general, struc-

turing should be kept to a minimum. Because in therapy groups people are expected to function differently than in "real life," some structuring seems to be necessary. Rogers, in meeting for the first time the encounter group depicted in the Academy Award winning film "Journey into Self," began as follows:

> I'm glad we all had a chance to have dinner together because it gives a little chance to get acquainted, at least a few of us; but I feel as though really, we really are strangers to each other in spite of that—with lots of geographical distance and occupational distance, and everything. And, I feel like saying just one or two things to start with, from my point of view. One is that this is our group. We really can make of it anything we want to make of it, and, for myself, I don't have any prediction, except that by the time we end Sunday afternoon, we'll probably know each other a lot better than we do right now; but how we may want to go about it, or what we want to do, that's really up to us. And I think that it is an opportunity to *be* in the group as fully as we can; maybe in some respects to try ways of being or ways of relating to each other that we never quite have had nerve enough to try before, where in ordinary life situations it seems like it's too impossible. In a sense, it's an opportunity to try out new ways of behaving with other people; there's that in it too: things that we have sort of wished we might be or do with others and never have quite had the nerve—maybe we will have the nerve here. I don't know, but at any rate from here on in, as far as I'm concerned, it's up to us. . . . Oh, yes, one thing I did want to say: I feel a lot of anticipation about this group; I really look forward to getting to know you. And at the same time, I'm apprehensive; and I don't think it has much to do with the lights and the cameras. I think I'm always a little apprehensive in not knowing what a given group is going to be like. I don't know who we are, how we're going to get along, whether anything is going to come of this. Ah, so I feel a very double feeling; I feel excited and full of anticipation; I feel a little on the scared side too.[11]

A similar approach is appropriate for therapy groups. Structuring is designed to give participants some idea of what to expect and what is expected of them, thus reducing initial anxiety and threat.

2. *Listening*. The therapist listens carefully to *everything* everyone says, focusing upon the feelings being expressed. This is an intense personal listening, to whatever the member of the group is expressing.

3. *Acceptance and respect*. Each member is accepted and respected as he is, as a person. There is no pressure for change, no attempt

to make the group "jell," "get down to business," begin expressing feelings, or to "speed up" the group process. There is no attempt to get each member involved, to force participation, to "psyche out" a silent member, or to delve beneath what persons say. Each person's contribution is taken at face value.

4. *Empathic understanding.* The therapist attempts to understand what each member is thinking, feeling, and trying to express. He attempts to place himself in the place of each person, so he can understand the personal meaning of what he is saying and feeling.

5. *Responding.* The therapist attempts to convey his understanding of what is said by his responses. It is not necessary, or desirable, or even possible, that the therapist respond to every statement by a member of the group, for to do so would tend to lead to the development of a two-way interaction. Group members respond to each other, and the therapist must allow for this. But, as a trained and experienced person, the therapist can often better understand what a member may be trying to say and can often, in communicating his understanding, put it in a clearer form, reducing the incoherence or lengthy attempts at expression. By responding to feelings rather than intellectualizing, the therapist can focus the group upon feelings. The therapist can sharpen differences among participants by bringing them out clearly, thus helping participants see their differences more clearly and engage in a more meaningful interaction.

The reader will recognize these methods of facilitating a group. They are the basic conditions of the individual therapy relationship. The group is no exception when it comes to them. As a model for good, open, honest interpersonal relationships, these conditions must be present in the group. While some groups might be able to function as a group without the presence of a therapist, since these characteristics are present to a greater or lesser extent in most individuals, their presence to a sufficient degree cannot be counted on. Groups without a therapist would at best be less efficient—that is, move more slowly. The therapist—as a trained person, an expert, and a constant model—provides a stability to the group as its members flounder and struggle in their relationships with each other. The therapist is thus necessary. He is the model for the conditions for a good interpersonal relationship.

The presence of the conditions provided by, and fostered by, the therapist leads to a nonthreatening, safe atmosphere in which people can become less defensive, less inhibited, less constricted, and more open, free, and honest. They can become more real, more human, and thus more the kind of person they are capable of being. And in doing and being so, they make it more possible for others to be so. They become *therapists* for each other. In fact, Yalom goes so far as to say that

> the curative factors in group therapy are primarily mediated not by the therapist but by the other members who provide the acceptance and support, the hope, the experience of universality, the opportunities for altruistic behavior, and the interpersonal feedback, testing and learning.[12]

The fact that group members become, to some extent at least, therapists for each other is an important element in group therapy, making it potentially more powerful and effective than individual therapy. This mutual therapeutic effect has, of course, two elements— one is the experiencing of the therapeutic elements in the behaviors of others, and the second is the experience of being therapeutic for others.

Both these elements of group therapy have been reported by members of groups as being important factors in their experience in successful groups. Dickoff and Lakin found that "more than half of the former patients indicated the primary mode of help in group therapy is through mutual support."[13] Clark and Culbert found that outcomes (as measured by the Walker, Rablen and Rogers' Process Scale) in a T-group were not related to the members' perceived personal relationships with the therapist (as measured by the Barrett-Lennard Relationship Inventory), but were related to the number of two-person mutually therapeutic relationships.[14] Berzon et al. found that among incidents considered most important by group members were feelings of positive regard; acceptance and sympathy for others; witnessing honesty, courage, openness or expressions of emotionality in others; and feeling responded to by others—incidents involving relationships with the therapist did not rank high.[15]

If the therapist is a model, it may be questioned why he doesn't model self-disclosure and self-exploration at the beginning of the group process. One reason, mentioned in the discussion of the therapist as a model in individual therapy (Chapter 7), is that therapy is for clients, not the therapist. The therapist does, of course, engage in some self-disclosure as the group progresses. While it might help for the therapist to model self-disclosure at the beginning, it is not necessary. Its importance can be emphasized through structuring with the group members prior to the beginning of the group. And as one member begins to disclose himself he becomes an example or model for others. As suggested in the discussion of individual therapy, the use of tape recordings or films prior to the start of the group process can be helpful in facilitating the progress of the group.[16] Yalom reports that "successfully treated patients, when interviewed at the conclusion of therapy, have usually expressed a wish that the therapist had been less aloof, more involved in the group. Yet none of the patients wanted the therapists to have contributed more of their personal lives or problems to the group."[17]

The research on the effects of leader or therapist self-disclosure in groups is contradictory. Therapists and leaders who are self-disclosing are perceived as likeable, friendly, trustworthy, and helpful.[18] However, self-disclosing therapists were perceived as less mentally healthy in all but one of the studies cited. In the exception (the May and Thompson study), the groups were encounter groups, not therapy groups. Although a study of T-groups by Culbert found leader self-disclosure to be facilitative, Bolman reports that "unexpectedly, trainer openness showed little relationship to participant learning" in a study of 20 trainers and 118 participants in T-groups at Bethel.[19]

The nature of the group appears to be an important factor. Therapist self-disclosure would appear to be less relevant (or appropriate) in counseling or therapy groups than in encounter groups. There are also a number of other variables that influence the effects of leader or therapist self-disclosure. Among these are the timing of self-disclosure in terms of the life of the group (whether at the beginning or early, or later after the group members have become close and have become comfortable with the leader or therapist). While it would appear that to be effective as modeling, therapist self-disclosure should come early, there is some evidence that group members (particularly in therapy groups) disapprove of early self-disclosure.[20] It is apparent that many factors must be taken into account in evaluating the influence of leader or therapist self-disclosure. There also seems to be some confusion between therapist self-disclosure and therapist genuineness, with evidence for the value of the latter sometimes presented as evidence for the value of the former.

There is a further function or responsibility of the therapist that it is necessary to consider because of certain practices of some leaders of encounter groups. This is a function that trained and experienced therapists automatically assume. Beginning therapists and students, however, perhaps under the influence of reports of practices of some encounter group leaders, may not recognize or assume this function. It is the responsibility of the therapist to protect members of the group from being hurt by other members of the group. This is, of course, implicit in the requirement that the group be a therapeutic experience for each member.

Some encounter group leaders apparently believe that the group is not successful unless members express strong negative or aggressive feelings towards each other very early in the process, and they therefore encourage, stimulate, or even provoke such reactions. This misconception is probably based on the fact that usually the first feelings expressed by group members are negative. They are usually directed toward the therapist or facilitator, however. But not all group members necessarily have repressed aggressive feelings towards other members of the group, though no doubt all of us will respond aggressively if provoked enough.

There are two reasons why early expression of uninhibited and indiscriminate expression of aggression or negative reactions toward other group members is undesirable. The first has been alluded to earlier—they can be harmful to the persons to whom such reactions are directed, who may be unable to understand or cope with them, and may be provoked to respond with negative reactions or attacks on others without adequate reason, resulting in later guilt and remorse.

Such negative or hostile reactions are often justified as being desirable because it is claimed they represent feedback to the person to whom they are directed, on the basis that they are responses to himself or his own behavior. However, it must be recognized that before the members of the group get to know each other their responses or reactions may be inaccurate or mistaken, based on misinterpretations or misperceptions. They are apt to involve projections. They are thus not true feedback. They include much that is based upon transference. Mintz notes that "transference, in the sense of distorted perception of others, is clearly visible in groups, as members misperceive other members initially, often on the basis of subtle resemblances to childhood figures."[21] Members respond to each other in terms of associations with significant persons in their lives or in terms of stereotypes. Mintz, in discussing the technique of having each person, fairly early in the group, select three people whom he likes and three of whom he feels critical, and to give reasons for these feelings, writes:

> Participants are encouraged to explore the extent to which their feelings are determined by distorted perceptions coming from past experiences, accidental resemblances, or prejudice. On the following day [of the marathon], when group members know one another better and when their behavior has become more open, they are asked to share any changes in their initial reactions. Typically, although a sense of liking is further enhanced by further acquaintance, initial critical feelings become milder and turn into approval.[22]

Thus it is unreasonable to expect the recipients of such early negative reactions to cope with them as accurate feedback and to learn about themselves from them. They are shocked, hurt, or at least, puzzled.

After the group members know and accept and understand each

other, such feedback can be helpful. Again, Mintz notes that "after an atmosphere of mutual warmth and concern is established, confrontation can occur which might be painful or even injurious under other circumstances."[23]

Early hostile or aggressive feedback or confrontation, while undesirable even in encounter groups with so-called "normal" individuals, is particularly dangerous in therapy groups. While normal individuals may be able to "take it" (up to a point, at least), clients are more vulnerable because they are especially low in or lacking in self-esteem and are easily threatened. Yalom points out that such individuals are not likely to give accurate feedback, either. Thus, "the therapist . . . must constantly modulate the amount of confrontation, self-disclosure, and tension the group can tolerate."[24]

There is another potential danger in groups that has not been adequately recognized. This is the power of group pressure towards conformity. Individuals are susceptible to the expectations and demands of others, and the majority members of a group can exert tremendous pressure on a minority or on a single individual. This is the reason some people do things in groups that they would not otherwise do. Under group pressure an individual may do things he does not want to do, which cause him pain and discomfort, and which may be damaging to him as a person, because he is led to believe they are "good for him," because he does not want to be different—"everyone else is doing it"—and it would be an admission of weakness or lack of courage not to do so. And sometimes, members who do conform experience considerable regret or guilt afterwards. Encounter groups often exhibit this phenomenon, and some leaders foster it, in the name of group esprit de corps or as evidence of group cohesiveness. Such extreme cohesiveness is undesirable and can have harmful effects on members who are coerced to conform to so-called group norms. In group therapy the therapist must be careful not to allow any member to be forced into doing something for which he is not prepared and which can perhaps be harmful rather than helpful. No member should be expected or required to do anything which he does not want to do. This applies particularly to self-disclosure. A group member must be permitted to remain silent and not to disclose himself if he doesn't feel ready to do so.

GROUP SIZE AND COMPOSITION

Group Size

There is general agreement that counseling or therapy groups should be small, though the exact number recommended varies from four to ten. Four is perhaps too few, and ten perhaps too many. The larger the number, the less time there is, on the average, for each member to participate or to talk, and the less interaction each member has with each of the other members. In a large group there is a tendency for members to direct communication to a few others (leading to the development of subgroups or cliques) or to the therapist. Another important reason for keeping the group small is the demands upon the therapist made by a large group. Interactions among members increase in geometric proportion to their number. It becomes very difficult for the therapist to be aware of all the interactions, including nonverbal interactions, and to be responsive to each member at the appropriate time.

Selection of Members

Much has been written about selection of clients for group therapy; most of it is based on clinical opinion rather than research. Whatever the problem, or kind of client, someone has reported success in group therapy. Differences in therapists, in the type of therapy, in outcome or success criteria, as well as in the composition of the group, are certainly significant factors in the differences reported. In spite of the lack of agreement and of research, most writers feel that selection is necessary and important.

Research on dropouts, who are for all intents and purposes failures and thus poor risks and to be excluded, indicates that they feel less disturbed psychologically (and thus probably not highly motivated) but more hostile than continuers, that they complain more frequently of somatic or physical symptoms, are less responsive to others, are subject to external stress or problems, and are isolates in the group. Dropouts appear to be low in psychological-mindedness and introspectiveness. They are lacking in openness, are self-defensive, insensitive to others, and unable to engage in self-disclosure or in interpersonal intimacy.[25] Yet it could be argued that these are just the kind of clients who need group therapy. In most groups, however, it appears that they are not sufficiently accepted by—or acceptable to—the other members to remain in the group.

The converse of the dropout's characteristics would appear to be desirable for continuation or success in group therapy—openness, sensitivity to others, ability to engage in self-disclosure and intimate personal relations. Ohlsen advocates a rigorous selection procedure, using a personal interview, to select such clients—clients who are ready for and committed to disclosing and exploring themselves and to listening to and helping others. He states that "the prospective client must convince not only the counselor but also himself that he is ready for counseling."[26] But while rigorous selection increases the likelihood of success in group counseling and may be justified if only a limited number from many applicants can be accepted, the desirability of a highly restrictive admission policy can be questioned. As in the case of highly selective procedures for individual counseling, the result is that the cards are stacked towards successful results, and those accepted are those who are less in need of help. In the case of group counseling, the factors used in selection, such as ability to disclose oneself and to verbalize problems, to listen to and accept others, are actually the characteristics which group counseling is expected to develop and should not be used too restrictively to reject applicants.

It would appear that selection should best focus on rejecting the few applicants who clearly are not ready to function in or to benefit from a group or who give evidence that they might prevent others from functioning in or benefitting from group counseling. This is, in fact, what many writers suggest. Bach, for example, recommends that persons with insufficient reality contact, with culturally deviant symptomatology, who are chronic monopolists or highly impulsive should be excluded from therapy groups.[27]

Yalom, on the basis of a survey of the literature, lists as poor candidates those who are brain-damaged, paranoid, narcissistic, hypochondriacal, suicidal, addicted to alcohol or drugs, acutely psychotic, or sociopathic.[28]

It would appear that concern with selection should best be limited to excluding those individuals who because of extreme characteristics (muteness, withdrawal, isolation, lack of any ability to relate to others coupled with fear of social contacts) are not likely to be helped but might even become worse in a group, and those whose extreme behaviors (impulsivity, aggressiveness, verbal dominance) are likely to interfere with the progress of other members of the group.

Group Composition

The issue of whether groups should be homogeneous or heterogeneous has not been settled; the situation appears to be similar to that which existed when Furst summarized it over twenty years ago.[29] Yalom agreed with Furst: "There appears to be a general clinical sentiment that heterogeneous groups have advantages over homogeneous groups for intensive interactional group therapy."[30]

The question, of course, is: On what characteristics is homogeneity or heterogeneity to be based? Such variables as problem or diagnosis, age, sex, intelligence, education, socioeconomic level, and culture and social origin could be bases for group composition. The problem of communication might suggest the desirability of some homogeneity. Persons widely different in age, intelligence, education, socioeconomic level and culture may have difficulty in accepting, understanding and communicating with one another. Yalom appears to favor somewhat homogeneous groups (though he doesn't specify in what variables) on the grounds that they foster cohesiveness, which leads to better outcomes. For some groups, relative homogeneity in age, and homogeneity in sex, may be desirable. Children in group therapy probably should be similar in age or developmental level, although if one purpose of the group is to develop mutual understanding between children and teachers, parents, or adults, then this would not be the case. Adolescents, particularly, might benefit from groups with older members. In some instances, however, single sex groups of adolescents may be desirable or useful.

But it could be argued that it is enough that all group members share the basic characteristics of human beings living in a common society, or segment of society, with its common problems. If the purpose, or one of the purposes, of group therapy is to develop facility in interpersonal relationships, then a wide variety of kinds of group members would appear to be desirable.

Extreme heterogeneity can perhaps create problems, but these need not be insurmountable. However, there is one caution that deserves attention. In the discussion of selection, it was suggested that extreme deviants should not be included in a group. Except for the very extremes, this might not apply to a group composed entirely of such persons—such as severely disturbed psychotics. The point to be made is that there should be no individual in the group who is extremely different from all the other members of the group in one or more characteristics that could interfere with communication with or acceptance by other members of the group. Bach's suggestion is appropriate here: "In general, we limit excessive heterogeneity by trying to place a patient in a group where he can find at least one other patient in circumstances which are similar with respect to some other central phase of his own life."[31]

Probably there is too much concern with the heterogeneity-homogeneity issue. Even when we achieve some homogeneity on some variables, sufficient heterogeneity remains on many other variables because of individual differences to keep the group from becoming dull, stale, uninteresting, unproductive, and unsuccessful.

There is one other point about group composition, which is related to the fact that group members become therapists for each other. It would appear to be desirable, if not necessary, that the group have at least one member who is able to listen to others, to accept and respect others, and to understand others, at least to a minimal degree, to supplement the modeling of the therapist.

It is not possible here to go into considerations of the place and duration of group therapy sessions, frequency of meetings, the life span of the group, and whether groups should be closed (fixed membership) or open (members leaving and new members admitted during the life span of the group). These matters are not specifically related to the nature of relationship group therapy.

SUMMARY

Relationship counseling or psychotherapy, with its focus on the interpersonal relationship between the counselor and the client, extends naturally into group counseling or psychotherapy. The conditions for therapeutic progress in individual counseling are also the conditions for progress in group counseling.

While group counseling is more complex than individual counseling, it is not qualitatively different. The vocabulary by which interpersonal relationships in groups are often discussed, such as the vocabulary of group dynamics, differs, but the concepts and principles appear to be the same as those involved in relationship therapy. The concept of group cohesiveness is used as an illustration.

Group counseling offers certain experiences to the client that are not available in individual counseling or psychotherapy. In the group, the client interacts with a variety of other persons, receiving feedback on his impact on them. He thus has the opportunity to learn how to interact with others in an actual situation. The client also may be helped by others in the group whose behavior is therapeutic; that is, they demonstrate respect and warmth, understanding and empathy, and honesty and genuineness. Finally, the client has the experience of being therapeutic or helpful to others as he learns and practices these conditions of facilitative interpersonal relationships.

If, as appears to be the case, many if not most of the problems that individuals bring to counselors or therapists are problems of, or related to, interpersonal relationships, it would appear that the treatment of choice for many if not most clients would be group therapy. However, there are some clients who may not be ready for the group relationship or who may have characteristics that do not allow them to benefit from a group situation or impede or block the progress of others in groups. Therefore, some attention must be given to the selection of clients and the composition of counseling or therapy groups.

NOTES

1 I. D. Yalom. *The theory and practice of group psychotherapy.* New York: Basic Books, 1970, p. 30.

2 *Ibid.,* p. 176.

3 R. L. Bednar and G. F. Lawlis. Empirical research in group psychotherapy. In A. E. Bergin and S. L. Garfield (Eds.). *Handbook of psychotherapy and behavior change: An empirical analysis.* New York: Wiley, 1971, pp. 812–838; Yalom. *Theory and practice of group psychotherapy,* pp. 40–43.

4 Yalom, *Theory and practice of group psychotherapy,* pp. 36–37.

5 *Ibid.,* pp. 231–241.

6 C. A. Mahler. *Group counseling in the schools.* Boston: Houghton Mifflin, 1969, p. 65.

7 W. C. Bonney and W. J. Foley. The transition stage in group counseling in terms of congruence theory. *Journal of Counseling Psychology,* 1963, **10,** 136–138.

8 E. E. Mintz. *Marathon groups: Symbol and reality.* New York: Appleton-Century-Crofts, 1971, p. 26.

9 W. C. Bonney and W. J. Foley. A developmental model for counseling groups. *Personnel and Guidance Journal,* 1966, **44,** 576–580.

10 C. R. Rogers. *Carl Rogers on encounter groups.* New York: Harper & Row, 1970, pp. 15–37.

11 In William Coulson. Inside a basic encounter group. *The Counseling Psychologist,* 1970, **2** (2) , 1–27.

12 Yalom, *Theory and practice of group psychotherapy,* p. 83.

13 H. Dickoff and M. Lakin. Patients' views of group psychotherapy: Retrospections and interpretations. *International Journal of Group Psychotherapy,* 1963, **13,** 61–73.

14 J. B. Clark and S. A. Culbert. Mutually therapeutic perception and self-awareness in a T-group. *Journal of Applied Behavioral Science,* 1965, **1,** 180–194.

15 B. Berzon, C. Pious and R. Parsons. The therapeutic event in group psychotherapy: A study of subjective reports by group members. *Journal of Individual Psychology,* 1963, **19,** 204–212.

16 C. B. Truax and R. R. Carkhuff. Personality change in hospitalized mental patients during group psychotherapy as a function of the use of alternate therapy sessions and vicarious therapy pretraining. *Journal of Clinical Psychology,* 1965, **21,** 225–228; C. B. Truax, D. G. Wargo, R. R. Carkhuff, F. Kodman and E. A. Moles. Changes in self-concepts during group psychotherapy as a function of alternate sessions and vicarious therapy pretraining on institutionalized mental patients and juvenile delinquents. *Journal of Consulting Psychology,* 1966, **30,** 309–314; C. B. Truax and R. R. Carkhuff. *Toward effective counseling and psychotherapy.* Chicago: Aldine, 1967, pp. 153, 362–363; I. D. Yalom, P. S. Houts, G. Newell and K. H. Rand. Preparation of patients for group therapy: A controlled study. *Archives of General Psychiatry,* 1967, **17,** 416–427; C. Whalen. Effects of a model and verbal instructions on group verbal behaviors. *Journal of Consulting and Clinical Psychology,* 1969, **33,** 509–521; K. Heller. Effects of modeling procedures in helping relationships. *Journal of Consulting and Clinical Psychology,* 1969, **33,** 522–531.

17 Yalom, *Theory and practice of group psychotherapy,* p. 103.

18 R. R. Dies. Group therapist self-disclosure: an evaluation by clients. *Journal of Counseling Psychology,* 1973, **20,** 344–348; O. P. May and C. L. Thompson. Perceived levels of self-disclosure, mental health and helpfulness of group leaders.

Journal of Counseling Psychology, 1973, **20**, 349–352; R. G. Weigel, N. Dinges, R. Dyer, and A. A. Straumfjord. Perceived self-disclosure, mental health and who is liked in group treatment. *Journal of Counseling Psychology*, 1972, **19**, 47–52; R. G. Weigel and C. F. Warnath. The effects of group therapy on reported self-disclosure. *International Journal of Group Psychotherapy*, 1968, **18**, 31–41.

19 S. A. Culbert. Trainer self-disclosure and member growth in two T-groups. *Journal of Applied Behavioral Science*, 1968, **4**, 47–73; L. Bolman. Some effects of trainers on their T-groups. *Journal of Applied Behavioral Science*, 1971, **7**, 309–325.

20 R. R. Dies, unpublished study. It should be noted that the leader or therapist self-disclosures that were strongly disapproved were expressions of negative feelings toward the group and its functioning. Disclosures relating to feelings and experiences external to the group were rated as potentially helfpul by the psychology students who were the subjects in this study. Thus, the content of the disclosures and, when they relate to feelings about the group, whether they are positive or negative, are important variables.

21 Mintz, *Marathon groups*, p. 26.

22 *Ibid.*, p. 51.

23 *Ibid.*, p. 133.

24 Yalom, *Theory and practice in group psychotherapy*, p. 369.

25 *Ibid.*, pp. 159–170.

26 M. M. Ohlsen. *Group counseling*. New York: Holt, Rinehart & Winston, 1970, pp. 103–104.

27 G. R. Bach. *Intensive group psychotherapy*. New York: Ronald, 1954.

28 Yalom, *Theory and practice in group psychotherapy*, pp. 157–158.

29 W. Furst. Homogeneous versus heterogeneous groups. *International Journal of Group Psychotherapy*, 1951, **1**, 120–123.

30 Yalom, *Theory and practice in group psychotherapy*, p. 193.

31 Bach, *Intensive group psychotherapy*, p. 26.

Index of Names

Abeles, N., 1
Adler, A., 20, 35, 37, 164
Alland, A., Jr., 35
Allport, G. W., 32
Anderson, S., 77
Angyal, A., 36, 164
Ansbacher, H. L., 35
Ansbacher, R. R., 35
Aristotle, 17, 20, 38

Bach, G. R., 193, 194
Ban, T. A., 164
Bandura, A., 138, 139, 143
Barrett-Lennard, G. T., 58–59, 80
Barry, J. R., 167
Battle, O. L., 140
Bednar, R. L., 180
Bender, L., 35
Berenson, B. G., 11, 50, 56, 58, 59, 61, 63–64, 68, 71, 75, 79–80, 86, 88, 100, 110, 111, 112–113, 113–114, 115, 116, 123, 124, 129, 154
Bergin, A. E., 64, 99, 164–165, 166–167
Berne, E., 62–63
Berzon, B., 188
Bibring, E., 35–36
Bierman, R., 159
Biestek, F. P., 58
Bills, R. E., 172
Binswanger, L., 20
Blocher, D., 4, 164
Bolman, L., 189

Bonner, H., 17
Bonney, W. C., 181, 182
Bordin, E. S., 2
Bower, G. H., 131
Brammer, L. M., 6
Bugental, J. F. T., 4
Buhler, C., 35
Burton, A., 11, 16, 90, 116, 150, 151

Carkhuff, R. R., 11, 50, 54–56, 57, 58, 59, 59–61, 61–62, 63–64, 65–67, 68, 69–71, 71, 75, 76, 77–80, 81–83, 84–85, 85–86, 86–89, 95, 99, 100, 110, 111, 113, 113–114, 115, 116, 123, 124, 125–128, 129, 130, 132–133, 134, 135, 137, 140, 154, 157, 159, 168–169, 188
Carroll, L., 8–9
Clark, J. B., 188
Combs, A. W., 19, 36, 37, 39–40, 41, 42, 131
Coulson, W., 186
Cuchetti, D. V., 112
Cudney, M. R., 84
Culbert, S. A., 188, 189

Day, W. F., 32
De Grazia, S., 16
Dickerson, W. A., 80, 139
Dickoff, H., 188
Dies, R. R., 189
Dinges, N., 189
Dollard, J., 35, 143

Doob, L. W., 35
Drasgow, J., 159
Dyer, R., 189

Eldred, S. H., 106
Ellenberger, H., 166
Ellis, A., 5, 24, 99
Eysenck, H. J., 99, 164, 166

Ferenczi, S., 117
Fiedler, F. E., 152–153
Fierman, L. B., 112
Foley, W. J., 181–182
Ford, D. H., 163–164, 165, 168, 170–171
Frank, J. D., 140
Frankl, V. E., 16, 20, 24
Freud, S., 20, 34–35, 98, 157, 164
Friel, T., 112–113
Fromm-Reichmann, F., 102, 105, 106
Fulkerson, B. C., 167
Furst, W., 193

Garfield, S. L., 64, 167
Gendlin, J . T., 64–65, 121, 170
Ginsburg, S. W., 23, 24
Glasser, W., 130
Golding, W., 36
Goldman, L., 8
Goldstein, K., 19, 36, 37, 38
Goldstein, N., 23

Hahn, M. E., 2, 4, 7
Halleck, S. L., 11, 16, 17, 26–27, 39, 159
Heller, K., 188
Herma, J. L., 23, 24
Hilgard, E. R., 131
Hoehn-Saric, R., 140
Houts, P. S., 188

Iflund, B., 23
Imber, S. D., 140
Ingham, H. V., 22–23
Itard, J. M. G., 39

Jacobsen, E. A., 144
Jacobson, L. I., 140
Jahoda, M., 16, 17
Johnson, S. L., 144
Jourard, S., 62
Jung, C. G., 20

Kanfer, F. H., 143, 144
Kell, B. L., 83

Kelley, E. C., 40, 41
Kiesler, D. J., 165, 170, 171
Kodman, F., 188
Krasner, L., 135, 142, 144, 149

Lakin, M., 188
Lang, P. J., 149
Lawlis, G. F., 180
Lawrence, D., 172
Lecky, P., 36–37
Lee, H., 50–51
Lee, N., 16
Leitner, L., 86
Levine, J., 112
Levitt, E., 99
Lifton, W. M., 179
Locke, J., 20
Love, L. R., 22–23

MacLean, M. S., 2, 4
Magaret, A., 143
Mahrer, A. R., 15, 16, 20
Mahler, C. A., 181, 182
Malamed, B., 149
Marlatt, E. A., 144
Martin, D. G., 110, 135, 136
Maslow, A. H., 17, 35, 37, 38, 41–43, 45
May, O. P., 189
May, R., 20, 35
Mayman, M., 166
Menninger, K., 166
Mickelson, D. J., 144
Miller, N. E., 35, 132, 143
Mintz, E., 181, 190, 191
Mitchell, K. M., 52, 58, 64, 86, 112–113,
    169, 170
Mitchell, R., 86
Moles, E. A., 188
Montagu, A., 19, 35, 36
Morrice, D. J., 144
Mowrer, O. H., 3, 5, 35, 80, 139
Mueller, W. J., 83
Murphy, G., 24
Murray, E. J., 140

Nash, E. H., 140
Newell, G., 188

Ohlsen, M. M., 179, 192–193
Orne, M. E., 151
Ornston, P. S., 112
Orwell, G., 93

Parloff, M. B., 17, 21, 23
Parsons, R., 188
Patterson, C. H., 10, 143, 158
Patterson, G. R., 159
Paul, G., 94, 164, 172
Pearson, L., 121
Perls, F., 38, 83
Phillips, J. S., 144
Pierce, R. M., 159
Pious, C., 188
Polanyi, M., 141
Porter, E. H., Jr., 111
Powell, W. J., 144
Pratt, J. H., 178
Pruyser, P., 166

Rachman, S., 164
Racker, H., 117
Rand, K. H., 188
Rank, O., 164
Razran, G., 141
Rogers, C. R., 6, 18, 19, 36, 37, 39, 40, 41, 42, 49, 50, 57, 58, 62, 71, 91, 110, 116–117, 117, 121, 124, 128–129, 131, 164, 170, 183–185, 186
Rosenthal, D., 23
Rosenthal, R., 94, 151
Rousseau, J. J., 20

Sapolsky, A., 144
Schofield, W., 153
Sears, R. R., 35
Shaffer, L. R., 143
Shapiro, A. K., 147–148, 149
Shaw, F. J., 143
Shoben, E. J., Jr., 143
Shostrom, E. L., 6
Skinner, B. F., 32, 43, 44, 93, 133, 142
Smith, M. B., 16
Snygg, D., 19, 36, 37, 39–40, 41, 42, 131
Spotts, J. E., 58

Standal, S. W., 56
Stefflre, B., 6, 7–8
Stevic, R. R., 144
Stone, A. R., 140
Straumfjord, A. A., 189
Strupp, H. H., 164–165
Sullivan, H. S., 52
Super, D. E., 3

Thompson, C. L., 189
Thompson, W. R., 140
Thorne, F. C., 24, 163
Truax, C. B., 50, 52, 54, 58, 59, 61–62, 64, 65, 67, 68, 71, 91, 99, 123, 125, 127–128, 132–133, 134, 135, 137, 140, 159, 168–169, 170, 188
Tyler, L. E., 3, 4–5, 7

Ullmann, L. P., 135, 142, 149
Urban, H. B., 163–164, 165, 168, 170–171

Vitalo, R., 144

Walker, D. E., 34–35
Wargo, D. G., 188
Warnath, C. F., 189
Watson, J. B., 32
Weigel, R. G., 189
Weisskopf-Joelson, E., 24
Whalen, C., 188
White, R. W., 17
Wilder, J., 24
Williamson, E. G., 18
Wolberg, L. R., 23
Wolpe, J., 16, 20, 99, 148
Wyatt, F., 99

Yalom, I. D., 179, 180, 181, 182, 188, 188–189, 191, 192, 193, 194
Yarrow, L. J., 39

Index of Subjects

Acceptance, 41, 44, 91, 123
  as aspect of respect, 58, 59
  in group psychotherapy, 186–187
  responses, 107
  and therapist self-disclosure, 80
Action dimensions, 75–92, 129–130
  and responsive dimensions, 50, 75, 89,
    100, 113–116
Adequacy, 39–40
Adjustment as goal of therapy, 16
Adlerian therapy, 83
Agape, 89–93
Aggression, 35–36, 44
  in group psychotherapy, 189–191
Allport's images of man, 32
American Psychological Association, 2
  Division of Counseling Psychology,
    Committee on Definition, 2, 3, 4
Ann Arbor Conference, 2
Anxiety, 44
  client, 122, 134, 135, 137
  in group psychotherapy, 182
  hierarchy, 136
  neurotic, 3
  in therapist, 98
Approach-avoidance conflict, 135
Attitudes of therapist, 97–98

Behavior therapy, 131, 135, 140, 142
  as teaching or reeducation, 10

Catharsis, 109
Choice, 32–33, 34

Clarification, 108
  and interpretation, 110
Client
  characteristics, 119–122
  communication, 121
  continuation in therapy, 167
  contribution to therapy, 170
  expectations, 102–104, 122, 140, 148,
    151–152
  faith in method, 121, 148, 152
  faith in therapist, 121–122, 148, 151–
    152
  feelings toward the therapist, 83–84
  irrelevant talk of, 105–106, 134
  motivation, 119–120, 167
  negative self-disclosure, 123–124
  perceptions, 51–52, 131
    of therapist conditions, 121
  self-acceptance, 128–129
  self-awareness, 128–129, 130
  self-concept, 128
  self-disclosure, 123–124
  self-exploration, 68, 123–128, 129, 183
  silence, 105, 136
  trust in therapist, 105, 122
  unmotivated, 120–121
  voluntary, 119–120
Client-centered therapy, 65, 103, 142
Cohesiveness in group psychotherapy,
  180–181, 191
Compassion, 41
Competence as goal of therapy, 17

Concreteness, 67–71, 108–109, 113, 114
  and client self-exploration, 68
  examples of, 71
  and generalization, 68, 108
  and interpretation, 68
  and labeling, 68, 108
  scale for measuring, 69–70
Conditionality, 57–58, 58–59, 91–93, 132–133
Conditions of therapeutic personality change, 12, 49, 49–71, 75–94
  as common elements in all therapies, 168–169
  as counterconditioning agents, 135
  as means for extinguishing anxiety, 135
  as outcomes of therapy, 128–129, 130, 152
  as reinforcers, 132–137
  as specific treatment, 11, 19, 27, 45, 152
Conformity, 16, 18
  in group psychotherapy, 191
Confrontation, 76–80, 114
  and core conditions, 77
  and empathic understanding, 77
  examples of, 79–80
  and genuineness, 80
  in group psychotherapy, 184
  and immediacy, 84, 86
  kinds of, 76, 77
  nature of, 76
  and respect, 77
  risk in, 77
  scale for measuring, 77–78
Congruence. See Genuineness
Continuation in therapy, prediction of, 167
Continuum of helping relationships, 9–12
  and diagnosis, 171–172
Control, 93
Core conditions, 49–50, 65, 72, 75, 76, 77
  See also Emphatic understanding;
    Genuineness; Respect
Counseling. See also Psychotherapy
  as cognitively oriented, 3–5
  definitions, 1–6
  educational-vocational, 3
  as information giving, 5
  and psychotherapy, 1–12
  techniques, 5–6
  vocational, 12, 157

Counselor. See Therapist
Counterconditioning, 135, 137
Creativeness, 43, 44

Demand characteristics, 151
Desensitization, 135, 137, 140, 172
Determinism vs. freedom, 33–34
Device for Automatic Desensitization, 149
Diagnosis, 163–173
  and continuum of helping relationships, 171–172
  in relationship therapy, 170–173
  resurgence of interest in, 163–165

Emotional disturbance
  nature of, 44–45
  origin of, 11, 36, 44
  unitary theories of, 165–170
Empathic understanding, 42, 50–57, 113, 114
  aspects or stages of, 52, 113
  client perception of, 121
  and client perceptions, 51
  and concreteness, 68
  and confrontation, 77
  discrimination vs. communication, 57
  examples of, 55–57
  and genuineness, 71
  in group psychotherapy, 187
  and immediacy, 84, 85–86
  and internal frame of reference, 51
  and interpretation, 110
  and listening, 100–102
  obstacles to, 52
  as reinforcer, 132–137
  scale for measuring, 54–55
  and sympathy, 50
  therapist preparation for, 53
  and understanding, 50
Encounter groups, 177, 178
Existential therapy, 3, 142
Expectations of therapist, 94, 98–99, 151
Extinction, 132
  of anxiety, 135
  of client talk, 109
  of irrelevant talk, 106

Freedom vs. determinism, 33–34
Friendship, and psychotherapy, 152–156
Fully functioning person, 40, 128

Gemeinschaftsgefühl, 42
Generalization, 108, 131, 137
  and interpretation, 68, 112
  as opposite of concreteness, 68
Genuineness, 41, 62–67, 113
  client perception of, 121
  and confrontation, 80
  and congruence, 62
  examples of, 67
  and immediacy, 86
  and impulsiveness, 64
  misconceptions of, 63–65
  phony genuineness, 64
  as a reinforcer, 132–137
  and respect, 58
  scale for measuring, 65–67
  and therapist self-disclosure, 80
Gestalt therapy, 83, 179–180
Goals of counseling or psychotherapy,
    3–5, 15–22, 26–27
  and behavioristic movement, 15
  client determination of, 26–27
  competence as a goal, 17
  and conditioning, 93
  general vs. specific, 20, 26
  as goal of life, 18–19, 27
  immediate, 20, 97
  levels of, 17
  mediate, 21–22
  psychological effectiveness as a goal,
    17
  self-actualization as the goal, 18–22,
    26–27, 44–45
  specific goals as by-products, 21–22,
    26–27, 131, 152, 169, 172
  ultimate, 17–20, 26–27
  variety of, 16
Group counseling. See Group psycho-
    therapy
Group dynamics, 180–181
Group guidance, 178
Group psychotherapy, 177–195
  aggression in, 189–191
  composition of group, 193–195
  feedback in, 191
  origin of, 178–179
  as preferred mode of treatment, 177
  process in, 181–191
  responsibility of therapist, 189–190
  selection of members, 192–193
  size of group, 191–192
  stages in, 181–185

therapist functions in, 185–191
  transference in, 190
Guilt, 44

Helping relationships continuum, 6–12
  and diagnosis, 171–172
Human relations training, 157–158

Immediacy, 83–89, 112
  and client feelings toward therapist,
    83–84
  and confrontation, 83
  and empathy, 84, 85–86
  examples of, 87–89
  scale for measuring, 86–87
  and transference, 85
Information giving, 5, 10
Insight, 68, 75, 76, 109, 113, 129–130
Integration as goal of therapy, 16
Internal frame of reference, 51, 98, 101,
    110–111, 112
Interpersonal relationships, 42–43
  disturbance in, 11
Interpretation, 110–112, 135
  and clarification, 110
  and concreteness, 68
  and empathy, 110
  as generalization, 68, 112
  and resistance, 112

Labeling, 100–102, 108
  and concreteness, 68
  and interpretation, 111
Learning and psychotherapy, 131–141
Listening, 99–102
  in group psychotherapy, 186
  and respect, 58
Locus of control, 42
Love, 89–93

Medical model, 142
Mental health, concepts of, 16
Minimum change therapy, 5
Modeling, 26, 138–141
Models of man, 32–34
Motivation, 36–38, 41, 44
  Gestalt concept of, 38
  Maslow's hierarchy, 38
  for therapy, 119–120, 121

Nature of man, 32–39
  as active vs. reactive, 32–34

Nature of man (*continued*)
   aggressiveness, 35–36
   as being in process of becoming, 32–33
   as controlled vs. free, 32–34
   humanistic view, 33
   as inherently good, 34–36, 129
   motivation, 36–38, 41, 44
   as a social being, 38–39
Necessary and sufficient conditions for
      therapy, 11, 49, 121, 152, 169, 171–
      172
   See also Empathic understanding;
      Genuineness; Respect
Neurotic anxiety, 3
Nonpossessive warmth. *See* Respect

Operant conditioning, 132–133, 134–136,
      138
Outcomes, 93–94, 99–100, 130–131, 166–
      167
   as by-products of self-actualization,
      20–21, 26–27, 131, 152, 169, 172
   client influence on, 119–122
   as identical with conditions, 93, 130,
      152
   as related to core conditions, 99

Perceptual theory, 131
Personal growth groups, 177
Personal identity, 4
Personality change, 4
Philosophy of life, 24–25
Placebo effect, 147–152
   and authority, 150
   and suggestion, 150
Positive regard. *See* Respect
Prevention vs. remediation, 4, 5
Probing, 112
Process in Psychotherapy, Scale of, 124
Psychoanalysis, 111, 142, 155
Psychological counseling, 7, 8–9
Psychological education, 158–159
Psychological effectiveness as goal of
      therapy, 17
Psychotherapy
   action dimensions of, 75–92
   common elements in, 168
   conditions of, 49–75
   and counseling, 1–12
   definitions of, 1–6, 19
   dimensions of, 49, 75
   drugs and, 5

   as an encounter, 90
   for better or for worse, 99
   and friendship, 152–156
   goals of, 3–5, 15–22, 26–27
   as a good human relationship, 152–
      153
   as love, 89–91
   necessary and sufficient conditions for,
      12, 49, 121, 152, 169, 171–172
   need for, 19, 27, 120
   outcomes of, 20–21, 26–27, 93–94, 99–
      100, 119–122, 130–131, 166–167
   phases of, 49, 75, 89, 113–116
   and philosophy of life, 24–25
   prediction in, 90–91
   as a profession, 153, 154, 156–158
   responsive dimensions of, 49–71
   as a specific treatment, 11, 19, 27, 45,
      152, 172
   spontaneity of, 90
   and teaching, 10, 25
   techniques, 5–6, 97–98
   unitary theory of, 168–170

Questioning, 68–69, 112–113, 129, 136,
      137

Rapport, 101, 105, 106
Reading problems and therapy, 172
Reassurance, 122
Reciprocal affect, principle of, 131, 140
Reflection, 107–108
Reinforcement, 141
   of client talk, 106
   conditions as, 93
   of human relating, 132–134
   of positive self-concept, 138
   of self-exploration, 134–137
   and the silent client, 105
   view of therapy, 131–137
Relationship therapy. *See also* Psycho-
      therapy
   and medical model, 142
   as necessary and sufficient, 12, 49, 121,
      152, 169, 171–172
   as a specific treatment, 11, 19, 27, 45,
      152, 172
Remediation vs. prevention, 4
Resistance, 112, 135
   in group psychotherapy, 182, 183
Respect, 41, 43, 44, 56–62, 113, 114
   aspects of, 58
   client perception of, 121

Respect (*continued*)
  conditionality of, 58–59
  and empathic understanding, 71, 93
  examples of, 61–62
  and genuineness, 71, 93
  in group psychotherapy, 186–187
  and listening, 102
  and love, 93
  as a reinforcer, 132–137
  scale for measuring, 59–61
  and therapist self-disclosure, 80
  and unconditional positive regard, 57–58
Responding, 104–113
  in group psychotherapy, 187
Responsive dimensions, 49–71
  and action dimensions, 50, 89, 100, 113–116, 129–130
Role Induction Interview, 140

Self-actualization
  aspects of, 39–44
  as basic motivation, 19, 36–38, 120
  biological basis for, 19
  conditions for, 12, 39, 49–94
  and emotional disturbance, 11, 36, 44–45
  as goal of life, 18–19, 26–27
  as goal of psychotherapy, 18–22, 44–45, 49, 131
  impediments to, 45
  as integration of specific goals, 20, 26–27
  and love, 90
  and need for therapy, 120
  as outcome of therapy, 20–21, 26–27, 93–94, 99–100, 128–131, 166–177
  and specific goals of therapy, 20–21, 26–27, 131–132, 152, 169, 172
Self-awareness, 128–129, 130
Self-concept, 128–129, 131, 138
Self-disclosure
  client, 123–124
    in group psychotherapy, 183
  therapist, 80–83, 113
    examples of, 82–83
    in group therapy, 80, 188–189
    modeling of, 139
    and respect, 80
    scale for measuring, 81–83
Self-esteem, 41, 44
Self-exploration, 123–129

and action conditions, 125
and approach-avoidance conflict, 135
examples of, 127–128
in group psychotherapy, 183
of negative feelings, 123–124
reinforcement of, 134–135
scale for measuring, 125–127
shaping in, 134–135, 137
Self-ideal, 76, 128–129
Sensitivity groups, 177, 178
Shaping, in self-exploration, 134–135, 137
Silence, 105, 109–110, 122
Social responsibility of psychologists, 159–160
Specificity of expression. *See* Concreteness
Spontaneity, 41
  of therapist, 90
Spontaneous remission, 99, 122, 153–154
Structuring, 102–104, 122
  in group psychotherapy, 185–186
Supportive vs. uncovering methods, 5

Teaching
  human relations, 157–158
  and psychotherapy, 10, 25
Techniques, 5–6
  as implementation of attitudes, 97–98
T-groups, 177, 178, 180
Therapeutic genuineness. *See* Genuineness
Therapist
  attitudes, 97–98
  and authority, 150–151
  commitment, 90–91
  concreteness, 67–71
  confidence in client, 115–116
  confidence in methods, 94, 151
  confidence in self, 94, 151
  confrontation, 76–80
  empathic understanding, 42, 50–57
  expectations, 94, 98–99, 151
  faith in client, 92, 115
  genuineness, 41, 62–67
  in group psychotherapy, 189–196
  immediacy of relationship, 83–89
  and irrelevant client talk, 105–106
  listening, 99–102
  and love, 89–93
  as a model, 26, 138–141
  and negative client responses, 123–124

Therapist (*continued*)
  patience, 105, 122, 130
  questioning, 68–69, 112–113, 129, 136, 137
  respect for client, 41, 43, 44, 56–62, 115
  responding, 104–113
  responsibility of, 98–100
    in group psychotherapy, 189–190
  and role playing, 62–63
  as a self-actualizing person, 93
  self-disclosure, 80–83, 113
    in group psychotherapy, 188–189
  silence, 109–110, 122
  and silent client, 105, 136
  structuring, 102–104
  in the therapy process, 97–117
  values, 22–24
Threat, 112, 122, 132, 133–134, 135, 187
Transference, 85, 109

Unconditional positive regard, 57–58, 91
Uncovering vs. supportive methods, 5
Understanding. *See* Empathic understanding
Unitary theory of emotional disturbance, 165–170
Unitary theory of psychotherapy, 168–170

Values in therapy, 22–27
  and goals, 22
  influence of therapist's values, 23
  self-actualization as, 19
  therapist awareness of, 24
  therapist dealing with, 24–25
Vicarious therapy pretraining, 140
Vocational counseling, 12, 137

Warmth. *See* Respect